Triumph over Tragedy

Irish women's true life stories

Triumph over Tragedy

Irish women's true life stories

Trina Rea

Gill & Macmillan

Gill & Macmillan Ltd
Hume Avenue, Park West, Dublin 12
with associated companies throughout the world
www.gillmacmillan.ie
© Trina Rea 2006
ISBN-13: 978 07171 4078 7
ISBN-10: 0 7171 4078 4
Typography design by Make Communication
Print origination by TypeIT, Dublin
Printed by ColourBooks Ltd, Dublin

This book is typeset in Minion 11pt on 13.5pt.

The paper used in this book comes from the wood pulp of
managed forests. For every tree felled, at least one tree is
planted, thereby renewing natural resources.

A CIP catalogue record for this book is available from the British
Library.

5 4 3 2 1

This book is dedicated to the women who made it possible.

The curtain is lifting. We can have triumph, or tragedy, for we are the playwrights, the actors and the audience.

JOHN MACAULEY, CHAIRMAN
— LEAGUE OF RED CROSS SOCIETY

Contents

Acknowledgements

I would like to thank the women featured in this book who shared not only their stories but their hospitality, patience and time. In all cases it would have been easier for them not to bother. There was no personal gain. But they selflessly agreed for one reason only — in hope that their stories might help others.

Also, my thanks to Gill & Macmillan and especially Fergal Tobin, who enthusiastically took on this book.

And of course, my family: Dad for his fulsome praise and blunt criticism; Michael for his support and high standards; Martin for always being on the other end of the phone happily willing to help with scanners, cars, maps, directions ...; and especially Mum, for her inexhaustible enthusiasm, support, blind belief, love, invaluable advice and proof-reading! I would be utterly lost without you. You're incredible.

Finally, Daire, this would not have been possible without you. Thank you from the bottom of my heart for everything. You helped me realise my dream of writing this book. I know this isn't the first or the last of many dreams we will share together.

PS. Lest I forget! IT genius Freddy Desmond retrieved this book from my corrupt, virus-ridden laptop a week before my deadline! Thank you.

Trina Rea, 2006

Introduction

I have come to dread reading newspapers. They seem to be filled with nothing but sadness, tragedy and hate. Day after day they dutifully bring us a barrage of horrific events — last night's rapes, murders, kidnappings, assaults, abuses, etc. We have in many ways become immune to such stories, as if the people involved disappear when we turn the page of the newspaper. But every now and again there is a story that stays in our consciousness and we find ourselves asking, What ever happened that person? Can people ever recover from such loss, such tragedy? How do they cope? Do you ever get over it?

Surely not, I thought.

But after two months of speaking with ordinary women who had been through extraordinary experiences of tragedy — from watching loved ones being murdered to enduring sixteen years of child rape and homelessness — two things were clear: firstly, you never 'get over' a tragedy of that scale and, secondly, what you choose to do with that tragedy, that grief, will make all the difference.

One woman told me that 'recovery' or 'getting over it' implies that after a certain time you get back to the way you were before, but nothing can ever be the same again. You don't 'get over', 'work through' or 'deal with' the tragedy. The tragedy deals with you.

This woman continued: 'For a time you have to surrender to the tragedy, the grief. Then, unexpectedly, you have to grab it with both fists, accept that it will be with you for the rest of your life but realise it's time for you to be in control of it, not it in control of you. It is in that moment of clear decision, of there not being a possibility that you will let it devour you, that you will be filled with courage to go on.'

Sometimes the triumph is simply being able to get up each morning. Yet other times, extraordinarily tragic experiences

inspire people to do things they might otherwise never attempt —
courage to take on a terrorist army, a government, a health board
. . . Such is the case with the women featured in this book, women
who have turned their profoundly negative experiences into
something inspiringly positive.

They hope their stories will help others who are going through
their own personal tragedies, no matter how big or small. They
hope their words will give reassurance that even in your darkest,
craziest, most dead-end moments, you are not alone.

Chapter 1

Branded 'a murderer'

Roisin McConnell

*The Tribunal . . . has come to the conclusion that
An Garda Síochána is losing its character as a
disciplined force . . . Ultimately, the gradual
erosion of discipline within An Garda Síochána is
a developing situation that will, sooner or later,
lead to disaster. It is no more than a statement of
commonsense that a member of An Garda
Síochána should be immediately obliged to
account for anything that he or she has done in
the course of a tour of duty or otherwise while
using the powers invested in him or her as a
member of the force.*

MR JUSTICE MORRIS, THE MORRIS TRIBUNAL*

'You're under arrest for the murder of Richie Barron . . .', that's all I
remember the detective saying, *says Roisin McConnell, the first
woman to be arrested for the murder of the Donegal cattle dealer.* I
was led to the police car. My voice broke as I shouted to my friend,
'Call Mark (my husband). Tell him what has happened to me.'

'Don't make a show of yourself, woman!' Detective Sergeant
John White snarled as he put me in the back seat of the unmarked
garda car.

Detective White sat on the left-hand side of me and another
detective sat on the other side. At least I think he was a detective —

---

* The Morris Tribunal was set up to investigate complaints involving a
  number of Gardaí in Donegal.

he was wearing plain clothes. Two uniformed Gardaí sat in the front. White turned to me and roared into my face, 'Richie Barron has been murdered and it was an animal who did it!' I knew he was referring to me. His eyes stared into mine. He must have seen my fear and confusion. I felt horrified by what he'd said. I didn't realise then that what would happen during the next twelve hours would change the course of my life forever. Things would never be the same again.

Hours earlier, Roisin had been enjoying a life that she and her husband, painter and decorator Mark McConnell, had worked hard to achieve. They had met five years earlier when Roisin returned from working in England to her childhood home in Raphoe. Raphoe is a small, pretty village in County Donegal, northwest of Ireland. She loved Raphoe; the familiarity of the place brought a contentment that only comes from home; each turn and face brought a happy childhood memory; she liked the way of life in Raphoe and chose to settle there. The young couple married after knowing each other for three years and a year later their son Dean was born. Life was finally where they wanted it to be.

Mark and I had been living with his mother and our new house was just finished so we moved in along with baby Dean who was one and a half. We were planning on having another child because I didn't want Dean to grow up on his own. We got on well with our neighbours. They're good neighbours, nice people. No one bothered anyone. We all kept to ourselves, and I imagined that was how life would continue.

Roisin's one regret is that on the night of 13 October 1996 she and Mark decided to drive into Raphoe. Roisin wanted to visit her mother in Raphoe and Mark decided he'd go to the pub for a quiet drink while he waited for her.

Mark dropped me off at my mother's at around 7 o'clock. As far as we were concerned we weren't even going out that night. Mark would just have a drink while I visited my mother and then we'd go home. At eight o'clock my sister dropped me off at the pub to meet Mark so that we could return home, but I decided to stay for a drink because my sister Caitríona and her husband were in the pub. It was an opportunity to catch up. At nine o'clock my sister's three children took my child down to their house because children aren't allowed in pubs after nine o'clock. Some other family members joined us: my two brothers, my cousin Charlotte Peoples and her husband. The craic was getting good so we stayed on. I phoned down to my sister's house to see how the child was and they said to stop phoning, he was fine, there was nothing to worry about.

Richie Barron came into the pub about eleven o'clock. He was a local cattle dealer. I knew him to see but not to speak to. He sat on a high stool on his own at the bar. We were sitting away from the bar, at a low table. Mark went to the bar to get drinks and then someone in our group drew attention to the fact that Mark and Richie Barron were having 'words' at the bar. I looked around. There were raised voices but the disagreement was over in a matter of seconds. No one took much notice — it seemed to be just pub banter, and the night continued much the same as before. Sometime later I got up from the seat to use the toilet. It was then that I noticed Richie Barron was leaving.

Roisin asked her husband why he and Richie Barron had 'words'. He said Richie tugged on the back of his shirt as he walked by and sarcastically said, 'You're some excuse for a McBrearty.' Mark didn't rise to it and told him to 'sit down', which he did. But he got back up and went towards Mark as if he was going to hit him. Someone stepped in and held him back and that was the end of it. Richie left sometime afterwards and went to another bar where he allegedly had a fistfight with another man.

Roisin's impromptu family get-together continued into the night. Her cousin suggested that they go across the road to The Parting Glass — the local nightclub owned by Frank McBrearty senior, Mark's uncle. Roisin's brother pointed to the time, noting it was 1 a.m. He said he wasn't going to pay the entrance fee for a mere hour. It was decided they would stay where they were if the barman would serve them one more drink and if not they'd go to The Parting Glass. The barman refused because his wife had come home from hospital that night. She had just given birth, and he was anxious to go home.

So they finished their drinks and sometime after 1 a.m. they left the bar and made their way across the road to The Parting Glass, stopping off at Sarah's Chipper to order food which they'd pick up on their way home.

Roisin and Mark arrived at The Parting Glass nightclub where they heard some songs which brought back happy memories of teenage years. They went and danced for a couple of songs before they sat down to have a drink. When they sat down a woman whom Roisin's sister knew joined the party. She had heard some news and in true small-town tradition she was anxious to share it.

'Did you hear Richie Barron has been knocked down by a car?' she said to Roisin's sister.

Roisin looked over at Mark who was sitting at the other side of the table. He hadn't heard the news over the loud music. Roisin decided not to tell her husband about Richie Barron's death until morning. She knew the news would shock him, more especially because he had had words with him that night.

As Roisin left the nightclub she was speaking to the owner, Frank McBrearty senior. Frank senior was on door duty that night. He enjoyed chatting to his customers, many of whom were regulars he knew by name.

'Is it true about Richie Barron?' Roisin asked him in a voice a pitch lower than usual.

'I believe he was knocked down and taken to hospital,' Frank said.

'So he's not dead?' Roisin asked.

'No, no, he's fine. I heard it wasn't that serious,' he said.

Mark overheard the conversation and interrupted, 'What are you talking about? Who has gone to hospital?'

Roisin told her husband what she'd heard.

'Trust me to have an argument with Richie Barron before something like this should happen,' he said regretfully. Roisin consoled him by saying they'd have news in the morning of how he was doing.

Mark went next door to collect their chips and they arrived home to her sister's house where Dean, their son, was sleeping. They decided to stay the night because they didn't want to disturb Dean's sleep.

The next day it emerged that Richie Barron was in fact dead. It was said that his death had been caused by a 'hit and run' and that there was a white car involved. Roisin and her husband owned a white car but so did many other people in the area.

To Roisin and Mark's astonishment they heard that the Gardaí had questioned people in the community about Mark's movements on the night of the 'hit and run'. They asked their friends and family a myriad of pointed questions: 'What was Mark McConnell wearing on the night of the hit and run?' 'What time did he leave the pub?' 'Who was he with?' It was then that the speculation and rumours began to circulate around the village of Raphoe.

The Tribunal was disturbed by the manner in which the movements of the McConnells were investigated by members of An Garda Síochána. It was also concerned with the ease with which the suspicion of murder was arrived at in respect of Mark McConnell based on the discrepancies perceived by the investigating members.

MR JUSTICE MORRIS, THE MORRIS TRIBUNAL

Roisin was concerned that Mark's name was being tarnished, so she visited his parents' house and spoke of her concerns to his father. Mark's father phoned Raphoe Garda Station and told Sergeant Hannigan about the rumours. He said he couldn't do anything to stop them. Mark put on a brave face and said, 'Sure they'll find someone else to talk about next month.'

We tried not to take any notice of the local gossip, yet we knew that when we walked into shops and people would go quiet, we knew we were being talked about. We had peace in knowing we had done nothing wrong and I knew the truth would come out in the end, *says Roisin.* Things settled down when it was announced that a murder weapon had been found. The case was no longer classified as a 'hit and run'. It was now a murder investigation. We thought it was a good thing that a weapon had been found because they would be able to fingerprint it and identify the killer, or at the very least rule out Mark. Then it emerged that the guards hadn't actually found any murder weapon. Yet unexplainably the case was still classified as murder.

It became commonly known that the Gardaí knew exactly who had murdered Richie Barron and arrests would be imminent. Roisin and her family felt relieved. The arrests couldn't come quick enough. No one wanted murderers walking around the small community of Raphoe. Roisin wondered as to the identity of the murderers. After all, Raphoe was a small place where everyone knew everyone and a stranger would have stood out if s/he had been present on the night of Richie Barron's murder. So who could it be?

On 14 December 1996 Roisin McConnell and her family received the answer to that question. The identity of the suspected murderers was revealed when the Gardaí did a swoop to arrest those concerned. This revelation brought little comfort to the McConnells, for it was Roisin and her extended family who were arrested for the murder of the local cattle dealer, Richie Barron.

The morning of my arrest started out like a typical working day. My two friends collected me from my house at about 8 a.m. and we drove in the direction of the Fruit of the Loom clothing factory where we worked. We were driving for about a mile when at the barracks in Raphoe we noticed a garda checkpoint. Though Raphoe isn't very far from the border of Northern Ireland, this was nonetheless an unusual place to have a checkpoint.

We thought there must have been an accident because it was winter and the roads are often icy in these parts. We joined the small queue of cars but we wondered why the Gardaí waved to the car ahead of us to go on, yet seemed to be stopping us.

A garda came around to my side of the car and peered inside. I was in the back seat and my two friends were in the front. Through the fogged window I could see his eyes focused on me. I let down the window. He nodded towards me, 'Are you Roisin McConnell?'

Immediately I thought there must have been a crash and someone in the car belonging to me must be dead. Each member of my family flashed through my mind. I had left my husband and baby at home in bed so I knew they were alright . . . I thought of my mother, my sisters . . . my heart was beating fast. I just wanted him to tell me what was wrong.

I nodded my head, 'Yes, I'm Roisin McConnell.'

'In that case, step out of the car,' he said with pronounced authority. 'You're under arrest for the murder of Richie Barron.' To be quite honest I don't know what he said after that. I could see he was still talking but all I could hear were those few words ringing in my ears. I stared at him in astonishment. I felt like someone had stolen my breath. I couldn't breathe, let alone speak . . .

The thought of Roisin being arrested for murder was preposterous to her and to anyone who knew her. The gentle, law-abiding citizen hadn't received as much as a parking ticket in her life. She kept herself to herself and enjoyed the simple things of life: seeing her son take his first steps; decorating her new home for Christmas; spending time with her family.

The unmarked garda car drove quickly to Letterkenny Garda Station. Roisin's legs felt weak. She wondered would she be able to stand up when the car stopped. She wondered did Mark know yet. Was he on his way to sort things out?

Detective White didn't let up. He roared at Roisin, accusing her of Richie Barron's murder. His voice seemed to reverberate around the full car. The robust yelling had nowhere to escape to. The windows grew thick with the heat of his words. Roisin felt the tears well up. Her throat grew tight and dry. She swallowed hard, afraid to react or move. As the car sped around sharp country bends she struggled to keep her balance. She didn't want to knock against either of the men who sat on each side of her. She felt vulnerable and overwhelmed. A hundred thoughts whirled through her head:

'How could they think I killed Richie Barron? Surely they've spoken to the other people who were in the bar on the night of Richie Barron's death. These people can verify that I was in the bar at the time of his death.'

When I stepped out of the car in front of Letterkenny Garda Station, Detective White changed his demeanour and approach. He cleared his throat and in a calm and measured voice he asked, 'Roisin, do you believe in God?'

I looked at him and said with sincerity, 'Aye, I do.'

He replied something like, 'That makes two of us then.' I tried to take comfort in these words. Sure he must be alright if he believes in God.

It was about 8.40 a.m. by the time Roisin entered Letterkenny Garda Station. As she was being read her rights her two car-pool friends arrived back at her home to tell Mark, her husband, what had happened. On the way to his house they had stopped off at Roisin's sister's house. They thought it would be a good idea to have a family member break the shocking news to Mark. Roisin's friends and her sister arrived at Roisin's house to be met by swarms of Gardaí and detectives. It soon became clear that Mark was also being arrested for the murder of Richie Barron.

Roisin's sister went into the house looking for baby Dean. He was only one and a half and quite attached to his parents, particularly his mother. She realised he would be distressed by the situation. She found a ban garda and explained that she would look after Dean because he wasn't good with strangers. The ban garda went to the detective and told him her request. He refused and instead arrested her as an accessory to the murder of Richie Barron.

Mark stood with his son Dean in his arms. The child clung to his father, burying his face in his father's chest, sensing these strangers didn't belong in his home. Dean was in his pyjamas. Minutes before he had been fast asleep in a cot beside his father's bed. Both father and son had been woken by Gardaí banging on the bedroom window. He had been frightened by the sudden noise. He held onto his father so tightly that he wouldn't have fallen even if his dad had let go. Mark's gentle hold turned to a firm grip when the garda announced without consideration for the child's reaction, 'Hand your son over. We'll take him from here. You're going to prison.'

'I'm not giving you Dean. You can drop me down to my

mother's house and I'll give Dean to her to look after . . .' Mark voice was firm and uncompromising. Dean became distressed and ultimately the Gardaí agreed with Mark's suggestion. They realised they had no other choice, short of pinning Mark to the ground and ripping the child from his arms.

Roisin didn't know her husband had been arrested. She sat patiently in the interrogation room in Letterkenny Garda Station and tried to be as helpful and co-operative as possible so that this obvious mistake could be rectified. The memories of that room are as fresh in Roisin's mind as they were on the day of her arrest.

It was a small boxroom with a wee table in the centre; two plastic chairs on either side; a grey filing cabinet — nothing else except a window at the side that looked out onto bushes. There was a harsh light in the centre of the room and the door was kept closed.

The detectives read out a statement that I had given some time previously when they had called to my house. It detailed where I was on the night of Richie Barron's death. The Gardaí weren't happy with my statement and wanted to know why I hadn't given detailed answers.

In my head I played over that night's event: The Gardaí called to our house at about 11 o'clock at night to take a statement from Mark and me. It had been a long day because we had been decorating our new house. I was tired and preparing to put Dean to bed.

One garda took a statement from Mark in the kitchen and another one took a statement from me in my bedroom. They obviously wanted to take our statements separately so they could compare both versions of events. As I was talking to the garda Dean was running around the room looking for attention. I was distracted by him. I just wanted the garda to leave so that I could put my son back to bed and get a night's sleep.

If I was truthful I didn't pay much heed to the garda's questions. I saw them as a formality — they were talking to everyone in the community. I answered the questions quickly and in a general way. If I'd known I was a suspect I'd have gone into greater detail and given my undivided attention, or if I'd known that detail was what was required I'd have gladly given it.

I remember when the Gardaí were leaving we told them if they wanted more information just come back to us at any time. Mark and I had been brought up to trust in the law, to respect the law. The law wasn't something we questioned.

Looking back I think the Gardaí had a plan from day one. They wanted to frame Mark and his cousin Frank McBrearty junior for the murder of Richie Barron and treat me and my family as accessories. We were convenient suspects because Mark had had words that night with Richie Barron and the Gardaí also had an old score to settle with Frank senior who had years earlier reported a garda to his superiors. Yet the fact of the matter is that even if Richie Barron was murdered, we couldn't have done it because we were in a public place at the time. The only problem was that all the witnesses in the pub who placed us there and who backed up our statements had also been arrested by the Gardaí and told to have nothing to do with us.

Roisin's solicitor arrived at Letterkenny Garda Station. He was brought into the interrogation room to sit with his client. He requested a copy of the statement that had been taken at Roisin's house and a copy of the memo that had been taken when she arrived at the station. He was told he would be given a copy. Sergeant White went to fetch it. In the interim Roisin's solicitor advised her not to sign anything. When Sergeant White and Garda Dooley returned to the interrogation room they refused to hand over the statements. Thereafter Roisin's solicitor was asked to leave. When he left Sergeant White told Roisin to sign her statement. On her solicitor's advice she refused. Sergeant White and Garda Dooley looked knowingly at each other.

Sergeant White had not expected this gentle woman in her thirties to disobey him. He became irate, his face went red, the veins on his neck protruded as he screamed: 'Your baby is going to be taken away from you. You'll never see him again. He will be put in the hands of the State. And do you know why? Because you're going to prison for seven years. And so is your husband. You'll never get your child back. Never,' he hissed with equal amounts of rage and disdain for the woman who sat before him trembling with fear.

He went through my statement, line by line. He asked me the same questions over and over. Sometimes he would shout the questions, sometimes he would lean down towards me and ask them in a normal voice, suddenly breaking back into a roar. I answered everything in detail. There were no inconsistencies in my answering. It's easy to remember the truth. It's lies that trip people up. He had questioned and re-questioned me a 'hundred' times. There seemed nowhere else for him to go. I could sense his frustration. He wanted me to trip up. He paced the room like a trapped animal looking for a way out. His pacing stopped suddenly. He took a long hard look at me, cleared his throat and spat on the wall with anger, as if talking to me disgusted him, as if I quite literally left a bad taste in his mouth. Then he left the room, slamming the door behind him.

I kept telling myself, 'You have nothing to be afraid of, you have done nothing wrong.' I tried to stay strong. I thought of my son and my husband Mark. I was glad when lunchtime came and they took a break to eat. I wasn't hungry but I was given food, gammon, I think. I couldn't really eat. The moment lunch was over they came back into the room.

'You're nothing but a murdering bastard,' began the barrage. White was so aggressive and angry that froth formed in the corners of his mouth. He stood directly in front of me while he shouted. His face was inches from mine. I could feel his breath on my face. I could smell what he had just eaten. He was so worked up that he spat when he talked. The spittle landed on my face. I wiped it off but he didn't back off. I felt intimidated, frightened, trapped and humiliated. The shouting, screaming and questioning continued: 'What time did you enter the pub? What time did you leave? How can you be sure of the time? Who was there?' As the hours grew so did the severity of the technique.

Roisin had not previously been acquainted with Sergeant White. He was not a local guard. She thought perhaps he had been brought down from another garda station especially for this investigation, so no doubt he was keen to show his worth. Roisin tried to explain that she had never been accused of anything before. She had never broken the law. Her record, as her family's, was completely unblemished.

Sometime in the afternoon a ban garda entered the interrogation room. She sat in the corner. She didn't say anything. I thought they might lay off a bit when she was there. They didn't. There was no shame in them. No sense of humanity. I wondered had they wives, sisters, daughters. How would they like it if a man treated their loved ones like this?

Some time later Detective Superintendent John McGinley came into the room and White left. McGinley asked me, 'What's going on now, Roisin?'

I replied, 'They're trying to say I left the pub at 12.30 a.m. but I didn't leave until sometime after 1.10 a.m. I know this for sure because my brother referenced the time when we discussed going across the road to The Parting Glass. *The time frame was crucial, as Richie Barron died at about 1 a.m.*

'I'll put a scenario to you of what really happened on the night of Richie Barron's murder,' McGinley proposed. 'Let's nickname your husband Mark "the big fat pussycat", and we'll call his cousin Frank McBrearty junior "Rambo". "Rambo" knew Richie Barron would be walking home from the pub, so he went up the road to look for the cattle dealer and "the big fat pussy cat" followed him. When "Rambo" saw Richie Barron he picked up a piece of timber from the side of the road. This piece of timber would later become his murder weapon. When he saw Richie Barron approaching he ran up to him and hit him over the head. One slap and he was dead. Then "Rambo" and "the big fat pussy cat" ran down the road, threw away the bit of timber and went back into the disco in The Parting Glass. Isn't that what happened?'

'That's a load of rubbish,' I said. I thought this must be how the Guildford Four felt when they were being set up for a crime they didn't commit. 'I'm not answering any more questions,' I said.

McGinley replied, 'You're just like an IRA woman. That's the way the IRA talk.' He kept smirking and laughing as I grew more distressed. McGinley wasn't aggressive like the others. He was more the laughing type.

White re-entered the room, after what I presumed was his tea break. 'Well, did she confess yet?' he asked.

'No, she did not,' McGinley replied, unsurprised.

'I know what the murdering bitch deserves! A cell!' White said in a savage voice of intent.

White had left the door of the interrogation room ajar. I could see my mother outside. She looked like she had been there for a while. For whatever reason they allowed me to talk with her. A guard brought me a cup of tea and my mother entered the room. The ban garda stayed in the room with us. I don't think my mother knew what to say under the circumstances. She put one hand on mine and touched the cup of tea that had been placed before me.

'It's stone cold,' she said.

'It doesn't matter. I didn't want it anyway,' I uttered.

'They've all been arrested. Mark . . .' She listed my family members, anyone who had anything to do with us on the night of Richie Barron's death, from the sister we stayed with to the cousin whose father owned the local nightclub.

'Is Mark here?' I asked.

'He is. And Charlotte has been brought into the interrogation room next door,' she said. Later Charlotte would tell me how terrified she felt because my sobs could be heard outside as could White's treatment of me.

'You know you've done nothing wrong,' my mother said. 'The truth will come out in the end.'

The ban garda who stayed in the room interrupted, 'Could there be a possibility that Mark could have sneaked out the front door of the pub when you were sitting there having a drink with your friends?'

'No, because I would have missed him and when he wasn't with me he was in the pool room. I know because I had to go through it to get to the toilet and I saw him there.'

When my mother's visiting time was up the ban garda came and sat with me. She was nice enough to me. I think she felt sorry for how I'd been treated. She had no cigarettes left so she had one of mine.

'Do you know where Dean is?'

'Your son is with your mother-in-law. He's fine,' she said in a kind voice.

Then Dooley and White came back into the room. The ban garda put out her cigarette, got up from the table and sat on a chair in the corner. I didn't move. I had just lit a cigarette. White shouted, 'Put that fag out!' I obeyed.

'Get the hell up out of that chair. You've been in that chair all day.' As I was standing up he kicked the legs out from under the chair. The chair went flying. I kept my balance. I stood beside the filing cabinet. I leaned against it because I felt like I was going to faint with fear.

'Stand up straight. Don't lean against anything.'

I had never been around any type of violence. Kicking the chair from under me frightened the life out of me. Nor had I ever been shouted at by a man in an abusive manner. It was another world, something I had only ever seen on TV.

Nothing could prepare me for what happened next. White and Dooley stood on either side of me. I was clammed in between the two of them. White shouldered me as hard as he could. I staggered and fell against Dooley and then he shouldered me back as hard as he could and I fell against White who would shoulder me back once more. They continued to violently push me back and forth between them like ping-pong.

'You know what you are, McConnell? You're a disease. No one wants to touch you, or be around you. You're the devil,' they said as they pushed me back and forth.

I used all my strength to push one of them away from me and I ran to the other side of the room. I thought this isn't happening, this can't be real. I looked at the ban garda but she avoided my eyes.

Then they started shouting abuse about my family, 'Your husband is riding such a person . . ., do you know that?' Then they spoke vulgarly about him, things I wouldn't repeat. The young female garda who had until now sat passively by stood up and walked out. My eyes followed her as she exited the room. This made me feel hugely unsafe. Why didn't she say something to them? Maybe she was afraid of them too.

White threw photos on the table. Dooley nodded to White. White lifted the photos and held them before Roisin's face. She glanced at them. She could see there was blood in the photos but didn't want to look at them in closer detail because she guessed they were of Richie Barron's body.

I closed my eyes. When I opened them one of the detectives was holding the photo in front of my face and the other detective was switching the light on and off. I felt disorientated. They continued to roar at me, 'You murdering, dirty bastard.' 'You're Satan.' 'You're the devil . . .' The shouting and abuse went on for an indefinite amount of time. They insisted that I look at the photos. They described in detail what each picture depicted.

Finally I looked at one picture. I thought if I looked at one they might leave me alone. What I saw in that one photo still gives me nightmares today. The photo was of Richie Barron's skull. It had been cut open and it was resting on a bloodied white pillow. I think it must have been a post-mortem photo.

'Look at this!' they shouted. 'This is the handy work of your husband. He did this, didn't he? Answer me!'

I ran away from them to another corner of the room. I was shaking. I thought I was going to vomit. When I moved they started passing crude sexual comments. They asked me vulgar, dirty questions. Stuff like, 'Are you riding Frank McBrearty senior or Frank McBrearty junior? Or are you riding both of them?'

It's so humiliating to be spoken to like that. And I just couldn't work out how anyone could do this to me. Why did they pick me? They had no evidence, no reason. They didn't even know me.

Roisin's father had died five years previously. White was aware of this and said, 'Pray to your dead father and ask him about Richie Barron.'

I looked at White and he shouted, 'Bless yourself, Roisin.'

So I blessed myself and I prayed with all my heart to my dead father. I asked him to help me. White said he was going to say a prayer to Richie Barron.

'Were you speaking to your dead father?' White asked.

'Aye, I was.'

'What did he say?' White asked.

'He told me to continue to tell the truth, and to tell you that I have been telling the truth all day.'

Upon hearing this White turned into a madman. He banged the table with his fists. He was spitting and shouting, 'You dirty, lying, murdering bastard. Praying to your father and then lying!'

'Please leave me alone. Please leave me alone,' I cried with a desperation I had never before experienced.

'You are Satan, that's who you are, commonly known as the Devil, you're evil . . .' White yelled, 'Your father is in heaven but you'll never see him again because you're going to hell for what you did to Richie Barron. The devil belongs in hell and that's the place for you.'

White walked up to me until his backside was facing me. He lifted his leg the way a dog would lift his leg if he was about to go to the toilet. Then he farted straight into my face and laughed. He wanted to disrespect and humiliate me in any way he knew how.

'Someone in Raphoe is going to murder you. You're going to be stabbed. And when you're dead and buried I'm going to come to your grave and spit on it,' White said with cold madness in his voice.

I couldn't believe that a sane person would say such a thing. I felt he was unstable. I felt he was going to hit me. He wasn't in control of his temper.

'I'm going to be sick. I need to use the toilet,' I blurted out.

A guard came and escorted me to the toilet.

My head was banging with the pressure of the day's events. I couldn't even think clearly any more. I stood in the toilet cubicle and thought, how am I going to go back into the room? I felt defenceless. On the way back from the toilet Martin Leonard, my custody guard, said, 'You don't have to go back into that room.'

Leonard must have been able to hear what was going on or maybe he could see it in my face and demeanour. Either way he asked, 'Do you have any complaints?'

'Them two boys in there have been pushing me around the room and abusing me,' I said with a faint hope in my voice that he might help me.

He turned around, laughed at me and said in a sarcastic voice, 'Would you like the doctor?'

'No. You're all the same', I said.

'I suppose you're not going to sign this release form either?' he asked.

'No, I'm not,' I said.

The ban garda who had been in the room earlier asked, 'Who will I phone to collect you?'

'Phone my brother and my sister. They'll come down for me,' I said, exhausted and shaken.

'For what it's worth, I believe you,' she said in a low but sincere voice. That stuck in my head.

Then I saw Mark. I thought he was going to prison because he was wearing clothes that the Gardaí had given him.

'It's okay,' he said. 'We can go home.'

'Where are your clothes?'

'The Gardaí took them for forensics,' he said.

I was too distraught to say anything more. I just wanted to get out of there.

The Tribunal is much concerned by the lack of any independent body to receive legitimate concerns about Garda behaviour. The provisions of the Garda Bill need to be reviewed by the Oireachtas, so as to satisfy the legitimate disquiet that arises from the Tribunal's study of the documents in this case. All queries were ultimately forwarded to the Garda Commissioner, who received minimal co-operation to his enquiries from all ranks serving in Co. Donegal. The question kept recurring in the Tribunal's mind: To whom do you turn? Whatever measures are put in place must ensure that there is, indeed, a body to whom people with legitimate concerns are able to turn.

MR JUSTICE MORRIS, THE MORRIS TRIBUNAL

———

The extended family of Roisin and Mark who were arrested endured mistreatment at the hands of the Gardaí and yet no one was charged. The next day Roisin's sisters tried to convince her to go to work.

'You have to go in and hold your head up high. You're an innocent person. You have nothing to be ashamed of,' they coaxed. But after 12 hours abuse, mistreatment and intensive questioning Roisin didn't feel up to returning to work.

Roisin then began to have trouble sleeping and started having nightmares. Every time she closed her eyes all she could see was the picture of Richie Barron's skull, split open with blood coming out onto the white pillow in the morgue. She went to a local doctor and explained what happened to her in the station and how the experience had distressed her so much she couldn't sleep at night. She asked him to prescribe sleeping tablets so that she could get back into a routine of sleeping at night. He wasn't her usual GP and he felt it was better for her to deal with her experiences and not resort to sleeping tablets.

Roisin now wonders if she had managed to get sleep would she have been able to handle what happened to her. But after a week of not getting any sleep she began to fall apart.

I felt violated by the experience. I became paranoid. I thought the detectives were following me, watching me and that everyone was talking about me. I couldn't bear to go outside. It was like I was living in a nightmare that I couldn't wake from.

People who I expected to support me didn't. I soon found out who my real friends were and sadly I didn't have many. Then I really started to go downhill. I wouldn't even talk aloud. I whispered when I spoke because I was convinced that the detectives were listening all the time. I felt like I was going mad. I wasn't capable of looking after my son.

Mark brought me to my own GP. Within moments of seeing me he admitted me to the local psychiatric hospital. I was like a zombie. I was driving myself demented trying to work out why the Gardaí did what they did to me. And I was also trying to figure out who could have killed Richie Barron. These two questions never left my head. I interrogated myself trying to find answers.

I remember on the day that I was arrested I said to the Gardaí, 'If you want to find out who killed Richie Barron you should get to the root of where the rumours started about my family. If you find out who started those rumours you'll find Richie Barron's murderers.' This statement seemed to make the Gardaí very uncomfortable. They played it down and tried to silence me. I knew I had hit a raw nerve. They knew it was themselves who had started the rumours. They knew they were trying to frame me.

Mark brought me into the psychiatric hospital but I didn't really realise what type of hospital it was. I remember putting on my nightdress. I remember seeing a man I knew. He was in a union I belonged to. He was also a nurse in the hospital. He was shocked to see me. 'Roisin, what on earth are you doing here?'

'I don't know, I think it has something to do with Richie Barron,' I said in bewilderment. I couldn't even explain past events. Everything was tangled in my head. I know now that I was having a mental breakdown.

The hospital ultimately had to force the medication into me

because I didn't trust the doctors. I would shout and make accusations. I thought the doctors were detectives in disguise. I thought they were trying to kill me. Usually I'd be wild with embarrassment at the thought of speaking out. I'm not the type to raise my voice or draw attention to myself. I wouldn't deliberately insult anyone. But I just got sicker and sicker. I was going down, down, down — there was no getting me up. I was at the bottom ... I don't think the hospital really knew what to do with me. My mental breakdown was as severe as they come.

I remember on Christmas Eve my sister came in to see me and I begged and pleaded with her to take me home. Then I saw her husband talking to some of the nurses and I whispered to my sister, 'What is your husband doing talking to those detectives? Is he in on it?'

I remember other patients who were ill were cutting and burning themselves. I remember saying to myself, 'Ah, they're just pretending to be sick. That's not real at all.' There was a TV in the room and I didn't believe its content was authentic. I thought the hospital was showing bogus shows and that the news readers were lying. I also thought the hospital was trying to poison me.

Roisin desperately wanted to leave the hospital. She noticed patients who got better were allowed dress in their normal clothes. She managed to get some of her clothes back and got dressed. She went down to the canteen and as she sat there she saw a hospital worker walking towards her pushing a trolley. As it was coming towards her, in Roisin's mind it was getting louder and louder. Finally it was as loud as a steam train and Roisin felt like her eardrums were going to explode. She felt terrified because she thought the trolley's force was going to kill her. She ran back to her room, put on her nightdress and got back into bed. She couldn't cope. She knew she was a long way from being ready to wear her normal clothes.

It was hard on Mark to see me like that. He was trying to cope with what was done to him during his arrest, and at the same time he was trying to keep a brave face on things for our son. I'm sure he was frightened in case the woman he married was gone forever but he never let on. He supported me without judgment and loved me unconditionally. He truly lived the words of our wedding vows, 'for better or worse, in sickness and in health'.

Roisin's breakdown manifested itself in many ways. 'I thought I was the . . .' Roisin pauses unable to continue, unable to say the next word. Her voice breaks as she starts the sentence again, 'I firmly believed I was the . . .', this recollection is the most painful for Roisin. The tears roll down her face as she says the word that has been evading her . . . 'the devil'. The memory she is revisiting is something she has worked very hard to forget and something she does not speak about.

While in custody Roisin was consistently told that she was 'the devil' and these words wouldn't leave her.

I remember the priest came around the hospital with Holy Communion. He offered it to me. I wanted to receive but I couldn't. I said, 'Father, I can't receive Holy communion because I'm the devil,' and that was what I firmly believed. It's unbelievable how your mind can change. It was as if someone else had taken over my body, as if I was on the outside looking at this woman who wasn't me.

The line between sanity and insanity is very fine. I went from being normal one day to having a breakdown the next. And the worse mistake was not getting sleep in those early days. Night after night I lay in bed replaying and reliving everything that happened in that garda station. I'd toss and turn all night and then I'd hear a noise in the house. I'd lie frozen to the spot, convinced it was the Gardaí in my house coming to arrest me again, more especially because they had Mark's house keys; they'd taken them from him when he was arrested. I felt unsafe in my own home.

I was also sure we were being watched because the Gardaí knew what was going on in the vicinity of our house. For example, Frank junior was building a house next door. He hadn't yet connected electricity and we lent him a key to our house so that he could temporarily hook up his house to our electricity. I had forgotten we had given him a key, because it was some time earlier that the exchange had occurred. Yet when I was being questioned the Gardaí reminded me of it.

They kept asking me, 'Who else has a key to your house?' And I said, 'No one'. Then they said, 'You're lying. Frank junior has a key.' And they were right. He had. There was no way they could have known unless they were watching us.

They also made reference to a personal conversation that had taken place between Mark and me, in our house. They knew details of this conversation even though neither of us had ever repeated the conversation. I felt they couldn't have known unless they had a listening device in our house. I remember before I went to hospital I searched the house for bugs. I took apart a perfectly good clock because I was sure there was a listening device inside it. I found nothing.

In hospital Roisin underwent a series of treatment. Nothing worked. Finally, as a last resort, the hospital had to give her shock treatment, only used in severe cases when talk therapy or drug-based treatment fails to work. She was sedated for the treatment and afterwards she began to recover.

Roisin had been in hospital for almost two months when she was finally allowed home for a weekend visit to see how she would cope. Her family watched her carefully to see if she could differentiate between the world she had built up in her head and the way things really were. She went home for good the following weekend. She was on the mend even though she was on over ten tablets a day — three anti-depressants, valium, sleeping tablets and other tablets for calming the thoughts in her head. Roisin felt she would be able to move on with life but then she had a relapse. She went back to the hospital and they treated her through counselling.

Roisin tried hard to resume a 'normal' life but she suffered from severe head pain. It felt as if someone was drilling at either side of her head. The hospital assured her it wasn't from the shock treatment, rather from the stress that was being caused by sustained harassment from the Gardaí and isolated incidents of harassment from the family of Richie Barron.

The harassment became so intolerable Frank junior decided to sell his house which was next door to Roisin and Mark's home. He placed an advert in the paper with the details of his house. Soon afterwards posters appeared around the town which stated,

'Murderer's house for sale. No offers refused. Owner for
Mountjoy.'

Defamatory slogans were also painted on the road, 'Murdering
McBreartys', with arrows painted on the road towards their house.
Elsewhere the slogan was painted 'Murdering McConnells', also
with arrows painted beneath it on the road.

Can you imagine driving into town and seeing this type of stuff?
recalls Roisin. It's no wonder we didn't want to leave the house. I felt
so utterly humiliated and helpless. We couldn't control what was
being done to us. I often thought about leaving the country
altogether. We thought about moving to England or the States but
if we left it would be a sign of guilt, and we had nothing to feel
guilty about.

For Roisin and her husband some of the harassment became
violent. We went to Raphoe one night to see Mark's mother. On the
way back I told Mark to pull into the petrol station shop to buy a
half stone of potatoes for the dinner the next day. Mark went into
the shop. Dean was sitting in the back of the car and I was in the
passenger seat in the front. I didn't know how to drive at the time.
Myself and the wee one were chatting. He was mad to chat because
he was learning new words all the time. Then I heard a scuffle
coming from behind the car. I looked out the back window of the
car and as I did someone fell against it. It was Mark. I jumped out
of the car and Mark was on the ground roaring that his leg was
broken. Two boys, Stephen Barron and Paul Barron, the son and
nephew of Richie Barron, were battering Mark as he lay on the
ground, hitting him and kicking him with all their force. The
nephew grabbed me by my wrists. I was screaming, 'Get away, leave
him alone, leave him alone,' but he held me back until they were
finished with Mark.

Richie's son asked, 'Who is your private investigator
investigating?' Frank McBrearty senior had hired a private
investigator to try and find out who had actually killed Richie
Barron. If the investigator had been left alone and had been allowed
to get to the truth we might be better off today and the Barrons
might also be better off.

Finally Richie's son and nephew left Mark alone. I don't know if
the guards happened to come on the scene of if someone called
them but they appeared almost immediately. Martin Leonard, who

was my custody guard, was one of the guards present. All he was interested in was checking if our car tax and insurance was paid and up to date. He wasn't one bit interested in Mark or why he was lying on the ground with a broken leg and cuts. An ambulance was called for Mark and one of the Gardaí drove Dean and me home in our car. Then I went to the hospital to see Mark. He had a broken jaw, he had to get a plate and pins in his legs and he was very bruised and sore. I wondered where all this would end. Would one of us end up dead?

A couple of months later a summons came for Roisin and Mark, binding them to the peace, even though the members of the Barron family had already pleaded guilty to the assault.

The Gardaí consistently sent our family summonses for various 'made-up' crimes. They wanted it to appear to the courts that we had many criminal convictions, that we were trouble makers . . . It made their claims that we were murderers more plausible. Each court case was thrown out. The DPP wouldn't entertain these bogus claims and accusations about my family. But nonetheless the summonses continued to arrive.

The delivery of one summons in particular stands out for Roisin. At 11.45 p.m. White and O'Dowd came to Roisin and Mark's house with a summons. Mark answered the door.

'You put my wife in hospital. I don't want you calling at our door at this hour of the night,' Mark said.

'Your wife's guilty conscience put her into that hospital,' White said. Then he read out the summons in a loud voice so that I could hear. He left the house laughing. Coming to our door at that time of night was the last straw. I couldn't live there any more. I had no peace, always expecting them to arrive with a new summons, a new accusation. I insisted that we move out that very night. I packed a few things and Dean and I moved in with Mark's mother.

There is an absence of any willingness to accept any responsibility but, rather, a desire to shelter behind the fact that they [the Gardaí] were acting on an officer's orders. The phrase 'covering your back' has cropped up more than once.

MR JUSTICE MORRIS, THE MORRIS TRIBUNAL

———

'We made complaint after complaint about the way our family and our extended family were being harassed by Gardaí.' Frank McBrearty senior told the Morris Tribunal that on weekend nights the Gardaí would set up a checkpoint approximately 100 yards from his nightclub, starting at 11 p.m. and all traffic coming into the town would be stopped. This would continue until about midnight or later on some occasions. Then shortly after 2 a.m. the Gardaí would set up two checkpoints, 100 yards on either side of his premises (nightclub). They would stop all cars coming out of the venue's car parks, the occupants of which would be patrons of the nightclub. The customers were being harassed so that they didn't return to the nightclub again.

Defamatory leaflets, posters and business cards about the nightclub were circulated around the town. The leaflets and flyers read: 'The murdering McBreartys, see them live, father and son, at Frankies Nightclub, on 15 March 1997 . . .'

Soon it became difficult for the successful venue to book its usual array of national stars. People didn't want to be associated with 'trouble'. Punters didn't want the hassle of going through a checkpoint or being diverted out of their way to get home or to the McBreartys' venue.

Certain Gardaí were implicated in planning and executing this campaign against the McConnells and their cousins the McBreartys. In a note of an interview between Detective Garda Richard Caplice of the Carty investigation team and Mr William Doherty on 21 October 1999, Mr Doherty is quoted as having said, 'John White gave me a bundle of leaflets which said "Come and see live on stage father and son, the murdering McBreartys" etc. I spread them around Raphoe.'

In a subsequent statement furnished on 3 March 2000, Mr

Doherty stated: 'About March 1997, I think roughly, I was asked by John White if I would do a job. I said what? He said distribute these leaflets around Raphoe. He handed me a bundle of leaflets and told me not to leave my prints on them. This was at my house at Doorable. The leaflets read: "The murdering McBreartys, see them live on stage with Joe Dolan at 12 p.m. Father and son, Oh Daddy I killed a man, don't worry son I did too, keep your mouth shut and say nothing, I'll look after it, where money talks the truth stays silent, old Russian proverb . . ." or words like that. I distributed them that night around the streets of Raphoe . . . It was around 3 a.m. I spread them all over town and the people got them next morning. Frankie (McBrearty senior) went mad. It was the talk of the town next day. I can't say who printed them only they were given to me by John White and he gave me £100 to put them around.'

Detective Sergeant John White has denied any involvement in the production or circulation of the leaflets.

In a seven-month period Frank McBrearty's bar manager noted 138 inspections by the Gardaí of the premises. The inspections were almost exclusively on weekend nights, with often more than one inspection per night. Gardaí would remain on the premises for an extended period of time.

> *In common with the situation uncovered in 1993–1994, the situation through 1996 to 1998 shows appalling management coupled with the manipulation of facts and circumstances in order to present to Garda Headquarters, and to the world at large, an untruthful appearance of honesty and integrity in the Donegal Garda Division. The Tribunal reiterates that it has been lied to repeatedly by former, and serving, Garda officers.*
>
> MR JUSTICE MORRIS, THE MORRIS TRIBUNAL

Mark and Roisin stopped going out because when they did they felt harassed by the Gardaí. When Mark was in his uncle's nightclub a particular garda made hand gestures as if hitting someone over the head. Mark felt this was an attempt to provoke a row. Later on that evening Sergeant White and Garda O'Dowd stared at him and acted in an intimidatory manner.

Even though Roisin and her family had not been convicted of any crime she felt their reputation continued to be tarnished by this type of innuendo, rumour and harassment.

Ultimately good news came from evidence gathered by Frank McBrearty's private investigator, Billy Flynn. From telephone records, Billy Flynn was able to prove that one of the blackmail/extortion phone-calls that had been received by Charlotte and Michael Peoples had come from Garda John O'Dowd's house. The Peoples were cousins of Roisin's and had also been arrested for the murder of Richie Barron. This particular phone-call was part of a series of phone-calls made after 8 p.m. on Saturday, 9 November 1996 to the Peoples' home. Michael Peoples' recollection was reiterated during The Morris Tribunal:

My wife Charlotte told me I was wanted on the phone. I took the phone and a male voice, who spoke with a local accent, asked, 'Are you Michael Peoples?'

I said, 'That's right.'

'Remember the carry-on that you were at on Sunday night?' the male voice said.

'What carry-on?' I said

'You killed Richie Barron, I seen ya — I seen you and your wife outside The Parting Glass at twenty past one. You drive a bread van and you're the only one in Raphoe who carries a baton in their van,' the caller said.

I thought it was a wind-up. Then the caller added, 'I seen ya, ya go running down the field, I seen ya hitting Richie Barron with the baton and running down the field.'

'You're only talking shite,' I said.

'You're going to Mountjoy. You'd better get your hole ready. I want money [or] I'm going to the Guards,' he claimed.

I told him to fuck off and hung up the phone.

About a half an hour later I answered the phone again. It was the same man.

'Are you going to take me serious?' he asked.

We had a conversation for about three or four minutes and he demanded £2,000 and to take him serious. On advice from the Gardaí I played along and offered him £1,000. He said to meet him at the pub at the Whitecross with the money. He said he would be wearing a black leather jacket, a white Levis T-shirt and brown corduroys. I agreed to meet him.

In total Michael Peoples received four extortion/blackmail phone-calls between 8.05 p.m. and 10.30 p.m. During this time he phoned the Gardaí at Raphoe station to report the incident. Detective Garda Pat Flynn was on duty and answered the phone at about 8.30 p.m. He remembers being alone in the station at the time. He went out to the Peoples' house and told them to 'Keep cool. If you get another call play along.' He refused to go to Whitecross where the money was to be exchanged; he felt no one would show up. Michael and his father-in-law went on their own but no one showed.

The phone records show that one of the extortion calls was made from Garda O'Dowd's house. He claims not to have made it as he was at work at the time in Raphoe station.

The garda station records show that Garda Collins signed himself and Garda John O'Dowd off duty in the Station Diary at Raphoe Station at 10.30 p.m. on 9 November 1996 (the day of the calls). Yet in a statement Garda Collins is almost certain Garda O'Dowd was not present in the Station at 10.30 p.m. when he signed both of them off duty. He couldn't remember working with Garda O'Dowd on the day of the phone call, claiming Garda O'Dowd must have told him earlier to take him off duty at 10.30 p.m.

It was subsequently noted that the entries in the station records had been altered with Tipp-ex. Garda Collins said he did not know who changed the entries or the reason for changing them ... Garda O'Dowd subsequently asked for a transfer to another station. The transfer was granted but he never showed for his new post and cited 'severe stress' as the reason for his on-going absence.

Roisin may never get answers to her many questions but as the

Tribunal reaches its final stages more information is becoming available. As Roisin explains:

It has since been alleged by counsel for the Tribunal that it was Garda John O'Dowd who accidentally killed Richie Barron in a 'hit and run'. He and his colleague had been drinking on the night of Richie Barron's murder and afterwards O'Dowd got into his car and drove even though he was drunk. It has been alleged that he accidentally knocked down and killed Richie Barron and then fled from the scene. This supposition is strongly denied by Garda John O'Dowd.

In the last module of the Tribunal, Senior Counsel Peter Charlton said to John O'Dowd, 'If we are to believe everything we have heard about you then we can only believe one thing and that is that it was you who killed Richie Barron in a hit and run.' I think that says it all, *says Roisin in a voice that takes no satisfaction in repeating the assertions.*

> *Garda Pádraig Mulligan and Garda John O'Dowd failed to cooperate with the Garda authorities by answering the simple question as to where they were at the time of the accident. They were supported in this by their Garda Representative Association representative Garda Martin Leonard. They should have had no difficulty in accounting for their whereabouts. There was no justification for refusing to answer this lawful question honestly.*
>
> MR JUSTICE MORRIS, THE MORRIS TRIBUNAL

———

Roisin decided to take a civil action against the Gardaí for how she had been treated. She wanted justice and a firm acknowledgment that what was done to her during her interrogation was wholly unacceptable. When her court case came about, the State, on behalf of the Gardaí, made her a financial offer of compensation; they didn't want to go through a court case because the details of her case would be brought into the glare of the media. Roisin didn't want to accept the offer. She wanted her day in court. She wanted the Gardaí to be forced to apologise. However, her doctors strongly advised her to settle outside of court because they felt a court case could set her back. They made it clear to Roisin that she needed to finalise her case because it was imperative that she move on with her life and regain her full mental health. During this time it emerged that her medical records, which detailed notes of how she was treated in Letterkenny garda station, had gone 'missing' from the hospital. There was strong speculation that they had been stolen.

The State then made a second, and substantially larger offer to Roisin. She settled for in excess of €500,000, knowing that the other members of her family would make sure their court cases were heard in public.

> I didn't care so much about the money. I just wanted people to know what the Gardaí were capable of. I wanted them to be shown up for what they are. I wanted them to be brought down. And I trust that this will still happen. The whole truth will come out in the end. It always does.
>
> After the settlement I felt a great sense of relief. And as the doctors predicted, I started to get better. I never received an apology from the Gardaí or the State. They said the money is an apology because they're admitting that they did wrong. The Minister for Justice has promised an apology when they get to the bottom of their own tribunal investigations. For now he has told me that he knows I told the full truth and that I did nothing wrong.

In an eight-year battle for justice, Roisin, Mark and her extended family, with Frank McBrearty senior and Frank McBrearty junior at the helm, have contacted three Ministers for Justice, Nora Owen, John O'Donoghue, Michael McDowell; dozens of TDs; three Attorneys Generals, Michael McDowell, Dermot Gleeson and David Byrne; the Director of Public Prosecutions, Eamonn Barnes; and the Garda Commissioner;

explaining again and again how they were set up by the Gardaí for a crime that they did they not commit. They have managed, against much opposition from the Minister for Justice, to help bring about a Tribunal of investigation into why they were framed by the Gardaí.

Roisin and her extended family are nearer to the truth and justice than ever before. For them it is the beginning of the end of a miscarriage of justice that not only tarnished their names but stole their lives for eight years.

My life has changed utterly. I've changed utterly. I didn't just lose years of my life. I lost part of myself. I use to love nothing more than going out, even if it was only into the shops, but now I don't like going out. Most of the time when I need something from the shops Mark will go for me. Other times I'm strong enough to go on my own.

To be honest I find it hard to go into the local town. I think of all the damage it has caused me. It's strange because I loved growing up in Raphoe. It was and is a great place but it makes me sad now because it's not the same place for me as it used to be, not since all this happened. It divided the whole town, those that believed us and those that didn't. I don't really go to the pub anymore. We have our family around to the house instead. I like it that way because I know I'm safe. No one can accuse me of anything.

The lesson I learned is that your family is the most important thing in your life. They are the only ones you can depend on. I think I mightn't be here today if it wasn't for my family, especially Dean. He gave me a reason to live and he kept me going. When I came out of hospital Dean was a hyper child and that was a blessing because he needed constant attention. He didn't give me a second to think about what had happened.

I also learned not to trust the Gardaí. Before this happened I believed in the law, I believed in the Gardaí, I trusted them to protect the innocent. If this happened to another family I would have probably believed the Gardaí over the family, though in saying that I wouldn't have stopped talking to the family involved.

Roisin is beginning to pick up her life where she left off eight years ago. Her greatest sadness was that due to stress, medication and her breakdown she was unable to conceive another child which she, Mark and Dean so longed for. Especially Dean. He would beg his mother not to return his little cousins when they came to visit. He even asked his mother if she could adopt a child, which is something Roisin and Mark considered, but Roisin felt her past mental health illness would go against her in the application process. Roisin feels that Dean has missed out on a lot by not having a brother and sister.

A couple of months ago Judge Morris made a statement saying that my family and I were innocent of any wrongdoing . . . We knew we were innocent but to hear him say those words lifted a huge weight from my shoulders. I had waited for a long time for someone in authority to validate our innocence. They say your whole body reacts to what's going on in your life. I got sick when I was mistreated by the Gardaí and likewise when I heard these words from Judge Morris I felt well for the first time in ages. A month later I found out I was expecting our second child. I say it's a miracle because I was sure I would never have another child. Dean and Mark are over the moon.

I hope when my children are grown up our justice system will be more just. At the most basic level some rights have to exist for those arrested. After all you're innocent until proven guilty. If you're arrested you should have your right to have your solicitor there the whole time. Your interview should be recorded by video cameras and you should be allowed a copy. While I was being questioned nothing was recorded. Indeed notes were taken only on two brief occasions.

There was a time when an apology would have been enough for this family, but now it's about something far greater. It's about naming, shaming and imprisoning those who broke the law, and proving that those in uniform are not above the law. It's about getting firm assurance that the most sinister, ruthless and malicious case of garda corruption in the history of the State can never happen again; that no other person or family will be victims of a garda conspiracy; it is about hearing the State and the Ministers for Justice, who delayed in bringing these matters into the open, finally apologise. It's about reforming the whole justice system which failed in its job to uphold the law and protect its people.

> *It is said that the truth sets people free. However, even if this were a complete solution, it is not enough. It is hoped that this Report may become a focus for considering whether the wrongs done in Raphoe might not be replicated elsewhere unless action is taken. It is hoped also that by attempting to come as close to the truth as the Tribunal has been able, with the assistance of those who have appeared before it, including unrepresented parties, some peace will now be restored.*
>
> MR JUSTICE MORRIS, THE MORRIS TRIBUNAL

Chapter 2
Waiting to die

Linda Reed

> *Life is an error-making and an error-correcting process, and nature in marking man's papers will grade him for wisdom as measured both by survival and by the quality of life of those who survive.*

JONAS SALK

Two seventeen-year-old lads were sitting at the table in that little flat. They were chopping and slicing some powder. It was white and they were bent over it, concentrating on the task at hand. They had a look on their faces that was usually reserved for children on the night before Christmas.

'What's that?' Linda inquired.

'Ah, girls can't have any of this!'

That was it, it was like a red rag to a bull. I was having it. That night I took heroin for the first time. My teenage friend who lived in that flat with her newborn baby took it too. She hated it, never did it again and her life turned out one way. I was seventeen, I took it, loved it and continued to do it and my life turned out another way.

Eight years later Linda lay in a prison cell in Frankfurt, Germany. She heard the following words announced over the intercom, 'Would Linda Reed please get ready to see the doctor.' The news that was soon to be imparted to her would change her life for ever.

The cell was unlocked. I walked, with the accompanying guard, along the long corridor to meet the doctor. To me it was like watching a reconstruction in a movie. Everything was in slow motion. I entered the room where a blond female doctor was waiting for me. A nurse was sitting to her left which was most unusual. Usually the doctor would be on her own. This alerted me to the fact that there was something wrong. I sat down and the doctor said, 'I'm sorry but I've bad news. You've tested positive for HIV.'

The doctor continued to talk. I could see her mouth moving but I couldn't comprehend anything she was saying. Somehow I caught the most important detail, 'You have three years to live.' Then I was returned to my cell to sit alone. Prisoners with HIV don't share cells. This was a blessing but also a curse because it meant that I had no one to talk to.

The only thing that prison gives you in abundance is time, time to think. And Linda couldn't have but played the movie of her life over and over to try and understand why and how she come to be in this situation. Where would she be now if she hadn't tried heroin on that fateful night?

That first time I took heroin it wasn't really how it made me feel, it was more what it didn't make me feel. It numbed my emotions. I didn't feel anything. I didn't feel bad about myself and I didn't worry about how I looked. As I walked into the Belfield university bar for the first time in my life I didn't care what anyone thought. I felt a security and confidence that didn't come with being 17. At last I felt at home in my own skin.

It was a feeling of freedom from her problems and hang-ups; an escape from being trapped inside her own person; a person who, though much loved and belonging to a secure family unit, suffered from low self esteem; a person who was very clever and academically gifted but who lacked confidence; a person who was beautiful, who had every reason to be loud and vivacious but instead felt shy and out of place.

Up until this point Linda had dabbled with hash, but she never intended taking it any further. She tried heroin because it was there, it was something new, exciting and mostly because she didn't know the true consequences — that it would lead to over a decade of turmoil, hurt and devastation. For Linda and others of her generation, the 'Just Say No' and 'Heroin Hurts' posters weren't a big enough deterrent. Nor was having parents whose utmost ambition was to protect and love their daughter.

> I couldn't have asked for better as far as my parents were concerned. I had a very safe and loving childhood. My mother was and still is the best in the world, a magnificent person. At a great cost to herself she put everything into our family. I have fabulous childhood memories — trips to the pine forest, the beach . . . special family outings.

Linda attended the local convent school, Sion Hill, for both her primary and secondary education. She loved school and did well without doing much work. Each day when she came home from school her mother would be there waiting with freshly baked brown bread and homemade soup. She couldn't have loved Linda any more than she did.

As a child Linda enjoyed nothing more than sitting quietly in the corner reading. She was a very serious child who took everything literally. Her dad would call her his 'little philosopher'. He had high standards for himself and others and Linda admired him and wanted to make him proud.

> Mum was very socially conscious. She would send us around to the old people in the neighbourhood to check that they were okay. She helped the local Travellers who lived in caravans without running water and amenities. She'd drop into them and they'd drop into us. I remember during the Christmas holidays one of the Traveller families she knew had lost their home. Their caravan had been burned down, so on Christmas day Mum invited the family around to our house. She warned us to be polite and nice to them. They arrived and had baths and food. That is just one example to show the type of person my mother is — selfless and kind to the core.
>
> I was the eldest of five sisters and one brother. My sister Wendy was the first to be born 18 months after me and I was very jealous of her, and then the others all came along and I really felt hard done by. I found it hard to get my mother on her own and I loved nothing more than when it was just the two of us.

Linda's mother had a lot of trouble during child birth. Linda was her only normal delivery; her other children were delivered by Caesarean section. Each pregnancy brought with it toxaemia and illness for Linda's mother and by association extended stays in hospital.

Linda's mother would hire child-minders to look after her children while she was in hospital and while her husband was at work. She chose people who she thought would be kind, often young girls who were pregnant and might not have had anywhere else to go. However, she didn't know that some of them were 'quite psychotic'. Which brings Linda to the other story of her childhood where memories aren't so happy.

One child-minder cut herself with a razor blade and set about showing Linda how to do the same. Linda still has a scar on her arm from this incident. When her mother found out what was going on she immediately dismissed the girl. But there were other incidents with other child-minders that Linda didn't tell her mother about until it was too late. Probably the worst involved a child-minder who would lock Linda and her siblings in the garden during the day when her father was at work:

I remember distinctly climbing in the window to get oranges off the table because we were hungry. I remember seeing the stick and hairbrush on the table with which she used to bash us. I was terrified but I didn't get caught on this occasion. The child-minder would warn us, 'If you tell your father anything you will reap the consequences because remember he has to go to work and it will be just me and you,' so I didn't tell about the bashings.

On one occasion the child-minder opened the back door and called me in. She ordered me to go to the corner shop for her to buy cigarettes. It was a hot summer day and we were running around the garden in our underwear. She pulled a summer dress of mine down from the clothesline. I can still see that dress. It was blue with a white diamond pattern. I followed her into the kitchen and she pulled the dress on over my head and fastened it quickly. I guess I was about seven years of age. I suddenly became aware that it was crawling with earwigs. Up until this I hadn't been particularly frightened of earwigs. Of course I didn't like them, but when I saw the dress was crawling with them I hurriedly tried to get the dress off. The child-minder got the wooden spoon, threatened me with it and would not allow me take the dress off. I had to stand there until every earwig had crawled or fallen off the dress. It was a terrifying experience for a child.

I remember lying on my bed and crying until I was almost in convulsions. This experience was in sharp contrast to how my mother treated us. Even now when I see an earwig I feel like they're in my hair and on my body. I can feel them crawling. There were other cruel incidents like this which meant that my memories of childhood are mixed. Perhaps they had some effect on creating the insecure teenager who turned to drugs, but they can't be wholly blamed for how I turned out.

These negative experiences had little effect on Linda's academic abilities. By the age of eleven or twelve she was taken out of Sion Hill, the local convent school, and brought to University College Dublin for IQ tests. Her school deemed her to be exceptionally bright. She scored high in the tests and was skipped ahead in school, from fifth class to second year. This meant she had to make new friends among older peers. After a couple of years she grew close to her classmate Mary who came from a troubled background where her father was an alcoholic. Linda wanted to enjoy the freedom of her older friends and peers and rebelled against her parents when they refused her permission to go to teenage discos.

———

By fourteen Linda had gone from being a quiet, studious model daughter to being wild, truant and rebellious. Linda, Mary and a group of male friends would get served in pubs. They dabbled with hash and skipped school. Then Mary became pregnant by one of Linda's best male friends. Mary's parents didn't want to know. They kicked her out. Linda decided to run away with her and stayed away for three weeks. She finally agreed to return home but would go to Mary's flat when she was meant to be at school, and it was there that innocent teenage experimentation with drink and hash progressed to heroin. Linda's Leaving Certificate was now approaching. She was rarely in school but still managed to pass the examination. However, she had abandoned her dream of becoming a vet.

Linda's two best friends now had a baby together and had less time to spend with her, so Linda made some new friends through when she met her future husband, Darren. Darren, like Linda, was becoming more and more dependent on heroin.

Around this time Linda was involved in a bad car crash. She was pushed through the windscreen of the car and was blinded in one eye. The crash was not her fault and she would receive compensation which would give her financial independence. So she moved out of home in the leafy Dublin suburb of Blackrock into a flat in nearby Dalkey which she shared with Darren. Within a short time of moving out of home she became totally dependent on heroin. It was an expensive habit to keep so one of her suppliers suggested that she should deal to her friends who were already using. By doing this she would be able to feed her own habit free of charge. Linda finally agreed to become a dealer though she had a policy of not pushing drugs on anyone who wasn't already using.

> Up until this point my parents didn't know I was doing heroin, though they knew I was doing hash. One night my mother came up to the flat and said she had been told categorically that I was using heroin and that I was dealing. I lied through my teeth, denying it point blank. At this stage I didn't look like a heroin addict and I hadn't any marks from needles because for the first four years of using heroin I smoked it off tinfoil. She left, believing I was telling the truth.

Then things started to really go down hill. Linda was arrested for dealing and her parents were summoned to the station. This time there was no denying it. She had track marks on her arm from injecting heroin. She'd been caught red-handed and she was now facing a court case. Her parents brought her to St John of God psychiatric hospital to detox. It would have been more appropriate if Linda had been admitted to the unit that dealt with alcohol addiction (as there was no drug addiction unit) but she was placed in what she calls 'the lock-up ward' with people who were mentally ill. Linda had her court case coming up and her parents thought it would help her case if she'd been seeking treatment. Naturally, they also hoped the treatment would work.

I sat on the step waiting to see the doctor in St John of Gods. I presumed I was going to get methadone to ease me off heroin. I was shown into my room and was given Largactyl — it's a strong sedative with nasty side-effects. This medication is banned in most countries so I'm surprised it was given to me. After I was administered the drug a nun came into my room to pray with me. I wanted to tell her that I has lost touch with my spirituality and didn't feel much like praying, but when I tried to speak I couldn't because my jaw was locked from the medication.

The next three weeks were a blur: I have a vague memory of being in a room where people were shovelling food into their hair, taking fire extinguishers from the wall . . ., it was as you would imagine a mental institution. The medication made me irrational. For example, one night I went around to the waste paper bins and emptied them all into a bag, carrying the bag as if it were a suitcase of my clothes. I told the nurse that I was off home. Needless to say I wasn't allowed home. While I was in the hospital I received no counselling, no proper therapy, just sedatives. So as soon as I got out I started using again. It was actually the first thing I did. However, I did escape a prison sentence.

Linda's addiction had such a profound effect on her parents' relationship that it nearly broke up their marriage. Her mother would drive around the city at night time looking for her daughter, picking her up off the streets if she was in a bad way. She would do everything she knew to stop Linda from taking drugs and to stop people from selling them to her. She would be out all night and the next day she would be so tired she could hardly stand up. Her other children were very confused and hurt. They got a very hard time in school from their classmates who would say thing like 'Do you know your sister is a drug dealer?' Her husband felt he was losing his wife, but ultimately their love was strong enough to keep them together.

On one of the many occasions that Linda had gone missing, her mother and sister searched the streets of Dublin and finally went back to Linda's flat. Once again there was no answer from the door and there were no lights on, so they broke in. Inside they found Linda collapsed on the floor, almost unconscious. She was malnourished and living in utter squalor. With great difficulty they got her into the car and brought her home. The doctor was called and said she had pneumonia and was severely dehydrated. She hadn't eaten in a long time and was unable to take solid food. Her mother fed her with a tea spoon for days until she began to build up her strength. As soon as she was strong enough to stand up she got dressed and left the house to get more drugs. Finally Linda's mother realised her daughter was a hopeless addict. She was devastated because she thought she couldn't get her daughter 'back'. She had a ferocious sense of responsibility towards her and if anyone could have stopped Linda from using it was her mother and she never gave up on her.

> The hurt I caused everyone, especially the people I loved most like my mother, is incomprehensible. I don't know why my family didn't give up on me. I feel so ashamed. I was just so driven to get drugs, nothing would stand in my way.

Linda and Darren's flat was raided for drugs on a regular basis. Linda was arrested three time in total but avoided going to prison. The raids were so frequent that normality disappeared, so when Linda found out she was pregnant, she and Darren decided to move to Frankfurt in Germany where he was confident he could get work with a friend who was already established in the building trade in Germany.

Derrie, Linda's daughter, was born and at last Linda and Darren had a good enough reason to give up drugs. Darren moved over first to get work and somewhere for them to live. Though Linda was unaware of it, at that time Frankfurt had the highest rate of drug imports in Europe, so it wasn't an ideal place to start a new drug-free life. However, Linda saw it as a second chance to get it right, to be a proper mother to her new-born daughter.

Darren found work in Frankfurt but hadn't secured

accommodation by the time Linda's lease on her Dublin flat expired. So initially Darren and Linda lived with their friend Peter and his German wife, Hanna. Darren would often not return home until late at night. Linda grew lonely being in the house on her own and in a country where she couldn't speak the language.

———

Looking back Linda realises that moving to Germany was making a geographic escape from the problem. But of course the problem wasn't confined to one country. It was within her and Darren.

When she arrived in Frankfurt Darren had been clean for three months but Linda had been using so she had to deal with detoxing on her own. Two weeks into her detox Darren arrived home and said he had 'a little treat' for Linda. He handed her some heroin which she willingly accepted. Linda doesn't blame Darren and says if he hadn't brought heroin home that night it would have only been a matter of time before she found it herself.

'Where did you get it?' I asked Darren.

'Down by the railway station. But you're not to go down. It's a dangerous, unsafe place and it is also the red light district,' he said.

Of course within a short space of time I went down and scored gear. The sheer scale of the drug scene there was unbelievable. Coming up from the railway station there are three streets running parallel, each about a mile long, and a park at the other end. At any time of the day or night there were hundreds of addicts milling around, buying, selling, shooting up, over-dosing, dying. The police monitored what was going on but it was too big for them to completely stop and if they did try to stop it then it would go underground and they wouldn't be able to monitor the situation at all.

Prostitution was also prevalent because it's legal over there and many women use it as a means to support their habit, something that was rare in Ireland. In Ireland few addicts would admit to being prostitutes. Instead they would boast about stealing or cashing false cheques. It was seen as being okay to steal but not okay to sell your body, and I think that's the way it still is in Ireland.

Ninety per cent of the women I associated with in Frankfurt were 'sex-workers' — prostitutes — though I prefer the term 'sex-workers'. Ultimately they got involved in sex work to support their habits and they weren't embarrassed by it. That was the way it was and they thought it was better than stealing. At least what they had to sell was their own. That was fine with me but it wasn't something I was prepared to get involved with. Not ever.

At first Linda could support her and Darren's habit through her compensation money. She would take her new-born daughter, Derrie, in a buggy and make the trip to the railway station where she'd buy heroin. However, she knew it was getting to the stage where she would have to start dealing again because the compensation money was quickly running out.

Once you become a heroin addict your life becomes a vicious circle. When you wake up in the morning the first thing you think about is where will get heroin from today. It's a never-ending wheel of destruction and nothing else matters. I can't put that point across strongly enough. You lose who you are. You do things you would never ever normally do. For example, I stole from my family. On one occasion when they were at mass I stole jewellery — in particular a ring which I knew had huge sentimental value for my mother. My mother's life was put on hold because she was always trying to help me, and because of that the whole family suffered. But I couldn't stop myself. Heroin was all that mattered.

For the first year in Germany Linda hid from her parents the fact that she was back on drugs. She even came home on holidays that year and during that visit she married Darren in a low-key ceremony. Six months later her second child was born. Linda named him Merlyn because he was the only magical thing that happened in her life around this time.

He was born with withdrawals so it was a very difficult start for him but there was no long-term damage. Things went really badly downhill from here. I started selling during the day and Darren would stay at home and mind the children. Darren didn't deal at all. I did all the dealing, to support both our habits. He said it was best that I do the dealing because I'm better with people, a good talker. I get on with everyone. And that was true. It was my decision in the end.

I stopped all contact with my family in Ireland and they didn't know how to contact me. I was selling drugs in the red light area and it was a very violent scene around there. I would get knives put to my throat and people could rob my gear, but not even that was a big enough deterrent to make me stop.

As I was selling I got to know the girls who were involved in sex work. Sometimes I would stay out all night trying to sell gear and sometimes I wouldn't be able to sell enough because someone else would have better gear or whatever. On such nights the girls would say, Why don't you just go with a punter? I would say, No, you don't understand. I'm Irish and I'm catholic. I can't do that. I could never see myself doing something like that. The thoughts of it were abhorrent.

Then one night things got really bad. It was five in the morning. I'd no money. I hadn't sold any gear, so not only did I have no money for drugs I had no money for food for my children. I said to myself I'm going to do it, I'm going to go with a punter. But I also said to myself, there is a little part of me that I won't sell, that I will keep hidden and safe away from this sordid life. That was important, to be able to disconnect part of my mind, my heart, from what I was about to do. I know other women who have been sex workers and they're alive but they're so damaged and bitter they don't have a life. That part of myself which wasn't damaged by the situation meant I had something to build upon in later years.

In the beginning I didn't tell Darren I was working on the streets. I remember the night I told him. We were sitting in his car. He had come to find me and he asked me straight out. He seemed shocked when I confirmed that I was a sex worker but he didn't ask me to stop. I was annoyed because how did he think I was managing to support two habits, his and mine? Our relationship deteriorated after this. I found it too difficult to be intimate with him and he was insistent that I should be.

I found that I couldn't manage both my relationship, the children and the life I was leading. I couldn't work as a prostitute by day, and then make the forty-minute bus journey home to be a loving wife and mother. I began to go home less and less. I neglected the kids, leaving them with Darren even when they were sick. I remember Darren coming up with the kids, looking for me. They were crying and asking, 'Mammy, when are you coming home?' The weight of guilt was too much but the drugs had taken over. I was using cocaine as well as heroin.

In Frankfurt there are 'hotels' which offer rooms to hire by the night or by the hour. Some of the sex workers lived there at a cost of around €60 a night. Alternatively, every time you brought a 'client' into a room the hotel owner charged the client about €10. I started staying with friends who rented rooms in these hotels and eventually moved in and paid on a daily basis.

———

Five years had passed and Linda's parents knew she was using again. They came over to Frankfurt to try and find her.

I was standing on a road in a real rough part of the red light area. I saw my parents walk past me but they didn't see or recognise me. They walked past me. My mother and father stood 12 feet before me with their backs to me. I turned around and ran. I knew that if they were in this part of town they knew I was working as a prostitute. For that whole weekend I kept getting messages, 'Your parents are looking for you. They're not cross. They just want to see you.' I couldn't face them so they had to go home without talking to me. Then my brother came over about six weeks later, and as brothers do, he made sure he found me and made me get in touch with my parents. They wanted to help me but I didn't want to be helped. Nothing mattered, nothing but heroin.

By this stage the Frankfurt police knew who Linda was. They knew she was a sex worker and they'd picked her up a couple of times. One day they came to her door. She had a large quantity of drugs on the table. She didn't know the policeman had looked in through the keyhole of the door and seen that she had taken the drugs from the table and stuffed them down her jeans. They came in and trashed around looking for drugs. There were syringes lying around. She had just filled a syringe and was about to shoot up so her jeans weren't fully fastened, because she was about to inject herself in the groin. The policeman put his hand down her jeans and produced the drugs. He said, 'Oh Linda there is no way we can help you this time. You're going to prison.' Linda asked him if she could shoot up just one last time before he took her away. She knew this policeman and he had been kind to her in the past. He said, 'There is no way I can let you do that.' She asked again and just said, 'Please, please', and injected herself in the groin. Then she was taken away to prison.

> It was scary going to prison in a foreign country but at least I now had a working knowledge of the language and I knew another woman who was in there. She was a few cells away from me. When I arrived there she talked to me and told me something of what to expect. This girl's name was Darra. She was a sex worker. We had worked together on previous occasions.

Linda was brought to the prison's hospital wing where she became very ill detoxing. The vomiting, shaking and fits that she experienced were so bad that bars had to put at the side of her bed to stop her from falling out. This was coupled with a complete inability to sleep for seven days. All Linda could think of was how she would make contact with the outside world, how she would let Darren and the kids know what had happened. Finally, she was allowed to write a letter through the probation officer, telling Darren what had happened. Darren did not reply. Instead he returned to Ireland with their children. Linda was left alone with no contact from the outside world.

While in hospital Linda was tested for HIV, a test she had tested negative for months previously. By law all sex workers were tested for STDS and HIV on a regular basis. A mobile health unit would come to the hotel and inspect each sex worker's health screening book to make sure it was up to date, and if wasn't up to date the women would be tested there and then.

Linda had to wait for about ten days for her test results. Reality began to sink in that she had taken risks, not in terms of sharing needles but through sex work. Most sex workers are responsible about protecting themselves, but there were men who would come back hour after hour offering double, triple pay to have sex without a condom. On occasion Linda was really stuck for money to buy drugs and she took chances.

Linda's detox was so debilitating she spent longer in the hospital wing than was usual. One night a new inmate was admitted to her hospital ward. Linda immediately recognised her as she lumbered in. Her name was Anna Rose. She was a giant of a woman, a big, masculine, rough dike, the type of person people didn't mess with or befriend. She wasn't a heroin addict but did a lot of pills and drank excessively. Linda remembers she always had a knife in her hand which she would do tricks with, spinning it around. It would make people feel uncomfortable and they'd say 'Be careful or you'll kill someone.' That night she had done just that.

The nurse saw that Linda was still awake, unable to sleep because of the detox. She asked Linda to talk to Anna Rose, to keep her company. She was the last person Linda wanted to talk to but Anna Rose came and sat on her bed so she had little choice. That night Anna Rose had taken more pills and alcohol than usual and fell into a deep sleep. She woke up in the middle of the night to realise that at some point that night she had stabbed her partner to death. Upon realising what she'd done she went straight to the police to hand herself in after which she slit her wrists, such was her sense of regret and guilt. That night she opened her heart to Linda and Linda listened and comforted her. For the three and a half weeks Linda was in the hospital wing Anna Rose made two more attempts to kill herself. She just couldn't live with what she had done.

When both Linda and Anna Rose were moved to the main prison wing Linda found she had an important ally. When anyone thought about giving Linda a hard time Anna Rose would make it clear that Linda was 'alright' and was to be left alone. Anna Rose was the type of woman people listened to, out of fear rather than respect.

Linda got so caught up with getting used to prison life that she totally forgot about the HIV test until she was brought to see the doctor for her result.

In those days HIV equalled AIDS which equalled death. I had seen people I knew go into prison and test positive for HIV. They'd come out and a few months later they're get really sick and disappear. I saw so many people die from AIDS. There was no treatment in the 1980s. We didn't even differentiate between having HIV and AIDS. Either way you were going to die.

A couple of weeks later Linda unexpectedly got released on a suspended sentence. She thought there was no point in changing her lifestyle because either way her life was over. She became very ill with a kidney infection. It became so bad that she collapsed and went to see a retired doctor with whom she was acquainted. She chose to go to him because she hadn't money to go anywhere else. He gave Linda some antibiotics and let her stay at his house. She was so ill she phoned her mother from his house and told her that she wanted to go home. She gave her mother the address of where she was staying. But by the time her parents came over and called the doctor she was gone. However, the doctor told Linda's parents she was HIV positive. Linda's parents thought he was a nice man. They didn't realise he was also a punter.

Linda's mother persuaded Linda's father to come with her to look for their daughter and to bring her home. They arrived in Germany with no idea of where she might be. It was going to be like finding a needle in a haystack. They were tired by the time they finally got to a hotel in Frankfurt so Linda's father suggested they get something to eat, sleep and start the search in the morning. But Linda's mother had a feeling that Linda was nearby and insisted they begin the search immediately. They walked to the centre of Frankfurt and Linda's mother spotted her daughter. She couldn't believe it. She thought it was a small miracle to find her so easily. Linda looked terrible. Her eyes looked big in her thin, haunted face. Her mother felt the only thing that could bring them through was love and prayers. She didn't realise worse was still to come — they couldn't persuade their daughter to come home.

Linda's parents tried to help her get a new passport so that they could get her home, but by now Linda didn't want to know. She doesn't remember much from her parents' visit except the shock and worry on her mother's face, and how her father just looked towards the ground a lot. There was no anger or tears, just worry.

All they wanted to do was help Linda, who didn't want to be helped.

> I was out of it at that stage, using huge amounts of drugs, more than ever before. I was living recklessly. I stopped caring about everything. I really treated them badly, like when they'd come to my room there would be dirty needles and syringes lying on the table … They bought me some clothes. We had a couple of meals together.
>
> It was all very surreal, because I would only allow them help me on a superficial level.

———

Eight months later Linda was arrested for a second time. Knowing she had already had a two years' suspended sentence she felt sure there was no escaping a long sentence and resigned herself to the fact that she would die in prison.

> Simple Minds had released the song 'Belfast Child' around this time. When I heard it, it so reminded me of home, and everything that was good about home. The words made me feel so sad and lonely. It's such a heart-wrenching song to listen to when you're alone. One night in my prison cell I lay awake and cried bitterly. I said: 'God, if I could just have one chance to get my life back, I'd grab it with both hands, I won't let you down.' I had never asked God for help before and it didn't take long for my plea to be answered. I was deported home and did not have to serve my sentence.
>
> At the airport in Frankfurt I saw the man who was the main drugs supplier. He was wearing a suit and could have easily been mistaken for a businessman. He saw me being walked through the airport in handcuffs. We looked at each other but neither of us said a word.
>
> Where is he today? All drug suppliers end up in one of two places, a graveyard or a prison. There is nothing surer.

When Linda arrived at Dublin airport her parents were waiting for her and embraced her warmly. They drove from Dublin airport with Linda in the back of the car. She presumed they were taking her home but they weren't. They brought her to a hostel and told her she was barred from home until she could prove that she was clean and in control of her life. They had organised an appointment with a counsellor to help her on this journey.

Linda was shocked but for the first time began to understand the magnitude of the hurt that she had caused her family. The first thing she wanted to do was see her children but she didn't want to return back to their lives until she was sure that she could remain stable.

Linda began to spend her days in the counselling centre where other ex-drugs users and HIV victims came. She became great friends with Sam who was also HIV positive. As their friendship developed so too did his illness. Soon he was dying of AIDS. Each day Linda would go to the hospital to give him support and friendship. With each day she knew that what Sam was experiencing was what she would one day also experience. He was dreadfully ill.

Linda knew Sam would have visitors at the weekend so she told him she would see him the following Monday when she herself had an appointment in the hospital. When she arrived at the hospital on Monday she immediately asked the doctor, 'How is Sam?'

'Sam's dead,' he replied.

Linda couldn't believe that the man who was warm and alive two days earlier was now cold and buried in a grave. She had been such a big part of his life and she hadn't been there to say goodbye. She left the hospital and literally fell to her knees sobbing. Linda was still barred from the family home so her mother drove her back to Donnybrook where she had a small flat. She assured her mother she would be alright on her own. That night, after six months of being clean, she went out and used heroin again and used every day for three weeks until she had developed a habit again.

Linda knew if her family found out she would lose a

relationship and trust that she had been working so hard to rebuild. So she went to her family GP and asked him for help. He gave her a low dose of methadone to last a week and believed this would stabilise her habit. He warned her if she returned looking for more before the week was out he wouldn't be able to work with her. She took the methadone as prescribed and stabilised her habit. Now she was left with the quandary of whether or not to hide this from her parents. In the end she told them. They felt let down but slowly they began to understand the benefits of methadone. From that day to this Linda had been on the same low dose and has managed to stay off all drugs.

> Sometimes the doctor says to me, 'Would you not think of coming off the methadone?' I can't say I'll never come off it but I don't want to take the risk of hitting rock bottom again. I couldn't go there again. My body couldn't handle it. What does annoy me is when a kid has been a drug addict for six months and you see him being put on a high dose methadone maintenance plan without even being detoxed. Methadone maintenance is only for long-term chaotic users and should not be used otherwise.

For the first time in years Linda was in control of her life. So what she wanted to do more than anything else was rekindle her relationship with her children. This she achieved, gradually, though they continued to live with their father.

Linda wanted to learn everything she could about her illness so that she could empower herself and make sure she could live the longest life possible for her and her children. She went to the AIDS Alliance and read every piece of information she could find. She educated herself about her illness. There she met many others with HIV. She realised there was a huge problem with misinformation and lack of information. Soon ninety per cent of Linda's time was spent talking to patients of HIV, explaining to them what the doctors had already tried to explain. Not only did patients with HIV and AIDS not understand what the doctor was saying about their illness, the country in general didn't understand the illness.

This became evident in Linda's daily living when she was confronted with ignorance and fear.

When I was living in Donnybrook I would sometimes go to a local bar for coffee or a drink with my family. It was handy because it was near my flat. It was a nice, quiet and convenient place to go. I got to know the then manager. We would chat and have a few drinks together and I considered him a friend. One evening someone came in who was either related to him or a friend and we got talking. It emerged that she has found a lump on her breast and was terribly worried that she had cancer. She had been to the doctor and was terrified about what the results would be. She felt cancer was something she couldn't survive.

To empathise with her I told her about my situation. I told her I was HIV positive because I wanted her to understand you could get through difficult illnesses and have a life at the end of it. She didn't say much to me about it but she did look a bit shocked. The following day I came into the bar with my brother and the bar person wouldn't serve me. So, I asked, 'Why?' And he said, 'You know why!'

At the back of the bar, in the corner I could see the manager and the woman whom I had met the previous day. They were looking at me and whispering. I felt humiliated. We left and I've never gone back.

I don't blame the people in the bar. They didn't know any better and if they knew better then maybe they'd have done better. Even those who loved me most didn't know how to deal with HIV. When eventually I was allowed back home my mother had separate crockery and cutlery that were only for my use, and they were washed separately too. I had been used to helping my mother prepare dinner but she would always stop me if I picked up a knife to cut vegetables or whatever. One day after dinner at her house I set about preparing Zara's food. Zara was our black Labrador dog. My mother took the dog's food away from me. Finally I asked was she afraid that I'd give Zara AIDS. We looked at each other and burst out laughing. Things got better after that. We learned to laugh at my illness.

Soon the AIDS Alliance noticed a lot of people were coming to Linda for help and information. Like Linda they knew that education enables people and empowers them to make good decisions. The AIDS Alliance prevention education centre invited Linda to go to schools and hospitals and talk about living with HIV and to teach a drugs and AIDS awareness course. When Linda talked to young girls about drugs, AIDS and safe sex, she was amazed to learn that these girls were more worried about becoming pregnant than about catching a sexually transmitted disease. She couldn't believe that a baby was more scary to them than a lethal disease. Slowly she began to get the message through to them.

Linda believes that parents can best protect their teens by making sure there is two-way open communication, whereby the young people feel they can come and talk to their parents about anything. If a teen comes and tells you he/she has done something wrong and if you scream and impose extremely severe penalties, then the young person won't come to you again. And so thereafter communication is limited because the teen will want to avoid disappointing you, feeling that you just don't understand.

Linda also believes you have to be able to compromise with teenagers, to give them some freedom, because otherwise they will rebel and you won't know what they're getting up to behind your back. But parents must make their children understand that with freedom comes responsibility. One has to make sure that teens have the skills and knowledge to handle that responsibility. Handing teenagers leaflets about drugs or safe sex isn't enough. You have to empower them with high self-esteem and confidence. Linda strongly believes that personal development courses are something every young person should experience. It will help put them on the path of self-esteem. It will make them proud to be in their own skin and they will not feel the need to escape through drugs. It will help them have a mind of their own and conviction in making good decisions.

Linda's schools education programme wasn't confined to just teens. In 1994, through the International Community of Women Living with AIDS, she was asked to set up a support group specifically targeting women with HIV or AIDS. In the early days of HIV the people who were affected were gay men and drug users, so support groups for women were overlooked.

Linda set about finding HIV-positive Irish women who wanted to take part in a support group. She found forty such women, picked a date that suited everyone and arranged a room in the AIDS Alliance Centre. On the day of the meeting she sat waiting for the women to arrive. Sadly only one out of forty showed up. Linda couldn't understand it. These women had gone to the trouble of filling out a detailed questionnaire and had expressed a sincere interest in being part of a peer support group. When she looks back on it she realises it was because there was such a huge stigma attached to AIDS, and the very thoughts of entering a building with AIDS Alliance written on the door was enough to deter people. But this was not enough to deter Linda. She persisted and reorganised the meeting in another venue. The meeting was a success and continued to be so. These meetings were of more importance then because the women were 'waiting to die', there was no medication, no hope. People were in the dark. They had no one to give them hope. When medication came along people weren't hopeless anymore. They could look to the future with bright eyes once more.

———

Around this time Linda's children asked if they could come and live with her. She set about securing a family home so that her children could make the move. Derrie was then 15. She asked her mother many questions: 'Why is your women's group so important to you?' 'What are your tablets for?' Linda answered the questions truthfully but in a way that wouldn't alert her daughter to her illness. Derrie knew Mammy had to take tablets for her immune system and she understood the women in Mammy's group needed her support and she theirs. Linda had played out in her head the moment she would tell her children about her illness. It would be when they were old enough to understand fully. It would be at home, somewhere private and calm. She knew that time was coming near, at least for her daughter, and she planned the best way to tell her.

Derrie had other ideas about where and when she should be told and confronted her mother in the most unlikely of places.

My daughter and I were waiting at the bus to go to the supermarket to do the weekly shop. As the bus approached Derrie turned to me and calmly asked, 'Are you HIV positive?' She looked into my eyes in the way only a daughter can look at a mother. I knew I had to tell her the truth. I said, 'Yes, I am, love.' I went to turn around to go home so we could chat properly but Derrie didn't want to and stepped forward. The bus was packed with people. There were no seats. Everyone was squashed up against each other. She stood a couple of people away from me and looked out the window. We had only a few stops to go but I thought we'd never get there. Every second seemed like an hour. I looked at her and I imagined the questions that were going through her head.

We got off the and she walked a little ahead of me into the supermarket. I pushed the trolley and seemed to be just flinging in whatever came to hand. I just wanted to get out of there. Then Derrie began to question me but they weren't the questions I'd expected like — 'When will you die?', 'Do I have it?' These questions came later. For now her questions were, 'Does your mother know? Do my aunts and uncle know? Does my father know?' 'So they all know', she exclaimed. 'Everyone knows except me! Why am I the last to know? Does Merlyn know?' 'No, he doesn't know and don't tell him. I'll tell him when the time is right.'

Merlyn is younger than Derrie and I didn't feel he was ready to hear it. I wanted to protect both of them for as long as possible. A couple of days passed and I watched Derrie closely and talked to her about my illness. Then I noticed there was something wrong with Merlyn but he wouldn't confide in me. Finally, Derrie came to me and told me she had told him. I asked her what he had said. He had replied, 'You shouldn't have told me that. You shouldn't have told me,' and walked out of the room. She knew by his reaction that she indeed shouldn't have told him. So I spoke to him and we worked it out together as a family. It's good to have it out in the open and we deal with it in our own way, often by making fun of my illness — thankfully my children share my black humour. It makes me sad that they have had to deal with this. It has made them strong but I'm sure it has also made them hard — they're true survivors.

At the end of the day I know they've come out of it okay. They're both happy and successful in their own right. Derrie (22) works with a vet and is incredibly talented with animals. Merlyn (20) is really into computers and is about to start a course which will lead to a good job. They both moved out of home this year, to set up life in their own apartments. I'd love to have kept them at home with me for a little longer. I feel like I haven't had enough time with them even though they're both all grown up. My only regret is that I don't have other children just like Derrie and Merlyn.

My work has to some degree brought me into the public sphere. Of course it would be easier all round to just stay quiet but my children and I felt that by sharing our story with the public we can educate people about the realities of HIV, we can help in some small way to lift prejudices.

Linda has succeeded in educating many to the reality and truth about HIV and AIDS but that isn't to say ignorance and prejudices don't still exist. On Linda's 40th birthday she was joined by friends and family in a local bar. Great fun was being had as Linda and her friends danced, celebrating the special birthday, a birthday she thought she'd never see. Suddenly on the dance floor Linda found herself face to face with a big muscle man who walked right up to her, leaned into her face and said, 'Get out of here. We don't want your type in here. You druggie, addict, HIV bitch!'

I didn't want to cry, to get upset but of course I did. I can never believe how much it still hurts but I have to just let it go and move on. I meditate and rid myself of the negative feelings. One of the reasons I used drugs was because I feel things very intensely. There was a time I'd have changed this, wished I had a thicker skin, but now I see it as a blessing. Things can hurt me easily but likewise it's also very easy to make me happy. Little things that other people mightn't notice could make my day, like a beautiful view, seeing a little bird fly by. I'm never going to be very good at finding the middle ground on my feelings and I just have to accept that. Being the way I am means I have empathy for other people and that helps me to help others who are in my situation.

Consequently Linda won't let some burly man stop her getting her message out there, even if her work sometimes stretched herself too far, most especially when it involved giving one-on-one support to newly diagnosed HIV-positive women. She gave a lot of her self to this job, perhaps too much, by not only meeting the women face to face but giving them her home phone number so that she could be contacted day or night. This was coupled with working for the Drugs Task Force which funded Linda to design what became a successful training course for women who are having trouble accessing the health services.

––––

At last Linda found that she was doing something important and meaningful. But then as fate would have it life took a cruel twist and her health began to fail dramatically. She only had the energy to stay awake for a couple of hours. Her immune system was failing. The severity of the HIV virus was then measured by the number of T-cells Linda had in her body. A healthy person's would have about 1,200 T cells. The T-cells act as the soldiers against infection in their immune system. Someone with HIV would have far less. Linda knew that if her T-cells dropped below 200 she would start developing illnesses associated with AIDS (acquired immune deficiency syndrome). There are about 30 illnesses that people only get when they have little or no immune function left — illnesses like pneumonia. If you have two of these illnesses and your t-cells are under 200, the diagnosis is clear: you'll die shortly. Linda's T-cells were at 180 but she hadn't yet developed any of the illnesses associated with AIDS. However, she knew that short of a miracle she would soon be dead.

A miracle did arrive, in the form of the first ever drug for HIV — AZT. At first it was seen not only as a treatment but as a cure. The hype around this new wonder drug turned out not to be true, though the drug did help. Linda took it immediately and began to make progress towards regaining health. At one stage she was taking 36 tablets a day. She had to make sure she had the same amount of the tablet in her body at all times. This meant not only taking them religiously at the given times but also following the instructions on how to take them. Some had to be taken with food, some without . . .

> It was really mind boggling keeping track of all the tablets and the
> times and ways I had to take them. As one of the consultants said to
> me, 'People have trouble finishing a course of antibiotics, so you
> can imagine it will take some discipline.' You have to strictly adhere
> to the medical plan, do exactly as you are told — a terrible thing for
> an ex-addict to achieve! *Linda says with her trademark laugh.*

Medicine continues to make advances, albeit very slowly. Linda
accepted that they will never eradicate the virus and that even
controlling it is a constant race against time. Linda is now immune
to sixteen of the twenty drugs that are available. It frightens her
that no new drugs are coming on stream and that she might run
out of options. But she tries to live in the moment, not in the
future. That way she can stay positive and optimistic.

Linda combines western medicine with the best complementary
therapies and eastern philosophies.

> Complementary therapies are important. Even the doctors will
> agree that stress is the most damaging thing to your immune
> system, so anything that reduces stress is seen as a good thing. I
> believe it's important to treat the whole person so that's why I
> combine approaches. Western medicine looks at us like we're not
> robots made up of parts that need to be fixed. Eastern medicine
> looks at the whole person, the spiritual and emotional needs.
> Anyone I know who is doing really well with HIV is using both
> western medicine and holistic approaches.

The side effects and the long-term damage of Linda's
medication is becoming more apparent. She has nerve damage in
her hands and feet, she has lost the ability to grip with her hands,
and her feet feel like they're numb, a dead weight, as if she's
walking around on clumps of wood. But at night they go on fire
with severe pins and needles, which prevents Linda from sleeping.
She also has stomach problems, dry skin, dry mouth, has a
predisposition to heart problems, diabetes, osteoporosis. Also her
body weight has been redistributed; fat is deposited around her

body's organs whereas other parts of her body are left with no fat or 'cushion', leading to bed sores.

Her treatment is controlling the virus but it is at a cost. The other problem with the treatment is resistance. The virus mutates and changes so the drugs become ineffective. Hence one has to keep changing drugs. Linda is multi-resistant. It's a constant race to find new drugs so that she can stay a step ahead of the virus. There is a small group of people working on gene therapy. Some people who were diagnosed with HIV never got sick, never developed the symptoms. They seem to have something different in their gene pool which protects them. Science is trying to establish the make-up of the gene so that they can replicate it synthetically. Linda believes giving more and more toxic drugs isn't the answer. She feels the stigma of HIV/AIDS is still the worse thing about the disease.

I know it's hard to make people understand about the disease. For a long time I too believed a lot of what was said about HIV-positive people. I almost felt that I didn't deserve to be loved, that I was untouchable. And that loneliness was the real killer. When I was diagnosed I thought no one would ever want to go out with me, no one would ever want to make love to me because I've HIV. Then I met Conor a few years after I came back to Ireland. We would go to gigs together and I knew he liked me and I liked him but I knew I had to tell him about my illness. I told him I was positive and explained that all we could ever be was friends. Then two different traumatic events in both our lives seemed to draw us together and everything changed.

One night I was due to meet Conor at a gig. I arrived but he didn't turn up. This was out of character for him, so I was a little worried. I decided to go home and took a different route than usual. I took a short cut through the tennis grounds in Dún Laoghaire. It's a well-lit area and I thought I'd be safe. But as I walked through the grounds I was rugby tackled by a large black man who assaulted and raped me. His strength was so fierce that he ripped my bra in two and tried to strangle me. I fought him with all my strength and got away with my life. It was a particularly vicious and violent attack. There was a huge appeal to try and find him and the story was covered on television, but he was never caught.

When my family came to hospital to see me they asked if there was anyone I would like to see. The only person I wanted to see was Conor. Unknown to me, Conor too had been rushed into hospital. He had collapsed and was diagnosed with diabetes. We supported each other through these events and soon after a relationship developed, we moved in together and began a happy nine-year relationship.

I remember there was a huge stigma around us. One night we were sitting in a bar and Conor had his arm around me and this guy, whom we both knew independently, came up to us and bellowed: 'Does he know?'

'Yes,' I replied.

He looked at Conor and continued, 'Well then, what are you doing going with her, that dirty bitch!' The guy was drunk but that doesn't excuse him. I just cried. It's hard to know how to deal with this situation other than to walk away from it. This man wasn't the only one who thought I shouldn't be in a relationship. Other people would say, how could I think of being with someone, 'It's like putting a machine gun to someone's head.' This of course isn't the case.

Now when Linda goes to this bar, the older people there who were once somewhat apprehensive about her are quite protective of her. By putting a face and voice with her illness they have come to learn and understand. Now they've got to know Linda and see that she is also Linda the mother, Linda the person — not just Linda with HIV.

I thought for a long time my life was a complete waste of time. What was I? A HIV-positive junkie who was going to die and all I've done with my life is hurt, now I mean really hurt, the most important people in my life. Now I look at the work I have done through the women groups, the one-on-one sessions with HIV-positive women, the schools educational lectures . . ., indeed with the people who have just crossed my path who needed help . . . and most importantly I look at my two wonderful children and I know my life hasn't been a waste. I'm very sure that where I am in my life is where I'm meant to be. Perhaps what went before was my training for this role. After all, the best path we have for learning is through painful, trying experiences, and it is only through these experiences that you can truly learn. Sometimes I think you learn more from failure than you ever will learn from success. Failure teaches you humility, strength and empathy.

For now life is panning along well for me. I'm happy and when I find myself in a bad or difficult situation I realise that it doesn't matter. What matters is how I deal with it and what I take from the experience. And that's the way I try to live. I hope I've learned from my life and I hope that what I've learned can save others from walking the paths I've walked. My story is now a public one, one that I hope will help people to understand HIV/AIDS a little better, one that will make people realise that it's not a crime to be HIV-positive. Most of all I've shared my story because when I die I don't want my children to feel ashamed that their mother died of AIDS.

Chapter 3
'Can I call you Mammy?'

Eilish Enright

> *Look the world straight in the face.*
>
> HELEN KELLER

One day I was at home making the dinner, watching 'Coronation Street' while waiting for the kids to come home from school. And then next day I was in prison for the abuse and molestation of my own children whom I would never see again. You watch films about this type of thing. They're often based on true stories about American women who end up in prison for a crime they didn't commit. But you never think this type of thing could happen an Irish housewife and mother. You never think someone can come into your home, take your children and lock you up. But they can. I know it to be true because they did it to me.

When I got married and had children I thought it was going to be the beginning of a happy-ever-after fairytale life. I loved being a mother and wife. I had four children one after another and was expecting my fifth but even at that stage of our marriage I could see that 'happy ever after' was not a likely ending.

My husband started to beat me. The beatings would occur regularly, every three days or so. He would always regret his actions, always apologise and promise me it wouldn't happen again. Of course it always happened again. Sometimes it was just a few lashes. Sometimes I felt like I was fighting for my life. The last beating had been particularly vicious and more so because I was pregnant and he could have killed the child. He dragged my by the hair and left me with bald patches. I had a black eye with cuts and bruises. I couldn't take it anymore. I had known for a long time that we needed to leave him but I didn't know where to start. I had no money or means of escape but I needed to get away from him for my children's sake.

I went to speak with a social worker and explained my situation. I told her how I needed her help to start again. She said she had no home available for five children and me. She advised me to go home and to try and work it out. I had no choice so I went home.

He was glad to see me but I think he knew he couldn't trust himself not to hit me again. It was as if he couldn't help himself. He walked out the back door of the house and said he was keeping his promise. He had promised if he hit me again he'd leave me and the kids in peace. I followed him out the door and watched him walk down to the garden shed. I heard the door being locked from the inside. I was afraid that he was going to harm himself so I ran down after him.

'Please open the door. We can talk about this,' I begged as I banged on the wooden shed door with my fists.

'No, I can't,' he said in a voice void of life. 'I promised you if I beat you again that I'd leave you in peace and that's what I'm going to do. Please tell the kids that I love them. I'm sorry,' he said.

'Don't talk ridiculous. Just come out and we can work through this.'

He didn't reply.

I heard the stool crash against the ground, immediately followed by the sound of my husband choking. I knew he had hung himself.

I was six months pregnant but I kicked and shoved the door to try and break it down. I knew my attempts were futile so I ran to get a neighbour. My neighbour ran ahead of me to the shed while I ran behind him out of breath. He reached up and looked through the skylight at the top of the door. His face turned white. What he saw inside filled him with shock and despair. Between us we broke down part of the door but it was too late. My husband hung from the roof with a rope around his neck. The police and ambulance arrived quickly but it was too late — he was already dead.

Thankfully the children were all in bed asleep, all but Richard (5), who had woken up when he heard the ambulance. He peered out the window and I can't begin to comprehend the shock he must have felt when he saw his father hanging from a rope. I'm sure it is an image that has stayed with him.

It was a huge trauma for a child to experience and Richard had behavioural problems after that. He was disruptive in class. He wouldn't sit quietly and get on with his work. In the end his teacher refused to have him in her class. It was hard to accept that he was so disruptive in school because he was well behaved at home, but I realised he needed proper help. I organised for him to go see a psychiatrist in St John of Gods in Dublin. I understood it was the best place to bring him. It was recommended that he attend a residential school for disturbed children. I agreed that we'd start it on a trial basis. The school offered him one-on-one tuition and attention. He flourished in the school and would return home each weekend.

When my husband left us I expected I would be on my own with the kids for the rest of my life. I never thought I'd meet anyone who'd want to take on five kids. Then I met Pat Murphy. He never hit me, he was prepared to take the kids on, and he was good to us — or so I thought — and I agreed to marry him. We had two beautiful children together, so I'd seven children in total.

In 1989, my husband suggested that we should relocate. He was confident that he could secure a better job and lifestyle in Wales. He chose Wales because he had family there who could help us find our feet. I agreed. I felt we all deserved a second chance at happiness. I had to take Richard out of school because I wasn't leaving any of my children behind. It was an adventure for all of us, a chance for us to start again after all we'd been through with my first husband.

When we arrived in Wales my husband's uncle offered us a home with him until we could secure a home of our own. In the beginning things worked out well. Pat got a job driving a bus and the children settled into school. I thought Richard might have adjusted to the local school because he had been doing so well but he was disruptive once more so I organised for him to go to a special residential school similar to the one in Dublin.

One night as we slept, a fire broke out in the house. Richard was the one who smelled the smoke and got everyone out of the house. The fire was caused by an electrical fault at the back of the fridge. The house was destroyed and we couldn't live there again so each of the children went to stay with neighbours and friends until we could arrange alternative accommodation.

Marcella (8) and Pamela (9) stayed with a neighbour. They told the neighbour that when their brother Richard came home at the weekends he pulled down their pants. The neighbour went to a social worker and reported the girls' claim. The social worker came and told me about the accusations. I just couldn't believe it because I hadn't seen anything but I promised to get to the bottom of it. I spoke to each of the children and asked them to tell me what was going on. They said nothing was going on. Richard had just been tickling them.

I wasn't sure what was going on because they had told the neighbour one thing and now they were telling me another thing, so I went back to the social worker and explained what they'd said. I asked her if she would talk to them individually to establish the truth. I felt they might find it easier to speak with a neutral person. I gave her permission to go to my children's schools and speak with them there. The social worker spoke with the children but she didn't reach a conclusion so the dialogue continued.

I thought long and hard about the girls' accusations. On the one hand I said — well Richard is a 13-year-old boy, he's in an all-boys school and you know the way young boys are . . . God only knows what they've been talking about. But I also knew my son and I just knew there was no badness in him. He would never want to hurt his sisters. He was a good child.

When Richard came home the following weekend I didn't take my eyes off him. I watched his every move. I could safely say he didn't do anything that caused alarm bells to ring. Little did I know that I was watching the wrong person.

I told the social workers that I saw nothing to cause concern, but they decided if Richard was allowed home at the weekends the rest of the children would have to stay somewhere else. I felt torn between my children. I didn't want to send the others away because then it would seem like I was punishing the girls for what they'd said. But then again I didn't want to stop Richard from coming home because it would mean that I didn't believe he was telling the truth. In the end I had to protect the majority so Richard stayed in school at the weekends.

In the interim the visits from the social workers continued and I supported them in every way I knew how. During one of the visits Joanne (12) made allegations against her step-father, my then husband Pat Murphy.

I heard about these allegations through the police. When I think back now everything is in slow motion. I had just finished preparing dinner and I was watching 'Coronation Street'. The children were due home from their session with the social workers. I was timing dinner to be ready for their arrival when an unexpected knock came to the door. I opened the door. It was the social worker who had been working with my children, but she was accompanied by the police.

She bluntly said, 'Your husband has been arrested.' The first thought in my head was that he must have been arrested for something to do with the bus. Maybe he was driving recklessly or something. Then she added in a cold and forthright manner, 'Joanne had told us that her step-father has been molesting her. We arrested him off the bus earlier.'

You could have knocked me down with a feather. I went from shock to hysterics in a matter of moments. I would have killed him with my own hands if I'd know he was hurting my daughter in such a manner.

The children, who were aged from 3 to 13, weren't allowed home. They were separated from each other and sent to different foster families, except for Michael who they placed in a mentally handicapped institution even though he was a perfectly normal eleven-year-old. You can imagine how confusing it is for children to be taken from their home and placed with strangers, but for Michael to be put in such an institution almost caused him to have a nervous breakdown. He was devastated. He asked why he'd been put into this institution; could they not let him home or even move him somewhere else. They promised they'd move him somewhere else if he told them the truth about what was going on at home.

I was in bits because I couldn't see the children to comfort them. I was only allowed to visit them once a week. Each Thursday they were brought to a central location where I was allowed a short while with them.

I was told before the meeting that I wasn't allowed to cry because it would upset the children. I wasn't allowed to be emotional. They warned me that if I cried the visit would be ended and I wouldn't be allowed to see them again.

During the first meeting Michael was particularly distressed. He begged me to take him home. The children cried and screamed and asked why they weren't allowed home with me. I tried to explain to them that I wanted to take them home but I wasn't allowed. I couldn't give them a reason because I hadn't been given a reason myself. At the end of the meeting I had to remain stone-faced and couldn't cry as each of my children was physically peeled off me. 'Mammy, do you not want to take us home?' one screamed as I walked away holding back the tears.

'I want you home more than anything. You have to trust me when I tell you I'm fighting this as hard as I can,' I promised.

Michael would sneak out of the institution to see me on Saturday mornings. We'd meet behind the swimming pool. He told me they were asking him lots of questions about me. Then one Saturday morning he didn't show up but his friend came with a note which read, 'Dear Mam, I can't get out anymore but I have the addresses of the houses the others are staying . . .' and there was a list of each of my children's names and addresses. '. . . Please come and get us and take us home. I don't understand what they want me to tell them. They're asking me questions about everyone, even the milkman . . ., please help me, Mam . . .'

I felt like I was letting my children down but I couldn't kidnap them no matter how much I wanted them home.

I had hired a solicitor to try and get my children back. He was going through the proper channels but before we could even reach a conclusion things took a sinister turn.

———

I had seen the children every Thursday for about five weeks. After my last visit the same detectives who arrested Pat Murphy came to my door. I thought they were coming to tell me about the proceedings against Pat Murphy. When I answered the door I was greeted with the following:

'Eilish Murphy, we're arresting you on suspicion of child molestation.'

'What! What are you saying?' I demanded, shocked out of my mind.

'Your children have made allegations against you,' the detective said.

I couldn't reply. I just looked at them. Was this really happening?

'You're Irish?' he asked.

'I am,' I replied.

'Are you Catholic?' he asked.

'I am Catholic,' I said, wondering where he was going with this.

'And tell me do you have a bible in the house?' he asked.

I immediately went and got the bible and put it on the table.

He looked at it and then at me, 'Are you prepared to swear on it?'

Without hesitation I put my hand on the bible and said, 'I swear to almighty God I never touched my kids in a bad way.'

When I finished speaking he picked the bible up off the table and flung it across the room as much as to say, 'That's worthless and your words are worthless.'

I said nothing. I was at his mercy, at the mercy of a man who had already judged me and found me guilty. He pointed at me to sit down beside the kitchen table. I obeyed. Then he told the police who were with him to get started. I didn't know what it was that they were meant to get started with but within seconds I was left in no doubt.

I sat and watched them rip my house apart. They pulled out drawers and threw the contents on the floor. They did the same with wardrobes and presses. I could hear things crash to the ground and break in other rooms. I didn't know what they were looking for and I didn't ask. I now understand they were looking for pictures or video tapes of my alleged abuse. Of course they found nothing in my possession because there was no such tapes, no pictures, no abuse. My house was like any other — filled with a life-time of possessions which I had once so carefully packed and brought from Ireland. To this day I don't know what happened the contents of my house but everything disappeared when I was taken to prison.

The detectives were angry that they found nothing. They looked at me with disgust on their faces. The detective came to speak with me again.

'We know all about you,' he said. 'You're the head of a paedophile ring.'

'The head of what?' I asked.

'Of a paedophile ring!' he said in a loud voice.

I didn't even know what the word 'paedophile' meant but I knew it was something bad from the way they said it. Finally I had to ask them. They said it was an organised group of people who sexually abused children.

'Your children have told us you're the ring leader of this group,' he continued. 'We are going to make you an offer. If you give us the names of the other people who are involved in the ring we'll give you a letter which will ensure you get a lesser sentence.'

'I can't tell you about any paedophile ring because there isn't one,' I pleaded.

'There is', he insisted, 'and there are seventeen children involved in it. We have testimonies from all the children who live around here,' they claimed.

That would have meant they had testimonies from every child on the street!

Finally, they took me away and brought me to prison. I was put in a cell and from then on it was presumed I was guilty. No one would entertain the fact that I might be innocent. They gave me a terrible time in the cell. I couldn't really sleep. I was terrified out of my mind. One night, in the early hours, a female detective came into my cell and woke me up. She was accompanied by a male detective. She said in a hurried voice, 'You have to get up and take us to your uncle-in-law's house. You said it was in that house that a faulty door fell on your daughter Nikita and that is how she broke her arm. We need to see that door but we can't find the house. Will you show us where it is?'

'I will,' I said getting up quickly, anxious to help with anything that could prove my innocence. The uncle-in-law had already verified what had happened in relation to the door. He had told the authorities that the door was faulty and that it had fallen on Nikita. He also confirmed that I wasn't even in the house at the time.

I got into the detective's car. They sat in the front and I sat in the back. The doors were locked and it was dark outside. They drove a distance and then one of them said, 'We don't believe you. We think you broke little Nikita's arm.'

'What?' I said, noticing we weren't going in the direction of my uncle-in-law's house.

'We think you grabbed Nikita's little arm in your hands and snapped it like a piece of wood. We know this is true because one of your children told us.'

The medical records would later verify that the break wasn't consistent with this story. The nature of the injury was sustained most likely by something heavy falling on her arm.

The cars continued to speed down unfamiliar roads. Finally they pulled in beside a river. I realised we were never going to my uncle-in-law's house. That was just a ploy to get me out of my cell without a fuss.

'We're going to throw you into the river unless you tell us the truth,' one of them said. 'I've told you the truth, I've told you the truth,' I said over and over again.

'You will be sent to Puckle Church Remand Centre in Bristol and we have people in there who are going to beat you from one end of the day to the next. That is what your life is going to be like unless you tell us the truth,' they threatened.

Again I pleaded my innocence and begged them to believe me.

'This is your last chance. Tell us the truth and we'll make sure you're looked after in Puckle Church. You'll serve easy time . . .'

'I'm telling you the truth . . . I don't know what else to say . . .'

I thought they were going to throw me into the river and say that I fell in trying to escape or something. I was terrified. This questioning went on for hours. I thought it would never end. Finally they drove me back to the cell.

I was refused bail and was on remand for six months at Puckle Church Remand Centre until my case came to trial. I kept telling myself that the truth would have to come out in court. That's what courts are for ... I believed in the judicial system.

My family in Ireland stood by me and came over for the court case. They knew better than to believe the allegations. I had no contact with Pat Murphy. He disgusted me. I couldn't comprehend what he had done. To think I shared a bed with him still makes me physically ill.

When I arrived in court Pat Murphy told the judge that I had nothing to do with the abuse, that I didn't know there was anything going on, that I was a good mother. It made no difference. Who was going to believe the likes of him? He pleaded guilty to the abuse. He told the police when they arrested him that he was waiting for them. He said he knew it was only a matter of time.

He was sentenced to 15 years but got out early for good behaviour. He never tried to contact me. He deserved everything he got and more. It's hard to believe that you can live with someone and think you know them but you never know what goes on in anyone's mind.

———

I feel now that I was unprepared for my court case. The first time I met my barrister was in court at my trial. I hadn't discussed my case with him but I didn't know any better. I hadn't been through this process before and I just accepted that they knew what they were doing.

The allegations against me were horrendous, and difficult to repeat. It was said that I stuck hot pokers up the children's bottoms. That I quenched my cigarettes against their skin. That I held my children down so that they could be molested and raped by the milkman. That my son was held down so that I could rape him. It was despicable.

Richard came into the courtroom. He testified behind a screen. He said that my husband held me down and that he was made to have intercourse with me and then I had to get up on top of him and do the same. When Richard finished his testimony, Joanne came into the courtroom. She was to reiterate her observation of the same incident. Their stories didn't match. When she was asked which house the incident occurred in she named a different house to the one that Richard had identified. She went on to claim she saw what happened through the bedroom window of the house, but there was no way she could have seen anything through a bedroom window because the house that she claimed the abuse occurred in was a two-storey house. Under questioning not one part of her story matched Richard's. It was clear that the truth was not being told. There was a hung jury and thereafter the jury was cancelled and a new jury was brought in for the next trial.

This time Michael came into the courtroom and sat behind the screen. He said that I held him down so that the milkman could bugger him and that afterwards I told him to 'go out to play'. When he was asked a question he hesitated in his answers as if he was trying to remember something that had been rehearsed. So much so that the judge stopped him and asked him if there was someone in the waiting room with him coaching him the answers. He said he was alone in the room. It would later emerge that there was a social worker in the room with him the whole time.

The milkman was also on trial for molestation of my children. I was only acquainted with him because the kids worked with him on a Saturday morning delivering milk. They took the job for some extra pocket money, in the same way that some kids deliver newspapers. They weren't forced to work with him. It was by choice.

The milkman stood up in court and said he had never been

inside the door of my house, that he was only acquainted with me and had never harmed my children. However, we were both found guilty of that one charge involving Michael.

The case continued the next day. They brought Richard in to tell his story. He reiterated the same story he had told to the previous jury. This time they didn't bring Joanne into testify. They knew her testimony would cast doubt on the veracity of Richard's recollection. I demanded that Joanne be called to testify but the judge said she was a witness for the prosecutor so we couldn't call her. I didn't understand the legal system and felt out of my depth and totally helpless.

The seventeen children who were previously alleged to be involved in the paedophile ring never emerged in court because they didn't exist. The prosecution never mentioned the earlier allegations that had been put to me, i.e. putting out cigarettes on my kids' bodies, breaking Nikita's arm, or the ordeals I was meant to have put them through with hot pokers. They didn't mention them in court because they knew they were untrue and medical evidence would have proven them to be so.

The milkman was sentenced to fifteen years and I was sentenced to six years. Our convictions were based solely on word of mouth, the testimony of two children. There was no medical evidence, no doctor's testimonies, no witnesses — nothing.

I felt like I was living through a nightmare. I didn't believe that it was real. It just couldn't be. I was in a state of confusion and shock. And the thoughts of going to Cookhamwood prison in Kent filled me with fear. It is a large women's prison, home to some of the most notorious killers. I realised I'd probably be the only Irish woman there and that I'd also be a target because of my alleged crime.

————

I arrived at Cookhamwood prison. It was a frightening place. You go to bed one night and you wake up the next morning to find Myra Hindley is your next-door cellmate. She didn't say much. She used to call me 'Paddy' because I'm Irish. She didn't say it in a malicious way. Lots of people in prison called me 'Paddy'. She looked normal until you looked in her eyes. They had an unnerving darkness about them, void of emotion. I kept out of her way.

When I first went to prison I had to share a cell. My cellmate was okay. She was in for grievous bodily harm. We had little in common except that we were both frightened of prison. We didn't know what to expect. I didn't know how I was going to survive. So I just tried to take one moment at a time.

If you behave well in prison you're rewarded so I was quickly given my own cell. It's good to have the privacy but it's also lonely. No matter what luxuries you're given, be it an extra pillow or a radio, it doesn't matter because at the end of the day you're still locked up. It's still prison.

Most of the women in the prison were armed robbers; there were a lot of drugs people and then some murderers. There was a woman who had killed her foster children. Their bodies had been found cut up in suitcases in Piccadilly. She totally flipped one day and ended up drowning herself in a basin of water.

Each prisoner had her own way of getting through her time. For some it was with the help of drugs. Others made sure they were feared. And then there was always someone who just couldn't adjust, who couldn't cope. I was determined I wouldn't fall into any of those categories.

The one thing that everyone in prison would agree upon is that there is nothing to look forward to, so I thought I'd make something for people to look forward to. I put on stage shows and entertained the inmates with singing and performances. Once I organised a 'Miss Universe' competition which went down a treat. I dressed up as the Irish entry, 'Biddy Diddler the dancer'. I wore pinstriped Wellington boots and a country style outfit and I won! How everyone laughed . . . For that one hour everyone, including myself, forgot we were in prison and that's how I kept going. I kept taking on new projects: a Christmas show, one at Easter, Halloween, New Year . . . And in between I tried to better myself. I did a course in hairdressing and then in bakery. The latter course helped me get a job in the kitchen as a pastry chef.

And the shows meant that the other inmates liked me. No one was going to hurt someone who brought happiness, an escape from the monotony of daily prison life. I made some friends in prison. I told them the truth — that I was innocent. They believed me because I had no reason to lie to them. Around this time I found out that my appeal had been rejected. I was gutted. That was my last chance discarded.

Then the inmates did something extraordinary. They started a writing campaign to have me freed. I remember they wrote to Ester Rantzen who had a chat show which carried a lot of clout. We thought she might draw media attention to my story. Then the authorities would have to review my case. It seems naïve in hindsight but we were desperate. Unsurprisingly, Ester Rantzen didn't reply. But this didn't deter the girls. They continued to write. The replies they received, though courteous, were unhelpful.

Not a day passed that I didn't think of my children, but I wasn't allowed any contact with them. They were all sent to different foster homes. I thought about them constantly. On each of their birthdays I lit a match as if it was a birthday candle and then I made a wish and blew it out. I always wished for the same thing: that I could be with my children. I wondered if they were having a birthday party, were they missing me too? I'd try to picture how they looked a year on from when I last saw them, two years on . . . I knew one day we'd be reunited but I just didn't know how or when . . .

My prison time wasn't as hard as it might have been for other people because at night time I was 'free' — I'd go out dancing, or I'd go home to be with my children or I might go for dinner or to the pub for chats with my sisters. At night I was never in prison. During those hours I was free. I visited these places through my imagination.

I might have physically been in prison but my imagination could bring me anywhere. In prison they can take everything from you but they can't take your memories, your mind, even when everything has been stripped from you — your dignity, your self respect, your children, your honour. Even then you have choices, and I chose to be positive, and that has made all the difference.

———

When I had completed two-thirds of my sentence I was allowed home leave from a Friday to Monday. I had served two years and two months. In that time my dad had died and I had missed the funeral. I'd never even seen him sick or got the opportunity to say goodbye. So I was anxious to go home to Ireland to at least visit his grave and pay my respects. Needless to say I was also desperate to see my mother and my family. I made the journey back to Kildare.

I stayed with my sisters. The weekend came and went and I was due back in prison. But I just didn't go back. I thought the police would be at my door within hours because the prison authorities knew the address at which I was staying. All they had to do was contact the local Gardaí. I waited and waited but no knock came to my door. Weeks turned into months and still no knock came. To this day I still don't understand why they didn't seek my extradition back to prison.

I wanted to clear my name. I wanted to get my children back. But I wasn't sure where to start. I was a fugitive which meant I hadn't the law on my side and I didn't want to draw it on me because I was enjoying each day of being at home. Just to do normal things meant so much to me.

I met a man with whom I began a relationship and we had a child together in the 1990s. Not long afterwards I received an urgent phonecall from my sister to tell me that Joanne, my daughter, had been in touch with her and wanted to contact me. Soon afterwards she phoned me. When I'd last seen her she was a little girl. I couldn't believe this girl of seventeen on the other end of the phone was my Joanne. It seemed like fate — that after all this time she should try to make contact with the family and she hadn't even known I was back in Kildare.

We talked for hours about everything, everything except the allegations. We must have talked 24 hours straight. It was a very tearful conversation. I felt overwhelmed with emotion so Joanne did most of the talking and I just listened. At the end of the conversation she said, 'Mam, can I come home?'

'Of course,' I replied enthusiastically. The following day I bought her ticket to come home from Wales. I was so happy to have her back. I thought it was the best day of my life.

A week later my two sons, Richard (19) and Michael (16), arrived unexpectedly at my sister Kathleen's house. Kathleen's house was always a base because she never moved, though the children hadn't been allowed to stay in contact with her. When she told them I was home they immediately wanted to see me. Kathleen phoned me with the news. I dropped everything and made my way up to her house. I couldn't believe I was going to see another two of my children. I walked into the living-room and I nearly died when I saw these two grown men standing before me. The last time I'd seen them they were little boys and now they towered over me. They ran to me and gave me a hug. I looked up at their faces and thought, 'Things can't get any better than this.'

I had wondered so many times what the children grew up to look like . . . and here they were standing before me. The moment I'd wished for was at last here. I couldn't take my eyes off them. They were both six foot two and handsome.

We shared tears and hugs and couldn't even speak, such was the level of emotion. Then we sat down and talked for Ireland. I was anxious to know everything I'd missed out on. Most of all I wanted to know who they'd been living with, had they been happy. They hadn't been so happy and that was hard to hear. I guess I was asking a lot of questions when Michael interrupted me and said, 'Can I ask you one question?'

'Ask me anything you want,' I said.

He looked into my face with sadness in his eyes and asked, 'Can I call you Mammy?'

I just cried with happiness. It was a very special moment and his words will stay in my head forever.

We stayed up all night talking. Every minute was more precious than the next. I didn't want the night to end. As with Joanne we spoke about everything except the abuse. Finally Michael broke down and said he was sorry and that he knew I did nothing wrong. 'But why did you say it when you knew it wasn't true?' I asked.

He explained to me that the social worker asked him again and again if I was involved in the abuse. She told Michael if he admitted it she would have him moved from the handicapped institution. Each time he asked to be moved she replied, 'Only when you tell me about what your mother did.' So finally he told her what she wanted to hear and he was moved from the institution within hours. He didn't understand the repercussions of this. He never thought I'd go to prison.

I told him that it wasn't his fault. I never blamed him or any of my children for what had happened. They were only children. It was adults who were in charge, who were relied upon for making sure that justice prevailed. If a child is told by adults that something is one way then he believes it because the adult is always in a position of authority, of power. Richard and Joanne then confided to me that they too feel they had been manipulated into making allegations. For example, a social worker would tell Richard that Joanne said she saw me being forced to have relations with him so he may as well admit it. Then they would go to Joanne and say Richard said you saw him being abused . . .

The children said they wanted to help me clear my name, so the next morning we went to the solicitor together. We told him our story and asked him to help us. He told me he'd see what he could do but he didn't promise me anything.

———

Three years had passed and the police hadn't come to take me back to prison so I thought they never would. I felt sure that I'd be able to clear my name through the legal process. But in the meantime I had four children who needed a proper home. The house we were staying in was too small. I couldn't afford a bigger one so I had to apply to the council for public housing. They sent a social worker around to see me and I didn't want to lie to him so I reiterated to him my whole story. I guess he was obliged to alert the authorities. Before I knew it the Gardaí were at my door taking away my youngest child, then only two. They brought me to Mountjoy prison where I was on remand for ten weeks.

Mountjoy prison was a nightmare. It was a hard time. I thought I'd never get out of the place. I would do another ten years in an English prison before I'd stay in Mountjoy prison for one night. I'm sure it would have been no worse than any other prison except for the fact that accounts of my case had appeared in the newspapers and the inmates believed I was a child abuser. Thereafter my life was made a living hell.

They did everything to intimidate me. They spat at me when I walked by. They hissed. On one occasion they came into my cell and urinated on my bed clothes and personal effects. I couldn't have normal visits with my family because they'd shout obscenities at me, they'd shout things like 'paedophile'. It was a lonely time for me. I had no one to speak with but I wouldn't give in to them. I didn't allow them to intimidate me. I came out of my cell during my recreation time. I kept telling myself, I'm not going to hide away, I have done nothing wrong. The guards were nice enough to me. I couldn't really chat with them but at least they prevented anyone attacking me.

While I was in Mountjoy prison a detective from Puckle Church

Remand Centre arrived in Ireland. She was one of the detectives who had previously brought me to the river and threatened to throw me in. I knew she would try to make things more difficult for me. She appeared in the court when my bail was being applied for. It wasn't expected that I would get bail because I had absconded. The detective confirmed I had absconded from the British prison. In court my barrister asked the detective whether, if I were successful in getting bail, she would ask for my passport to be handed in.

She said, 'That won't arise because she's not getting bail.'

My barrister repeated his question. 'I didn't ask you if she'd get bail. I asked you if you'd request for her to hand in her passport?'

'I'm telling you she's not getting bail! She's not,' the woman demanded.

The judge looked over at her.

'She's not getting bail,' the woman repeated once more.

My barrister sat down and whispered to me, 'That's it. You've got bail.'

'How do you know?' I asked.

'Before he could answer the judge said, "Bail granted".'

I gather the judge wasn't going to let a detective from another country sit in his courtroom and tell him what to do. It's funny the way things work out. The woman who came over here to destroy me ended up helping me. She was ripping mad. I couldn't help but smile, though my smile didn't last for long because the bail amount was set for €10,000. My family didn't have that type of money and I certainly didn't have it. Nonetheless they tried to figure out a way to get the money. In the end my sister Noreen put up her house as security. She knew I wouldn't run away. I wouldn't leave my children and I wouldn't let her down. She also knew that I was anxious to see my mother who had become quite ill. This took a lot out of her. So I went home but I had to sign on at the police station in Newbridge each day for the next three years (1995 to 1998).

Some local people were supportive of me but of course others weren't and there are the few incidents that stay with you. I remember girls whom I went to school with would snub me when they came face to face with me. One in particular would cross the street when she saw me approaching. I remember when I got out of prison I mustered up the courage to say 'hello' to her but she just looked at me and crossed the street. I told people I had an appeal but it meant nothing. I knew people were talking about me. I knew what they were saying. But I refused to hide away because I'd done nothing wrong.

One Mother's Day when three of the children were home I went to the pub with my family. One of my sisters got up to sing a song and when she finished people clapped. Then she said, 'Come on Eilish, you're next.' I started singing but someone in the pub turned up a radio until it drowned out my singing. I stopped singing. I felt humiliated. A woman in the pub turned to me and shouted, 'You! You've no right to sing on Mother's Day. You've no right to even call yourself a mother!'

That was it. I'd heard enough. I didn't reply but I stood back up and I continued to sing and they turned the radio up even louder and I sang even louder and I finished my song. And when I finished singing I sat down and finished my drink. Even though I might have felt like going home I didn't. I had as much right to be there as anyone else.

I felt more determined than ever and I was happy that my solicitor in Dublin put me in touch with another solicitor in London who agreed to take on my case in England. He warned me that we had a long road ahead of us. I never realised how long it would be . . .

While I was out on bail I wasn't allowed take home my baby, who was living with foster parents and called them mam and dad. I realised if I was ever to have a relationship with my baby I'd have to clear my name. Otherwise I wouldn't be allowed near my own child.

The measures I took next may seem drastic but I was left with little alternative. I realised my appeal would take years and years so I chose to go back to prison and finish my sentence. Otherwise I could be signing on in the garda station for the following ten years and at the end of it I could still have to go back and finish my sentence. The second reason was because my appeal had to be heard in a British court but if I set foot on British soil I'd be arrested and put in prison, and it could have been any prison.

I wasn't scared of going back to prison. I knew what to expect. I was prepared this time and I carefully packed my suitcase as if I was going on holidays. It was great to be able to arrive there prepared because the last time I had nothing but the clothes on my back. But no matter how familiar, prison was far from a holiday.

The process of getting back into the same prison wasn't as simple as just arriving at the door with my suitcase. I had to make a request to be put back into prison. I'm sure it's the first time that the judge received such a request but I wrote him a nice letter and explained to him why I needed to go back to prison. He granted me permission.

So after three years of being free I was extradited back to Cookhamwood Prison in Kent. The governor was at the gate to meet me. He had a smile on his face. He said, 'I've no hair left worrying about you.' I knew the governor well. I used to work in the orchard in the grounds of his home, picking apples. It was a job given to those who could be trusted. I had also been given the task of bringing handicapped people swimming three days a week. I felt that this was an admission by the prison that I was innocent; otherwise they wouldn't have allowed me to work with vulnerable people.

Before my appeal could be processed my solicitor had to take my case to the Criminal Cases Review Committee (CCRV). The CCRV looks at cases that have already been refused an appeal and decides whether or not another appeal should be granted.

I thought it would take them a few weeks to review my case but it took them five years. In March 2003 the CCRV contacted me to congratulate me that it had taken on my case. Accepting a case is not something the Committee does lightly, hence the long wait. In the meantime I had finished my sentence in prison and returned to Kildare where I was living with my children.

The CCRV carried out detailed research into my case. They reviewed all the old records, statements, testimonies and checked and rechecked everything. When they gathered enough information it was sent to the Court of Criminal Appeal who decided if there was a reason why my case should be overturned. They only needed to find one reason to have the case overturned but they found twelve reasons. The prosecution claimed they had video evidence of Michael's confession, yet when a copy of this video evidence was requested they couldn't produce it; they said there wasn't a video in the camera at the time of the interview. They also interviewed him for 6 hours and twenty minutes without a break — this in itself is not permitted. All the children were medically examined by a team of people and the evidence that the medical team found would have helped prove I was innocent. Yet it wasn't admitted or disclosed in court. In fact I was told that the children wouldn't allow medical examinations to be done on them. The social workers who were involved in the case refused to be interviewed by the CCRC. And there was no record of my previous appeal.

———

By this stage I had been reunited with most of my children. Marcella (19) had been in touch with a sister of mine and she allowed me to phone her. Slowly we built up a relationship. I was a stranger to her because she was nine the last time she saw me. She invited me to visit her in Wales and while I was there she introduced me to her other sister, Pamela (20). It was, as with the other children, a tearful reunion. I had missed out on such a big part of the girls' lives but I'm overjoyed to have them in my life now.

I realised it was going to be more difficult to find Patrick and Nikita because they had been adopted by two different families. I'm not sure why this was allowed because I hadn't given permission for these adoptions to take place. I began my search to find them. I felt I was certainly entitled to know if they were happy and well and with whom they were living. I didn't want to disrupt their lives. I just needed to be reassured that they were happy, but the authorities refused me their records.

It so happened that while I was looking for Patrick he was looking for me. He took leave from the British Army — he was serving in Germany — to come to Kildare in 2004 to find his mother. The only information he had to go on was my married name, 'Eilish Murphy'.

He got the bus to Kildare and walked up and down the street asking people did they know 'Eilish Murphy'. People here now know me as 'Eilish Enright' so the answer he received time and again was 'no'.

He spent the day searching but no one could help him. His bus was due to arrive to take him back to Dublin when he noticed some young lads in the square and thought he'd give it one last go.

'My mother's name is Eilish Murphy. She came from this town and I'm trying to find her. Do you know her?' he asked.

'Do you have a brother named Michael?' one of the boys said.

'I do', he replied, hopefully.

'And a sister named Joanne?'

'Yes, yes, that's right!'

'Ah, sure we know Michael. We'll phone him for you.'

The chap took out his mobile phone and called Michael. He told Michael there was a young man called Patrick who was looking for his mother. Michael came down immediately and met Patrick. He hadn't seen him in 9 years so it was a special and unexpected reunion. Patrick wanted to immediately meet me so Michael phoned me and asked:

'Do you mind if I bring a friend home?'

'Sure that's no problem,' I said. Then he mentioned that he wanted to get a taxi because he was in a rush to get home, so I said I'd leave out some money as I was going to have a bath and an early night.

I had a quick bath and was about to get into bed when I heard Michael arrive home. He came straight down to my room and knocked on the door.

'Mam, you have to come into the sitting-room and say hello to my friend.'

'Michael, I'm only out of the bath. I'm not in a fit state to be greeting guests.'

But Michael insisted and I didn't want to disappoint him. I walked into the sitting-room and Michael introduced his friend. 'This is Patrick.'

We shook hands and I welcomed him but I was anxious to get back to my room.

However, I noticed when I walked into the sitting-room that Michael's friend was staring at a fire screen I'd made. The front of the screen is made up of photographs of all my children. I noticed he was looking at one picture in particular. It was picture of my son Patrick when he was about 9 years of age.

Michael could see I was about to make a swift exit so he said, 'Well, Mam, has he changed much?'

'Has who changed much?' I asked, not understanding what he was on about.

Then he pointed toward the picture on the fire screen. I looked at the picture of Patrick and then I looked at this fine man standing before me and I let a scream out of me, 'Patrick?'

I was overjoyed; I hugged him and ran up and down the sitting-room like a mad woman. I couldn't contain my happiness. I ran in screaming to Joanne who lived next door. She was pregnant at the time and she almost had the child there and then with all the excitement.

My court appeal hearing was set for October 2005 but two weeks before my hearing I received a message from my solicitor in London telling me to call him urgently because he had some news for me. He was out of the office when I called and wouldn't be back till late that evening. His secretary knew me by voice because I'd called so many times before. She didn't know what news he had for me so I began to think the worst. Finally at a quarter to eight that evening the phone rang. It was my solicitor on the other end apologetic for the lateness of the call.

'The social workers have pulled out. They won't testify against you,' he announced.

'What does that mean exactly?' I said, afraid to jump with joy in case there was a 'but' coming.

'That means you've won your appeal. They're not going to challenge you,' he said.

I didn't know what to say, I felt such mixed emotions. For fifteen years the social workers put me through hell and now they weren't even going to face me in court.

The judge ordered for the milkman to be contacted so that he would know that his case was opened for appeal. I hate to think what that poor man went through. When he was sent to prison he left behind a wife and kids. It's horrendous. I'm sure the recovery has been one hell of a battle for him as it has been for me and my family. But the battle was worth it because on 13 October 2005 I finally cleared my name. It took a big weight of guilt off Michael's shoulders because he had blamed himself for my going to prison. Now we all have to look forward. We have been living in the past for long enough.

––––

The only thing that matters to me now is the only thing that ever mattered to me, and that's my children. Each of them is doing well and they make me proud and happy. My youngest child is twelve, is doing fantastically well at school and is very talented at sport. Just

Roisin and Mark McConnell   (© Photocall Ireland)

Detective Sergeant John White   (© Empics)

Roisin and Mark McConnell with their son Dean and new baby Jamie
(© Roisin and Mark McConnell)

Mr Justice Frederick Morris   (© The Irish Times)

Linda Reed with her mother (© Linda Reed)

Linda Reed (© Linda Reed)

Eilish Enright   (© Eilish Enright)

Detective Garda Ben O'Sullivan, colleague of Detective Garda Jerry McCabe
(© Press 22)

Ann McCabe with the bronze memorial of her late husband, Detective Garda
Jerry McCabe   (© Press 22)

An early photograph of Ann and Jerry McCabe   (© Ann McCabe)

Detective Garda Jerry McCabe in uniform   (© Ann McCabe)

The McCartney sisters   (© Photocall Ireland)

Robert McCartney   (© Pacemaker Press International)

Bridgeen Hagans, Robert McCartney's partner, with their sons   (© Empics)

Robert McCartney's funeral   (© Empics)

Janette Byrne during recovery   (© Janette Byrne)

Janette Byrne, one of the founders of Patients Together   (© Photocall Ireland)

Janette Byrne and her mother protesting over the A&E crisis

(© Photocall Ireland)

Mary Gough and Colin Whelan's wedding day   (© Mary Gough)

Mary Gough's Holy Communion   (© Mary Gough)

Marie Gough at home   (© AllPix)

after his second birthday, my baby was taken from me. I'm not sure if my child even remembers our life together, having lived with the same foster family for the last eight years. They are called Mam and Dad and their other children are brothers and sisters. They are all very happy and they're wonderful people. After my name was cleared I could have insisted that my child came home to live with me but I wouldn't do that because it would be too disruptive. All I want is for my children to be happy. What makes them happy makes me happy. I wouldn't force my child to come home. I said that I could be visited any time and now we're at the stage that we spend weekends together. It's sad that I've lost so many years of my child's life and that I wasn't allowed visits until my name was cleared. But we can't dwell on the past. We have to rebuild our relationship into the future.

Nikita is the only one of my children with whom I haven't been reunited. She was adopted by a family when she was seven. Her siblings have told me that they were brought together for her 'goodbye party', and that was the last day they ever saw their sister. We have been searching for her but it's difficult because she is now living under another name and I'm not sure if she'd even remember me. She was only three when she was taken away from me. I have hired a solicitor to help me fight for access to her adoption files.

When I go to Wales I'm constantly searching for her. I presume that's where she lives because that's where she was taken into care. I'm always searching for her in crowds, wondering could this or that girl be my daughter. I've no idea what she'd look like now. She'd be 20 years old now. I haven't seen her for 17 years. I wonder does she even remember me.

Once when my sister Kathleen and I were in a pub in Wales we heard a girl singing. I immediately thought I recognised the voice because the girl's singing voice was similar to my own. Then we saw the girl's face and myself and Kathleen just looked at each other because we were both thinking the same thing, 'It's Nikita.' She looked incredibly like my other daughter Marcella and was about the same age as Nikita would be. When she finished her song I went up to her and said, 'Nikita?' but she said, 'No, I'm . . .' So I just walked away.

Of course I have since found out that Nikita's name was changed when she was adopted so maybe this girl was my daughter. I still don't know her adoptive name but my solicitor is trying to get this information released to me. I wonder what she's doing with her life. Is she in college, or working? Does she think of me and her siblings? I'd love her to be reunited with us. I don't expect her to give up her new family, but there is so much she is missing out on in our family — family weddings, births, celebrations ... For example her two sisters Marcella and Pamela are expecting babies. They both married Welsh men last year. Pamela got married two days after I won my appeal, so that made it an extra special family day.

I see all the other children regularly. Each of them has been through hell and they all have their own story to tell, but I'm happy that they are doing well for themselves. Michael (27) successfully runs his own scaffolding business and lives nearby. Joanne (27) also lives locally and has three children; she's a full-time mum. Patrick (22) was based with the army in Germany but since he found me he has relocated to Kildare and works as a paver. Marcella (24) works in a bakery in Wales. She lives with her husband. Pamela (25) is a vegetarian chef in a hospital and is also happily married. Richard (30) lives in England. He's a handyman. My youngest child is very talented and could do anything in life.

This experience has tested us all. I'm not yet sure what I've learned because I've been too busy just getting through it. Sometimes when I think back on my story I don't know how I got through it. Sometimes you don't know your own strength until it's tested.

I'm not bitter about anything. In my heart I always knew the truth would come out. I just wasn't sure how it would happen. It was important for me to have proved my innocence because otherwise people would have continued to look at me with disdain and disgust. These looks were hard to take and led to a certain type of isolation which was a prison in itself, but that's over now.

I can't afford to carry hate ... This story has already taken away too much from me. I won't let it take what happiness is due to me. The main reason I've agreed to tell my story now is in hope that it can help trace Nikita, that one day she might know the truth about me. And I want Nikita to know we're searching for her. That I'm here for her day or night. I'm always ready, always waiting for her call.

I'm going to keep on searching for her. I have no intention of ever stopping. One day I'll find her. I need to know she's happy. I guess that's all any mother wants for her children.

Chapter 4

'In the end they always fall'

Ann McCabe

*No one ever told me that grief felt so like fear.
I am not afraid, but the sensation is like being
afraid. The same fluttering in the stomach, the
same restlessness, the yawning, I keep on
swallowing. At other times it feels like being
mildly drunk, or concussed. There is a sort of
invisible blanket between the world and me. I find
it hard to take in what anyone says. Or perhaps,
hard to want to take it in. It is so uninteresting.
Yet I want the others to be about me. I dread the
moment when the house is empty. If only they
would talk to one another and not to me . . .*

C.S. LEWIS

'Oh Jesus, Jerry!' shouted Detective Garda Ben O'Sullivan when he
looked into the rear view mirror of his garda car and saw a Pajero
Jeep with a bullbar approaching at unrelenting speed. The jeep's
driver and the man sitting beside him in the passenger seat were
wearing balaclavas and army combats. Their intentions were
obvious and imminent. They were going to ram the unmarked
special branch garda car that was guarding an An Post delivery of
money. Their aim was to seriously hurt, disorientate and
demobilise Detective Garda Ben O'Sullivan and Detective Garda
Jerry McCabe who sat in the garda car.

Seconds earlier, the garda car had come to a halt a short distance behind the An Post van which was delivering pensioners' money to the local post-office in the quiet tourist village of Adare, Co. Limerick. An Post driver William Jackson had already got out of his vehicle, opened the back door, and entered the rear of the lorry where the money was kept.

It was 6.55 a.m., a sunny June morning. The village was still asleep and there was nothing unusual to alert the suspicions of the veteran detectives. That was until the birds' morning chorus was replaced by the sound of a car engine devouring the road. By the time Ben had uttered the words, 'Oh Jesus, Jerry!' their car had been rammed at great force from behind. They had no time to react or take control of the situation even though the detectives were armed with an Uzi sub-machine gun and their standard issued firearms — A38 Smith and Wessons.

The impact of the crash snapped Ben's arm and forced his seat forward, pushing him against the steering wheel. Within seconds a Mitsubishi Lancer, which was driven by a man wearing a balaclava, crashed into the side of the garda car. The two men who were inside the jeep now stood at either side of the garda car brandishing AK47 Kalashnikov assault rifles. They began to shoot through the windows; the first blast hit Ben's shoulder; the second blew his hands off the steering wheel; and the third hit the side of his head. In all there were five armed men surrounding the garda car.

Ben fell over on top of Jerry who was in the passenger seat. He saw Jerry's hands go into spasms and his arm changed colours. He called out three times to his friend and colleague, 'Jerry? Jerry? Jerry?' There was no reply. He reached for his wrist to find a pulse. He realised his friend was dead. The bullets that hit Ben ricocheted through him and then hit Jerry. The results were fatal.

William Jackson had heard the impact of the garda car being rammed and the round of ammunition being fired. Terrified, he emerged from the back of the van. He held his arms high in the air and sat submissively on the footpath beside his van wondering would he be next. A gun was held to his head and a quick discussion ensued as to whether or not they should kill him. By this stage they thought both Gardaí were dead.

'Go, go, leave him,' one of the men shouted frantically.

Thereafter they ran to the getaway Mitsubishi Lancer, aborting their plan to rob the contents of the An Post van.

Ben heard their base radioing through to the car. He reached to pick up the radio receiver but his hand had lost all strength and the receiver fell to the ground. He had been hit with eleven bullets.

William Jackson ran to his aid and picked up the radio to call for help. Ben was about to fall into unconsciousness but was fighting it. He told the An Post driver what to do to stop the bleeding. William followed his direction and talked to him, trying to keep him conscious.

First at the scene at 7 a.m. was local curate Fr Denis Mullane, who whispered the Last Rites to Jerry. He was accompanied by local doctor Nick Van Kuyik, who quickly realised it was too late for Jerry. He had been hit by three bullets, one in the back of his throat and two in his lungs. He died of massive haemorrhaging. Jerry's body was left in the car. The doctor covered it with a blanket.

Ben O'Sullivan was rushed to Limerick Regional Hospital. His wife, Ann, a nurse at the hospital was not on duty, but rushed from the family home in Corbally. Ben suffered massive bullet wounds to his upper body and required emergency surgery. He was later transferred by Air Corps helicopter for further treatment in Belfast. Ben was of robust physique, developed through his involvement in tug-of-war competitions; this may have helped to save his life.

He was a well-respected member of the force. In 1994 he had received a gold Scott Medal for disarming a man who stood at Childers Road and pointed a loaded shotgun at motorists. He received a second gold Scott Medal after this robbery and is the only guard to hold two such medals.

——

Ann McCabe's voice understandably trembles when she speaks of her husband's death:

> I never expected that Jerry would die in the line of duty. He was dedicated to his job but he always put his family first. He would

never have knowingly put himself in the line of fire because he loved his family too much for that. He wouldn't have wanted to leave his five children without a father and me without a best friend, a husband, a confidant.

On the morning of Jerry's murder he got up as usual at about 5 a.m. He called out to me, looking for an ironed shirt. I pointed him in the direction of a selection of shirts I'd ironed the day before. He took pride in his appearance. After he got dressed, he made a flask of tea which he brought with him in the car — tea he never got the chance to drink. He gave me a goodbye kiss and said he'd back at 10 a.m. for his break.

He was particularly full of life and happiness that morning because in two weeks time we were due to go on holidays to Spain with two friends. The holiday had been planned for a while and we were really looking forward to it. Jerry was also looking forward to retirement. He would have retired earlier except he wanted to build up one more year of hours for his pension. He was excited about his future. He had always been interested in plumbing and electrics and did odd jobs for people. Demand for his work was so great that he planned to do it full time in retirement; he liked the flexibility of the hours.

The phone rang uncharacteristically early on the morning of Jerry's death. It was a family friend; he told me that there had been some type of accident in Adare. He didn't say anymore. I phoned the garda station in Henry Street in Limerick but I couldn't get through. It was odd that all the lines should be busy so early in the morning. I tried a few times and then I gave up. I wasn't unduly concerned that anything had happened Jerry.

Then the doorbell rang. I wasn't expecting anyone. I was still in my dressing-gown so I didn't rush to answer it. The ringing was polite but persistent. When I opened the door I saw a man standing there. I didn't notice the bangarda at that stage. The man introduced himself as Detective Inspector John Kerin from the Henry Street station.

'Are you Ann McCabe?' he asked.

'I am,' I said.

'I have bad news,' he said, pausing before he continued. 'Jerry has been injured.'

'How bad is it?' I asked, never thinking for a minute that he was already dead. He didn't break the news to me there and then. First he asked, 'Who is here with you?'

'My daughter Stacey and my son Ross,' I said. They were upstairs studying for exams. Stacey was doing her Leaving Cert and Ross was doing his Junior Cert.

Then he told me, 'I'm afraid Jerry's dead, Ann,' he said.

The children were coming down the stairs as he said it. I roared and screamed. The children were hysterical. Within minutes the house seemed to be full of people. They had brought great back-up for us, a doctor, a counsellor . . . But I don't remember much more after hearing the news. I went into total shock. I remember at some point during the day finding Ross with his head under the covers of his bed and that's how he stayed for the day. He couldn't bear to speak with anyone. He was only 15 and was terribly close to his dad. None of us could cope. It was too much.

My eldest son John is also a garda and he was on the same shift as his dad but he was based in Monaghan. He heard on the garda radio that a member of the force had been killed. He called the station in Henry Street. At first they wouldn't give him information and then he said he was Jerry McCabe's son, so they confirmed his dad was dead. He got into the car to come straight down to be with me. Someone had to drive him because he was too distressed to drive himself. He phoned me throughout the journey, 'Mam, I'm coming. I'm coming.' He had to stop the car along the way to get physically sick, he was so upset. But he was a tower of strength to me. Along with the Gardaí he took over the planning of the funeral. That's wasn't easy for him and I'll always be grateful.

I wanted to see Jerry but I wasn't allowed until the post-mortem had been completed. I hated the thought of Jerry lying in the garda car without his family being around him. I felt I should be with him. I didn't want him to be alone. He was in the car until 3 p.m. that afternoon. Then he was placed in a coffin and driven away by hearse for the post-mortem.

As Jerry's body was being taken away from the scene the Gardaí were already closing in on the killers. They had helicopters and roadblocks in place. The killers' getaway car was discovered on an isolated lane six miles from Adare. Inside the car they found a petrol bomb which had failed to detonate and burn out the car. Rounds of ammunition for the Kalashnikov, and plastic ties that were presumably intended to seal the bags of money, were also found. The Gardaí already knew who was behind the murder. Within half an hour of the crime detectives raided the homes of John Quinn, Kevin Walsh, Jeremiah Sheehy, Michael O'Neill and Pearse McCauley. None of the men was home.

> The sad and ironic thing about this whole affair is that Jerry not only knew his killer but also did him a good turn some weeks before the murder. Jerry's friend owns a garage and Jerry would often help him out. Kevin Walsh had left a car into the garage for a new engine to be fitted. There was some work still left on his car and Jerry obliged him and finished it. When Kevin Walsh came to collect the car Jerry wasn't sure what price to charge him, so he agreed they'd catch up with each other again. Little did Jerry know the next time they'd meet it would be to take his life.

––––

The men involved in the murder were on the run. They needed a safe house and decided to hide-out in the home of bachelor sheep farmer Patrick Harty (53) who lived near Toomevara in County Tipperary. At 9 a.m. on the morning of the shootings the five men arrived at Harty's door. Harty didn't personally know the men, though he had, with reluctance, previously stored two cars and a bag for two of these men. When he saw them he immediately thought of the Adare raid. Under pressure, and afraid, he agreed to let them stay. The men seemed on edge. They used his bathroom to wash. They told Harty they were taking some clothes. They burned some of their old clothes in the kitchen stove and they hid the car in the farmer's shed. Harty parked his tractor in front of it, afraid that it would be discovered.

When Harty came back into his house he saw the men's handgun and an AK47 rifle. The men asked him to go and buy cigarettes and Ordnance Survey maps for the midlands and Dublin. On his return the men studied the maps and seemed to formulate a plan. They were about to leave when Harty noticed they weren't taking the guns. They assured him someone would call for them. When the men left, Harty put the guns in plastic bags and sealed them with tape. He waited for nightfall before he went to a field and buried them. He then meticulously cleaned the house to remove fingerprints or traces of the men being there.

The men involved in the murder were known to the Gardaí as they were to Jerry. Jerry would have often given a couple of them a lift home to their caravans or wherever they were staying. He would have tried to help them, *recalls Ann without anger in her voice.*

Several hours after Jerry's death, the IRA issued a statement to RTÉ denying the killing or any involvement in the crime. The statement read: 'None of our units were in any way involved in this morning's incident in Adare. There was absolutely no IRA involvement — P. O'Neill.'

This statement was important because the general public believed the IRA to be on a *de facto* ceasefire and peace talks were set to begin on 10 June — three days' later.

The police believed this IRA statement to be false because tests on the bullets found at the scene proved they were from weapons that had been used in a similar IRA robbery two years previously, during which £94,900 was taken from an An Post van in Limerick. The government was briefed and assured by senior gardaí that the robbery bore all the hallmarks of the IRA. Yet the Government was reluctant to challenge the IRA's statement.

On 15 June the IRA retracted their original statement and issued a second statement, admitting that its members were responsible for the attempted robbery and the death of Jerry McCabe but stating that the killing hadn't been sanctioned.

Meanwhile a massive hunt for the killers continued. The first big break came on 9 June — two days after the murder — when John Quinn was arrested at his girlfriend's house in County Limerick. In his statement he gave an account of his part in the raid and also gave some details about the farmer whose house they used as a hideout. He didn't know the farmer by name but gave directions to his house. According to John Quinn, the IRA had sanctioned the robbery but not the killing. He claimed the OC of the IRA's Southern command had met with the raiders in a car park for last-minute planning before the raid.

The following morning Jeremiah Sheehy was arrested. He refused to tell the Gardaí anything. Thereafter he was released.

_____

These arrests brought Ann McCabe little comfort as she prepared for her husband's State funeral. On Sunday, 9 June 1996, an estimated 20,000 queued outside Thompsons Funeral Home on Thomas Street to sympathise with the bereaved family. It was one of the biggest funerals the city had ever seen.

It was a State funeral so everything was more or less taken out of our hands. It was such a distressing time that I have very little memory of the funeral itself. Each of my children found the day horrendous. I remember that Ian had to stand outside the funeral home. He couldn't bear to go inside. Mark, the second oldest, was inconsolable, and like the rest of us couldn't control his grief. Ross couldn't even get up out of bed. And Stacey, our only daughter, stayed in the house. She was particularly close to her dad. I remember how happy Jerry was on the day she was born. He turned to me and said, 'Ann, we've a princess in the house!'

The house and funeral home were filled with people offering support. Jean Kennedy Smith visited our home and gave me a special gift. It was rosary beads that had belonged to her late mother, Rose Kennedy, who died aged 103. I have prayed with them ever since.

Jerry died because of evil people, but his funeral showed me that the opposite of evil, pure goodness, is also alive and well. As we drove behind the hearse through the city streets thousands stopped what they were doing, came out of the shops, offices, homes and lined the streets. They stood in silence with their heads bowed as the cortege passed by. At a time of deep personal anguish, this gesture by ordinary decent people was intensely moving and comforting to my family and myself. It was as if, by their silence, and by their sheer numbers, the people of Limerick were saying that they had had enough, and that they were unwilling to give any form of support to crimes like this, no matter what their so-called political motivation might have been. It is to these people that I say, thank you. Their support and solidarity was so important.

President Mary Robinson and the then Taoiseach, John Bruton, along with thousands of mourners attended the funeral Mass at the Holy Rosary Church, Ennis Road, on Monday 10 June.

Jerry's son, John McCabe, read a message on behalf of his family in which he said: 'Dad's deep and abiding love for his children was obvious to everybody. Each one of us always felt very special to him and as we grew, our relationships with him developed into ones of friendship as well as family. I know that I speak for my sister and brothers, when I say that we have a tremendous pride in everything Dad did . . .'

The Gardaí videoed the funeral and gave a copy of it to each family member. I watched it over and over again. In the end the family had to take it away from me because I was watching it too much. It upset me so much so I don't know why I watched it. I guess I just wanted to be close to Jerry.

Every night for six months Stacey and myself visited Jerry's grave. The same two friends came with us and drove us each night. We would stare down at his grave and just cry. Then the dark nights came in and we realised it wasn't good for us to be going so often.

Now when I visit Jerry's grave I like to talk to him as if he's alive. I give out to him and tell him to come down here and help me! He's only over my shoulder. I know he's helping me because I wouldn't be able to get through all this on my own.

The way Jerry was taken from us has ruined many lives. None more so than Jerry's own father. For a long time after Jerry's death he couldn't bear to come into our house. He would stand across the road with his arms folded and look at our house. But the journey across the road was too much. Our house was filled with too many memories of the living Jerry. When, after months, he finally came in he said, 'But you know you're a great girl. I don't know how you cope.' Then the two of us ended up crying together.

Jerry was the first son, the third oldest in his family. He had four sisters and one brother. I firmly believed it was Jerry's death that killed his father; he died of a broken heart. In the end he was only in the hospital for two weeks and I was there with him each day. I remember one day near the end he said, 'Ann, turn around, there's Jerry and Lizzy!' Lizzy was his wife who died in 1977. 'Can't you turn around and look at them!' he demanded. I turned around and I said to myself 'If only'. They say that your loved ones come for you when it's your time. I like to think that's true, that Jerry was there and his mother Lizzy.

I like to think of Jerry in heaven with his mother and father. We would usually go to mass together and I remember once there was a ceremony about the damage that can be done by murder and by seriously wronging someone else for your own gain. Afterwards on the way home, Jerry turned to me and said, 'Well, I think I'm in the clear with God because I've never killed or knowingly wronged anyone . . .' Neither of us was overly religious but Jerry liked to go to mass and he'd give out if we missed it.

———

Gardaí soon identified and arrested farmer Patrick Harty. He was willing to assist the Gardaí. He realised he had unknowingly become a player in a serious crime. He gave the Gardaí a detailed account of events. Though he didn't know the names of the men involved, he was crucially able to identify them from police photographs. He identified Kevin Walsh, Pearse McCauley, Jeremiah Sheehy, Michael O'Neill as well as two men from Cork and Clare. Later Harty agreed to become a prosecution witness.

On 18 June, Michael O'Neill was arrested and charged with membership of the IRA and possession of unlawful firearms with intent to harm in Adare. In May of the following year Pearse McCauley was spotted by a detective inspector in Monaghan who saw McCauley driving a car. He took chase but McCauley got away. It would be five months before the Gardaí caught up with him again. They became aware that McCauley and his girlfriend were staying at the home of an IRA sympathiser near Renvyle, in County Galway. McCauley and his girlfriend were walking home along the beach at 3 a.m. when the Gardaí swooped and arrested him. At the time he was in the middle of a huge argument with his girlfriend. He continued to shout at her while he was being handcuffed and led away.

The Gardaí were also closing in on Kevin Walsh, who was by now Ireland's most wanted man and was believed to be the leader of the gang. A few months later he was found hiding out with a family in a house in Cavan. He had been living in this house for over a year and had tried to disguise his appearance. He'd changed the colour of his hair, wore glasses and had obtained a false passport. He didn't mix with the locals and only rarely left the house. When he did he carried a hand-gun. If a car passed him on the road he would turn the other way. Walsh had told the daughter of the man who owned the house that the murder wasn't planned, that no one was meant to get hurt but that one of the guns had got jammed on automatic.

However, these claims do not correspond with forensic evidence or with Ben O'Sullivan's account of events. The trajectory of the bullets meant there was more than one round fired from the gun. And Ben O'Sullivan's account suggests that the bullets were fired to kill both men. Yet it is possible that one of the killers lost control of his weapon.

Now that Kevin Walsh was under arrest the other raiders were brought together so that they could be charged for the capital murder of Detective Jerry McCabe. The trial date was set for the Special Criminal Court for January 1999.

It was believed that Kevin Walsh may have been the gunman who fired the fatal shots that killed Jerry McCabe and badly injured Ben O'Sullivan. Kevin Walsh was involved in another robbery in 1994 when he shot at Gardaí as his gang escaped from the scene. He is also believed to have links with the IRA's ruling army council.

Jeremiah Sheehy is believed to have been a low-ranking IRA member whose task was to provide back-up in the Adare robbery.

Michael O'Neill was a close friend of Kevin Walsh and was given the task of driving one of the getaway cars.

Pearse McCauley was deeply involved in the IRA and would have been considered a veteran who fought in campaigns in the North and in Britain. He had served time in prison for possession of a hand-gun but had been released early as part of the first IRA ceasefire.

The five men entered the Special Criminal Court with their heads held high, unfazed by the public's repulsion at their crimes. Pearse McCauley (34), Jeremiah Sheehy (36), Michael O'Neill (46), and Kevin Walsh (42), wore new grey suits and green ribbon symbols on their lapels — ironically the republican symbol for the early release of prisoners. The men pleaded 'not guilty'. They seemed unperturbed by the tension of the court and chatted with friends before everyone settled down for the beginning of the long-awaited trial. Ann come to the court for the sentencing. Walsh eye-balled her and showed no emotion.

It became clear that it was Walsh who master-minded the robbery. He knew the route of the An Post van because he, Pearse McCauley, Jeremiah Sheehy, Michael O'Neill and John Quinn had been carefully watching it for weeks. They planned to steal £100,000 to help finance the 'republican cause'.

On the seventh day of the trial the farmer Patrick Harty was brought forward to testify against the accused, but when he entered the witness box he froze and, shockingly, he refused to testify. It was obvious from his voice and demeanour that he was afraid but he wouldn't confirm what it was that he feared.

The presiding judge, Mr Justice Richard Johnson, said, 'Mr Harty, from the book of evidence you have evidence to give of an extremely important nature.'

'I'm sorry,' Harty replied, unable to offer an explanation.

His solicitor, Liz McGrath, apologised for her client's refusal to testify and regretted that he was unable to offer an explanation. She tried to indirectly insinuate that her client could have been intimidated. She said he was 'a bachelor farmer with no brothers or sisters and . . . lives alone at this farm in a secluded spot'. Nonetheless the judge sentenced him to eighteen months in prison for contempt of court.

His refusal to testify left the case in a serious predicament, resulting in the murder trial's dramatic collapse when four of the men changed their pleas from not guilty of capital murder to guilty of manslaughter and the malicious injury of Ben O'Sullivan; the fifth man had pleaded guilty to conspiracy to commit a robbery. That followed a sensational development when the State's prosecuting counsel indicated they were prepared to accept pleas of guilty to manslaughter.

In February 1999, Kevin Walsh and Pearse McCauley were each given a fourteen-year sentence, not the usual 40-year mandatory sentence which applied for killing a police officer. After his sentence was passed, Pearse McCauley smirked openly as he was escorted out of the court by prison officers. Jeremiah Sheehy was sentenced to twelve years, Michael O'Neill to eleven years, and John Quinn was jailed for six years for conspiracy to commit a robbery. The judge took into account that Walsh had expressed 'no remorse' or regret even though Sheehy, McCauley and O'Neill had.

By this stage the farmer Patrick Harty had been in prison for two weeks. His solicitor, Liz McGrath, appealed to the judge on his behalf. She believed he had been put under 'pressure' which resulted in him fearing for his own welfare. 'The only reason he has found himself before this court is due to his obliging nature and sense of loyalty to the past which was clearly manipulated.' The judge freed Mr Harty after he purged his contempt.

> That was hard to take. We were devastated by the manslaughter plea because I believe if you have loaded guns the crime is premeditated. So it should have been a murder trial, not a manslaughter trial. The difference in the sentencing would have been so significant. The final straw was when we heard Kevin Walsh saying he had no remorse for the killing. How could he not feel remorse for killing an innocent man?

———

> Jerry was only 52 when he died. He'd worked hard all his life and was looking forward to retirement. He had been by my side throughout everything. I met him at a dance when I was 22 and he was 24.
>
> What I most liked about him was the fact that he was always happy. There was never any hassle. Everything was easy when Jerry was around. 'No problem,' was his standard reply. We were married in 1967, two years after we'd started going out. We went to Spain on our honeymoon. And from that day to the day he died

there was never a cross word.

He was a good family man. He was known as the guard with the children because he always had the children in the back of the car with him. He loved being a dad and the kids were mad about him. He was particularly close to them. Himself and Stacey would dance around the kitchen together. I remember one morning Jerry was particularly spruced up going out to work and I must have commented because Stacey said, 'Daddy told me his secret.' He was providing security for a British politician who was visiting Ireland. I remember the politician said to him, 'You must be very high up to be given the job of escorting me.'

Jerry replied, 'No, I'm not high up, I'm at the bottom of the heap. Why do you think they have me looking after you!' The man looked shocked and then he saw a little smile on Jerry's face and the two of them burst out laughing. He realised Jerry was joking. Jerry loved harmless devilment, jokes. He loved to laugh. We miss that laughter. *As Ann tells this story she touches her necklace which is a gold plate on which an image of her husband has been printed. She assured me the image doesn't do her husband justice.* I guess people will think I'm trying to make a hero out of Jerry, but he was a hero to me and it's with those eyes that I remember him.

Jerry was important to more people than his family. I received thousands of letters of condolences; so many of them had a story to tell of how Jerry had helped them out in their hour of need. I had no idea that Jerry knew so many people or that he'd touched so many people's lives. There was one letter that was particularly touching. It was from a man who was drying out in a home for alcoholics. His hand was so shaky from years of drinking, or maybe from the detox, that he had to get one of the nuns to write the letter.

The letter told of the many times Jerry had helped him. He said he first met Jerry some twenty years earlier, that he was in a bad way at the time, and even though he knew Jerry didn't have much money he still never passed this man on the street without giving him a fiver or whatever he could spare. He was worried that the man would go hungry. Yet no matter what help was offered this man he couldn't curb his drinking but now in memory of Jerry he was trying to stop. If Jerry knew he'd be proud.

Those types of letters lifted me up in moments of despair and hopelessness. People who didn't know me thought I was holding things together but I wasn't. I became badly depressed. For a long time I couldn't even bear to face into town, and when I finally did I had to make sure I had someone with me because I would get panic attacks and might not even be able to cross the road. The pressure would be too much and it would all get on top of me.

There was a point when I thought I couldn't go on anymore. I remember the exact moment. I was walking into town over the new bridge. I was on my own, and my mind was a million miles away. I looked over the bridge into the water and I said to myself, 'What am I going to do? How can I ever get through this?' I just didn't feel like I could walk another step let alone deal with the rest of my days. As I looked into the river I thought it might be easier to leave my life . . . Then I heard from behind, 'Mum, are you okay?' I turned around and saw my daughter Stacey. She was on her way out from town. I thought it was a miracle that she should show up at the very moment I needed her most.

There are still moments of darkness, when you just want the pain to stop. But the solution I was looking at was a selfish one. I had to think of the people who were still alive, my children who needed me and I them. There are a lot of moments when I feel down but I make myself lift the phone and call a friend or organise to meet up with someone.

———

Since the sentencing Ann McCabe has been haunted by the possibility of the killers' early release under the Good Friday Agreement. As part of the Good Friday Agreement of 1998, which envisioned a future for both Catholics and Protestants living in peace and sharing power, more than 500 convicted members of the IRA and other paramilitary groups have walked free from prison. Concern grew amongst the McCabe family when Gerry's killers were moved from Portlaoise prison to the low-security prison at Castlerea, Roscommon, in 1999. As a result of this, Ann McCabe met the then Minister for Justice, John O'Donoghue, in December 1999, who reassured her that there would be no early release for the four killers of her husband.

A year later, the killers were transferred back to Portlaoise prison along with six other republican prisoners following an incident at Castlerea when a prison officer was detained against his will. They were later brought back to the open prison of Castlerea where they happily posed for pictures with Sinn Féin TDs in 2003. In Castlerea they enjoy homely surroundings in a bungalow complex called 'The Grove'. Each has his own front door keys and is able to order takeaway food, have personal shopping lists and on occasion leave the prison. They enjoy the usual home accessories such as CD players, televisions, DVD players, microwaves, washing machines, etc.

> They have all been allowed home on compassionate leave. I had always thought compassionate leave was only allowed in extenuating circumstances, like for a funeral or if someone in the family was seriously ill. But these killers were temporarily released for all types of reasons. One of the killers was released so that he could marry his girlfriend. She was from Cavan. She was a schoolteacher and a Sinn Féin Councillor. I believe, in all, the killers have been released 24 times.
>
> I shudder to think what would happen if I ever came face to face with Kevin Walsh. I wouldn't be afraid but I think anger would overcome me. Anger hasn't hit me yet, just loneliness and sadness, which I know will always be part of my life. I can't let the anger eat me up or I'll be in the scrap heap.

In 1996 the Taoiseach of the day, John Bruton, met with Ann McCabe and assured her that the killers would not be released early under the Good Friday Agreement. His successor, Bertie Ahern, gave the same assurance, as this was not a politically motivated crime. Those involved in the killing of Jerry McCabe were not on active service for the IRA because at the time the IRA was on ceasefire. Consequently, the killers do not qualify for release under the Good Friday Agreement.

In May 2004, Taoiseach Bertie Ahern said for the first time that he would consider the early release of the McCabe killers but only in the context of a total end to the Northern conflict, the IRA and its activities. He said not only would he consider it but he would recommend it to secure a deal. 'This is not a question on which I want to have any ambiguity. If we are to have a comprehensive deal, this matter will be part of it, and I would recommend that that be the case,' Mr Ahern said. He said he wasn't breaking the government's promise not to release the killers under the Good Friday Agreement, rather the release would be at the discretion of the Minister under the Offences Against the State Act. In December of that same year, Ahern confirmed in response to a question from Fine Gael's Enda Kenny that the IRA murderers of Garda Jerry McCabe were to be freed. It seemed that the very specific guarantees that had been given to Ann McCabe were hogwash.

The Taoiseach's statement forced Ann McCabe into a high-profile campaign to ensure that she achieved justice for her husband. She questioned the Taoiseach's authority and asked, 'Who is running our government? Is it Sinn Féin, or the IRA, or Bertie Ahern?' later adding, 'I don't want to go down as the person who stalled the peace process but I'm just very disappointed.'

In December 1999, the then Justice Minister met with me and promised there would never be any early release. After the meeting he wrote to me and reiterated that promise. His letter stated the following: 'I hope that the meeting provided you with assurance that there is no question of granting early release to those concerned, either under the terms of the Good Friday Agreement or, for that matter, on any other basis.'

Ann went on to point out the threats our nation faced if a paramilitary organisation could dictate to a morally weak government.

I felt huge pressure on my shoulders and that pressure came from the government. I knew they saw my dead husband and me as a stumbling block. The Taoiseach referred to 'an item' that was giving us great trouble. I took great offence that he would refer to my husband in those terms. He wasn't 'an item'. He was a human being, a dad of five, a husband, a brother, a friend . . . I remember one of the Cabinet who was involved in the debate over the early release said it would be a happy journey he'd make to Limerick to tell Ann McCabe that the killers of her husband were going to be released because it would mean progress for peace. I thought it was a terribly insensitive thing to say and showed how out of touch some politicians are with the public's wishes. I began to feel very low about the whole thing.

Ann McCabe is a shy and reluctant campaigner. She would much prefer to stay at home with her family and tend to the everyday tasks of daily life. She, like her family, is an intensely private person who hates publicity. So it was understandably hard for her to stand in the glare of the media spotlight, not to mention standing up against a government, a terrorist organisation and media commentators who bellowed from the top of their ivory towers about the 'greater good' and referred to Ann as the woman who could single-handedly collapse the peace talks. It seemed unlikely she was going to change the mind of the Taoiseach, at least not on her own.

Those were dark days. It seemed there was no light. Then something wonderful and unexpected happened. Hundreds of letters from all over the country started to arrive at my house. Each letter had the same message: 'Stand firm'. People began to speak out in support of me. The media reflected the public's wishes — to keep the men who killed my husband in prison. My daughter, Stacey, refused to go shopping with me because at every corner was someone else offering me strength, support and solidarity. They really lifted my spirits and helped me carry on. The government totally misjudged the fact that the whole country would get behind me. They could ignore me but they couldn't ignore a nation. They began to realise an early release would have grave consequences for their public image.

Around this time the killers issued a statement from prison, an apology for the killing of Ann's husband. The statement read, 'We deeply regret the death of Garda Jerry McCabe and the wounding of Garda Ben O'Sullivan during an IRA operation in Adare in June 1996. We deeply regret and apologise for this and the hurt and grief we have caused the families. There was never any intent to attack any member of the Garda Síochána . . .' The statement went on to claim that they were entitled to be released under the Good Friday Agreement and that 'they (the Government) have refused to do so and are now presenting our release as an obstacle to negotiations and an agreement. For this reason we do not want our release to be part of any further negotiation with the Irish government.'

Ann McCabe saw the statement as nothing more than a calculated public relations stunt, an effort to win sympathy. The men had nine years to apologise and they chose to say sorry only at this strategic stage. An apology means nothing to me. It won't bring Jerry back, and I don't think they will ever show real remorse. They don't know the meaning of it. All they are interested in is criminality and murder, and I can assure you that one of those four is quite capable, if released, of killing again.

The Taoiseach subsequently changed his mind and said that the 'early release of the killers of Detective Garda McCabe is no longer on the table and I don't see it coming back on the table. That position has now been endorsed overwhelmingly by the Dáil in its recent debates so I think the situation as far as I'm concerned is now closed on this . . . They won't be released on my watch.'

Of course I welcomed the news. It was a victory, at least for the time being. It's an issue we've had to fight since the killers were imprisoned. I know some people wonder why I bother but I'm doing it for Jerry. Just because someone dies doesn't mean you stop loving them, that you stop standing up for them. I need to stand up for Jerry, for the members of the Gardaí and for all the law-abiding citizens of Ireland. His killers weren't freedom fighters. They were common criminals and must be treated accordingly. Walsh didn't want the money from the foiled robbery to fund IRA activity. He wanted it so that he could finish building his house.

The fear of them being released early doesn't go away; it's always hanging over me and has compounded my grief. It shocks me to think that at one stage the killers were within an hour of being released, or so I've been told.

According to an opinion poll, conducted by Irish Independent/ Millward Brown IMS, Ann McCabe had been credited with hardening government and public opinion towards the IRA and Sinn Féin. The majority of the people polled said that Ann McCabe was right not to accept the early release of the prisoners. It is fair to say Ann McCabe won't go down in history as the woman who threatened the peace talks. Rather she will be remembered as the woman who could see how the sinister nature of, and dealings with, the IRA could threaten our democracy. This thought brings her little comfort.

It's a lie to say you ever get over a death like Jerry's. One day I might be up but then something will happen to trigger how much I miss him, and then I'm back to square one. But you have to go on. I feel that Jerry is with me, all the time, helping me along. I know he would be proud of me. I can honestly say that not a day passes that I don't think of him. He is constantly mentioned in our house. We like to talk about him. I have been in counselling for the last eight years and that helps a lot. It's okay to ask for help from professionals. They can throw some light on things.

I have kept all the letters of support I've received and I've tried to reply personally to each one. That's important to me because people lent me their strength when I hadn't any. When those low points hit me I re-read some of those letters. One in particular gives me peace. It was written by a man who lived next door to my ninety-year-old mother. He's a priest. His name is Father Joe. He wrote this quote:

'When I despair I remember that all through history truth and love have won. There have been tyrants and murderers and for a time they can seem invisible but in the end they always fall.'

Chapter 5

Trojan women

The McCartney sisters

A Kingdom founded on injustice never lasts.

SENECA

'Scum,' the sisters of Robert McCartney uttered. In any other part of the world this description for the men who killed their brother, the father of two little boys, would not cause a glance. This however is the Short Strand in Belfast, a place where the local IRA men are held up as heroes, the 'Robin Hoods' of the forest, protectors of the neighbourhood. They're not referred to as 'scum', or at least not publicly. To do so is to advertise your own death sentence. However, this mindset began to change when on 30 January 2005 members of the IRA killed Robert McCartney (33) and by association took on the might of his sisters. Five sisters who, in the face of intimidation and death threats, refused to stay quiet, women who refused to 'know their place', and who above all refused to let their brother's killers away with murder.

Paula (40) is the eldest sister and mother of five children aged 19 to three. She is a mature student at Queen's University, doing women's studies. She has put her studies on hold because there hasn't been time to attend lectures. Her personality is unwavering and passionate, she is brimming with gusto, and you know you'd tire first in an argument with her. She and her sister Catherine have been the main spokespeople for the family.

Catherine (37), lecturer in politics at a local college and mother of four, is the sister closest in age to Robert. It's easy to see why the

IRA men who visited the family home in the Short Strand must have felt intimidated by her, someone whose education and natural intelligence enables her to smell crap a hundred metres away. Her tone is flat, exhausted, yet packed with a strong determination. She doesn't think she'll be able to ever go back to her lecturing job; her focus has been and remains too firmly fixed on the fight for justice. She has made a big career sacrifice yet sacrifice is hardly a word that she'd use: 'My future now lies in human rights. You have no idea of the injustices that exist until you're in the middle of it.'

Donna (38) runs a gourmet sandwich bar. She has had to neglect her business because her focus is on getting justice for her brother. She has missed mortgage payments because there isn't time for finances, for everyday tasks. She saw the man who ordered the killing of her brother in the shops the other day. Once she and the people of the Short Strand looked up to men like him. Not any more.

Gemma (41) is a district nurse who, like her siblings, has had to take time off work. Her sister Claire (27) is a graduate of English literature and currently a trainee teacher. She has two children and is the youngest sister but every bit as committed.

Their parents are quiet and unassuming people, who watch their children's battle for justice on television. Their mother had to be given sedatives when she heard about the murder, such was her sadness and shock. She was abroad on holidays at the time of the murder and her daughters had to phone her to tell her the news. Their mother was too distraught to attend the funeral or month's mind.

Robert's fiancée Bridgeen Hagan (24), the mother of his two sons, is broken-hearted. She had been planning a big white wedding; instead she ended up planning a funeral.

Their faces tell of unrelenting determination, motivated by unyielding grief, sadness and a sense of justice for their brother.

The IRA have battled and negotiated with many people over the years and few have stood up to them, but we're prepared to stand up to them, *says one of the older sisters*. They'll rue the day they heard our names. We're not just fighting for Robert. We're fighting

for the future of his children, his 17 nieces and nephews, his ̖
niece and every child in this country. We're fighting so that the
will recognise that they cannot turn their guns and violence on th
inside and think they'll get away with it.

These words are indeed brave. In the ten years since the IRA
announced a ceasefire they have killed 179 people, Robert making
that figure 180. The IRA have also been behind at least 2,313
punishment beatings and thousands of other incidents of
paramilitary violence.

These statistics don't cause a flicker in the eyes of this
determined family. And why should they? After all, these are the
women determined to do what Margaret Thatcher, Albert
Reynolds, Tony Blair, Bill Clinton, An Taoiseach Bertie Ahern,
President George Bush, and the British Army failed to do — bring
the IRA to their knees. What these women have, that those before
them didn't have, is grief. Grief empowers them with courage,
enables them to keep going when others would have given up,
allows them to call upon hidden reserves of tenacity and
determination. This grief, combined with love for their brother,
has inspired them to make the world listen to their story.

Six ordinary Belfast women have led the 'people's revolution'
against the local IRA and their henchmen. Even though their stance
has been compared with taking on the mafia they will not waver.
These six women continue to challenge a private army with
dignity, intelligence and unending courage — all in the name of
bringing their brother's killers to justice.

————

The Short Strand has been home to the McCartney family for over
a hundred years. Their family home is situated in a Catholic
enclave of over 3,000 houses, surrounded by over 85,000
Protestant houses. The two neighbourhoods are separated on
three sides by a 60-foot high 'peace wall' that still marks sectarian
divisions. The wall is adorned by paramilitary graffiti denouncing
loyalist Protestant paramilitary organisations. The houses in the

Short Strand have triple-glazed fire retardant security windows and steel tiles on the roofs to protect them from the rockets — kitchen knives, tins of beans — that at one time were thrown over the 'peace wall'. The houses on the Protestant side have the same protection but it's easy to see and feel how it's the Catholic Short Strand that feels barricaded in, under attack, and has done so for the last hundred years.

This Catholic enclave, the spiritual home of the IRA, has been attacked on numerous occasions throughout the Troubles. Even when Northern Ireland was supposedly at peace in 2001 and 2002, the Short Strand's summer months were spent in a virtual state of siege, as up to 1,000 republicans and loyalists fought hand-to-hand battles in the streets and rounds of ammunition were exchanged across the 'peace wall'. And like before, the IRA were seen as the defenders who stood up against loyalist invaders. They were seen as 'heroic' men who acted as protectors. They were not people you referred to as 'scum'.

It's no surprise that the McCartney sisters can name those who killed their brother. After all, the Short Strand is a place where everyone knows everyone. What is surprising is that they're prepared to name them publicly.

For every action there is a reaction and ours is to name and shame the men responsible for murdering our brother, debasing his parents, taking a father from two children and leaving a fiancée with her heart shattered. We've no fear of the IRA. They can do no more to me and my family than what they have already done by killing Robert, *says Catherine*.

She describes the details of the murder:

Robert and his friend, Brendan Devine (31), called into the pub for a quick drink on their way home. There was a soccer match on the television. They had a pint and watched the match. There were some girls sitting underneath the television. The referee gave a card to one of the players . . . Robert didn't agree with his call . . . so he made some type of hand gesture in protest. The gesture was made in the direction of the television . . . One of the girls who sat underneath the television thought he was making the gesture towards her. She told her boyfriend that Robert had made a rude gesture towards her.

The girl's boyfriend and his friend approached Robert and accused him of the latter. One of these men was a senior IRA commander. Robert explained that he was making the gesture at the television, but nonetheless apologised and explained he intended no offence. He offered to buy the girl a drink but she said it was okay because she was with a big group. The man accepted Robert's apology but used the exchange as a chance to start an argument with Robert's friend Brendan Devine. Robert was not involved in the argument, which quickly got out of hand; shouting turned into pushing, which led to bottles being thrown. The senior IRA man's arm was cut by some broken glass. When he saw his own blood he went crazy, completely out of control. He gave a sign to kill Brendan Devine. The sign was in the style of a stabbing motion.

Then one of his men, who had a long and vicious reputation of extreme violence, grabbed Brendan Devine from behind, put his arm around his head and slit his throat from ear to ear. It was at that point that Robert intervened. With blood pumping from Brendan's neck Robert knew he had to get him to a hospital immediately. He stepped in to defend his friend and through sheer will he bundled him out of the bar. They were only outside the door of the pub when eight or nine IRA men came after them and reinforcements were called.

One of the men present was a former bodyguard for Gerry Adams and was shortlisted as a Sinn Féin candidate in an assembly election. This man left the scene and returned with a knife that had been taken from the pub. He passed the knife on to another IRA man who would later use it to stab Robert.

Robert and Brendan were pushed to the ground and an all-out attack ensued. Knives were visible, along with sewer rods, which the IRA members used to beat the two men. Brendan Devine had a bottle smashed over his head; he was stabbed twice; one of the wounds ran from his breastbone to his abdomen.

Robert was an innocent bystander. He was a peacemaker who would have tried to diffuse a row and we've heard that when he was murdered he had his hands in the air. *But his killers didn't seem to care, they wanted to kill for killing's sake.*

Robert's eyes were gouged out of their sockets by the force with which his attackers stamped on his head. He was stabbed in the stomach and kicked in the head repeatedly until it appeared he was dead.

Brendan Devine and Robert were left for dead on the side of the street. The IRA men ran from the scene, but first they went back to the pub and warned those present not to call an ambulance and not to talk of the night's events. They were told to remain silent. The bar was cleaned of blood and finger prints.

Meanwhile a police patrol car saw the two men lying on the street. They initially thought the men had collapsed from drink after the Bloody Sunday commemorations, so they drove on. On second thoughts they decided to turn back for a closer look. They immediately saw the blood and called an ambulance. More than nine hours after Robert was set upon, his body finally gave up the fight. We were devastated. It was a murder that didn't need to happen. Robert was an innocent man.

———

Robert's death was in stark contrast to his life, Paula remembers: 'Growing up we never saw any violence. None of us got caught up in any of that stuff because our parents took us out of the area each summer before the marching season began.' Another sister recalled, 'When we heard that the 'Orangies' were coming we knew we were off for a long spell to our Granny's house in County Down.'

Childhood innocence was such that the 'Orangies' were thought to be giant pieces of fruit intent on pursuing the family. As the children grew up it became clear that the giant fruit's mission was to burn them out of their homes. Gemma was only five when the troubles began. She presumed all societies were the same as theirs: homes being searched by the army, riots, kneecappings, fire bombs, shootings, kidnapping; and perhaps each neighbourhood had a private army; theirs was called the IRA.

Even though the Short Strand was pitted with problems, Protestants and Catholics lived cheek by jowl and there was an RUC barracks on our doorstep, still nothing much happened that we were ever aware of. The only violence we remember was what we saw on television. We were totally kept away from it all, *says Paula*.

My parents didn't want us to get involved. Not one of us threw bricks at the police, not one of us picked up a petrol bomb when it was like a hobby to most kids in the area. We left that to other people.

Robert always had loads of friends; unusually the friends he made on the first day at school were still his friends on the day he died. He didn't lose friends, he didn't fall out with people.

We had a magical childhood. Each of us was carefree. I have wonderful memories of Robert. I can picture us all running for the bus to school. Robert was a brilliant runner. He'd always get to the bus on time and hold it for the rest of us, *Paula smiles as she remembers back.*

Even though our parents both worked — our mother was a dressmaker and our father was a carpet fitter and upholsterer — they always made a lot of time for us. They had five wee girls and two young boys, and somehow they managed to make each of feel like we came first.

Then as we grew older our sibling friendships grew stronger and firmer. *When the sisters' only other brother took his life after a long battle with depression, it was Robert who held the family together. He was a tower of strength. Robert was someone they would call on in a crisis; he always said the right thing; he knew how to solve problems; he was a natural diplomat, good with people; and his family was the most important thing in his life.*

Paula recalls that the occasion which brought Robert the greatest happiness was the birth of his first son, Coneald. He firmly believed that Coneald was the nicest looking baby in the whole world. He'd turn to us and say, 'There's nothing surer but my Coneald is the best-looking McCartney.' He loved that little boy so much and talked about him non-stop until his second son was born.

He named him 'Brandon', in honour of his hero Bruce Lee, who had a son called Brandon. He loved nothing more than being with the children and Bridgeen. He took great pleasure in the little daily chores that are part of any child's upbringing — from bathing his sons to taking them shopping for clothes. He loved to spoil them;

he would buy them little designer outfits. Robert had been planning on taking Coneald over to England to see Liverpool play. He had picked Coneald's next birthday as the date of the trip.

Robert's children were going to have the same childhood as their dad. Already they had spent their summers on the same beach where the McCartney family spent their summers. 'I suppose he was just repeating what Mum and Dad did with us children. Now Robert's sons will never spend another day at the beach with their daddy, they'll never be held high, laughing on his shoulders, they'll never be spoiled, cuddled or helped through their life by their father and that's just wrong.' Their childhood memories are not what their father had planned for them.

He was bringing his boys up in an atmosphere of tolerance and understanding. He wanted them to feel secure. One can only hope that when they're old enough to understand they will feel pride, not anger, pride that their dad died defending a friend, that their mother and aunts' fight for justice made a whole country grieve for a man whose name will never be forgotten.

Robert's dedication to his family was mirrored in other areas of his life. He trained hard to become a bodybuilder, a training which must have helped when he sought a second job as a bouncer. He took this job so that he could save extra money for his wedding. By day he worked as a fork-lift driver and by night he kept law and order at the doors of a bar.

Robert and his fiancée were looking forward to their summer wedding. Bridgeen had started to look at wedding dresses for her walk down the aisle. She planned a big white wedding in the Hilton Hotel, ironically not far from where Robert was killed. Instead she found herself walking behind a wooden coffin that held not only the father of her children but her best friend.

———

At the funeral Robert's two little boys clung tightly to their mother, who held her head down as she cried silently. They walked with dignity behind the coffin. Up to 1,200 people accompanied them through the streets of Belfast. Those that could crammed into Saint Matthew's Church on the Short Strand. When the church was full the remainder stood quietly outside the church in the winter cold.

Father Seán Gilmore referred to Robert's murderers as 'evil' and spoke of the 'devastating and demoralising' effect Robert's murder would have on his family, his children and the community. He said the 33-year-old brother will stand 'shoulder to shoulder with his killers' before God. 'Murder, the taking of a life, has to be the worst action one person can do. A life, once it is taken, can never be given back again.' He continued by saying that taking a life over a disagreement in a pub was particularly wrong. 'In murdering Robert his killers have not only ended his life but they have changed forever the lives of his partner Bridgeen, his children Conlead and Brandon who will grow up without the support and guidance of a father. They have also changed forever the lives of his mother and father, Kathleen and Robert, who lost their last remaining son in the space of four years . . .' A family who were only beginning to come to terms with the loss of their first son.

The bar outside of which Robert was murdered remained open on the day of the funeral.

The funeral was made sadder by the fact that no one had yet been arrested for the murder of Robert though the names of those who perpetrated the act were commonly known in the community, *says Catherine.*

The sisters explain that on the night of the murders there were more than 70 people in the bar — but immediate intimidation and threats from the killers and their lackies means no one has come forward. Privately many of the people who were in the bar say the same thing, 'We have families. We can't get involved or we could be next.' It's widely accepted that people who were in the pub are too afraid to come forward and that many are members of Sinn Féin and the IRA.

There is only one toilet in that bar, yet all 70 people say they were either in that toilet or were too distracted because they were on their mobile phones. People didn't want to know, *sighs Catherine.*

The first thing that made us suspicious of a cover-up was when Joe O'Donnell, a local Sinn Féin councillor (and Deputy Mayor of Belfast) went on national television and said this murder was part of the 'knife culture'. It seemed like such a strange thing to say when everyone knew the IRA were involved. Even members of his own party were in the bar at the time of the murder.

The police went to raid the pub where the attack had happened. They said they had never seen any thing like it. The pub had been forensically cleaned. Even the ashtrays had been disposed of. There was a strong smell of disinfectant. There wasn't a print to be found. There was CCTV but the video had been removed. The clean-up was organised by the IRA, by people who knew about forensics.

Then politicians got involved in the cover-up. It was bad enough that the IRA killed my brother but by hiding the truth the politicians were sending a clear message: 'Your brother's life was worth nothing.' This is not what you expect from your elected representatives. It outraged us.

The police tried to carry out a number of searches in the Markets area. They needed to search suspects' homes. In particular they wanted to remove a washing machine which they suspected was used to clean the killers' clothes. But they were forced to retreat after coming under attack from a mob throwing stones, bricks and bottles. These youths were under orders to cause mayhem. When the police tried to return on a second occasion they were met with the same barrage of violence which obstructed them from doing their job and gathering evidence.

Sinn Féin's Alex Maskey went on television claiming that the police were using heavy-handed tactics . . . He referred to Robert as 'that man'. It was then that we knew Sinn Féin were being dismissive of the case, *says Catherine.*

Two nights after the disrupted searches the peoples of the Markets area joined with the McCartney family in a candlelight vigil. They stood in their hundreds to mark the spot where Robert was murdered. Their act was simply to show their silent solidarity with the family who sought justice.

Two senior republican men appeared at the periphery of the gathering and this led to angry scenes of disgust and disbelief. This was only a murmur of the strength of feeling that existed. Anti-republican graffiti appeared on a wall which was normally reserved for the police. The words 'PSNI scum' was replaced with 'IRA scum'. In the letters page of the *Irish News* newspaper the headline read 'Short Memories'. It referred to the people who wrote 'IRA scum', stating that they must have poor memories. Had they forgotten about 1972 'when members of the IRA defended the Short Strand and St Matthew's Church from being burned to the ground? The end result — a young man from the Falls Road paying the price with his life.'

The author of another letter, on the same day, empathised with the McCartneys' stance. S/he pleaded with those involved in the murder and those who were in the pub and have information not to '. . . sit in silence . . . or live in fear'. Yet ironically the author was too frightened to sign the letter with his/her name. So much for standing up and speaking out.

In the days following the murder, the family was in a state of shock that the IRA could murder someone who they knew was an innocent Catholic, who was not involved in any type of criminality and who kept himself to himself, a man who voted Sinn Féin because he thought they could deliver peace. Initially the family had no intention of speaking out but when they saw that the IRA and Sinn Féin were remaining silent, not assisting the murder inquiry, they felt they had little choice but to ask for help.

It wasn't like an overnight decision to start a campaign to fight for justice for our brother. It was just something that happened. Everything started to build up, it got dirtier and more sinister . . . We couldn't understand why witnesses weren't coming forward with information. At first we thought they simply felt intimidated, so we decided to go on 'Talkback', a BBC Radio Ulster morning show. We thought that if people heard how badly we needed witnesses they would be brave and come forward. Finally things began to fit together. You see we believed Sinn Féin when they said they weren't involved in the cover-up. I believed Gerry Adams when we met him, *says Paula.*

At the time of the murder Gerry Adams wasn't in the country. When he returned to Ireland he telephoned us. Actually you couldn't get him off the phone he called that many times, and in between we met him.

At first when we met him I thought he was going to help us. I believed him because I thought that after what we've been through how could he not show us humanity? Here was a man who could put real pressure on those who killed Robert. Here was a man who could order these killers to co-operate with the police. A man who had the power to make a difference, *says Paula.*

We gave Gerry Adams the names of those who were involved in the murder and the clean up. He sat with us as we went through each name. He knew some of the men. There was one in particular he said he didn't know. We now know for a fact that this is a lie because this man had been a personal bodyguard for Adams. We have even seen a photograph of the two of them standing shoulder to shoulder together. This person was the one who got rid of the knife that killed Robert. Adams promised to help us, *recalls Catherine, who never trusted him.*

Suddenly the phone calls from Adams stopped. The last time we heard from him was the Thursday before we went to the States to meet President Bush. I guess he thought that we were taking his place in the White House.

We now realise that Adams came to meet us for one reason and one reason only, to suss us out, *says Catherine.* He wanted to find out what we knew and what we didn't know and we were prepared to meet anyone who we thought could help us. It was around this time that Sinn Féin activist Cora Groogan made a statement. *In her statement she said she had been in the bar on the night of Robert McCartney's murder but had not seen anything of relevance.*

People can examine the statement and draw their own conclusions. Cora Groogan claimed: 'I got to the bar about 10 p.m. that Sunday. I was there for a short while. There was a commotion in the bar, but I witnessed nothing and left shortly after 11 p.m.'

What exactly was that 'commotion' which didn't even cause Cora Groogan to lift her head from her drink? It was the sound of men shouting, a vicious argument followed by bottles being thrown and broken, and finally Brendan Devine having his throat cut. All this happened inside the pub before Robert and his friend were attacked so badly they were left for dead directly outside the door. There would have been ungodly screaming, cries for help, for mercy, a significant amount of blood would have been around the bar and immediately outside it, a clean-up operation was ordered while the customers were still inside and they were directed not to call an ambulance. Difficult to miss, you might think, difficult to mistake for a bit of a 'commotion'?

The sisters claim that a taxi driver who gave Cora Groogan a lift to another pub heard her describe what happened inside the bar.

> The driver told me that she was agitated and said, 'There was a murder in there, bottles and glasses flying everywhere.' When he drove off she gave a sigh of relief.
>
> There were suggestions that Cora Groogan could have been a candidate for Sinn Féin in the then forthcoming local elections. She stood in Mid-Ulster alongside Martin McGuinness in the November 2003 Assembly Elections. Cora Groogan could be Minister in Stormont with responsibility for Justice, and how would the people of Northern Ireland feel about that given that she wasn't ready to uphold justice when the opportunity arose?

Almost a month after Robert's killing, the McCartney sisters met with members of the IRA. The meeting lasted five and a half hours:

> . . . five and a half hours of going around in circles, getting nowhere . . . I think they just met us so that they could say they had.
>
> I could tell that they thought they were going to meet a group of hysterical women. I'd say they were surprised that we were calm and knew what we wanted. One of them was sitting there almost hyperventilating. They said they were the Army Council. One was from Dublin, or somewhere in the South, the other one was from Belfast. *Bridgeen asked them a question which was keeping her awake at night, 'Why Robert?'*
>
> They couldn't give an answer. It doesn't take much in the Republican psyche to justify a murder. They could have claimed that he was a tout or that it was a punishment beating gone wrong, or that he was dealing drugs. You just have to be able to stick the mud and people will believe it. In Robert's case, they couldn't stick

the mud. They couldn't justify it or make up an excuse. They had to
come clean — there wasn't a reason. We made it clear to them that
the people who covered up the murder were as important to us as
the people who murdered him.

After the meeting the IRA released the following statement:

'. . . The IRA representatives gave the McCartney family a
detailed account of our investigation. Our investigation found
that, after the initial melee in Magennis's bar, a crowd spilled out
onto the street on the evening of 30 January. Four men were
involved in the attacks in Market Street on the evening of 30
January . . . One man was responsible for providing the knife that
was used in the stabbing of Robert McCartney and Brendan
Devine in Market Street. He got the knife from the kitchen of
Magennis's Bar. Another man stabbed Robert McCartney and
Brendan Devine. A third man kicked and beat Robert McCartney
after he had been stabbed in Market Street. A fourth man hit a
friend of Robert McCartney and Brendan Devine across the face
with a steel bar in Market Street. The man who provided the knife
also retrieved it from the scene and destroyed it. The same man
also took the CCTV tape from the bar, after threatening a member
of staff and later destroyed it. He also burned clothes after the
attack . . .

'Reports in the media have alleged that up to 12 IRA Volunteers
were involved in the events in Market Street. Our investigation
found that this is not so. Of the four people directly involved in the
attacks in Market Street, two were IRA Volunteers. The other two
were not. The IRA knows the identity of all these men . . .'

The IRA representatives detailed the outcome of the internal
disciplinary proceedings and stated in clear terms that the IRA was
prepared to shoot the people directly involved in the killing of
Robert McCartney.

The IRA believed this offer not to be sinister but to be a gesture
of goodwill to the McCartney family and to the community.

The McCartneys are ordinary, respectable people, determined

to uphold their decency. They go to great pains to make it clear they're only after justice as defined by the courts, not that defined by criminals. The sisters declined the IRA's offer. They were horrified by it. Gerry Adams tried to smooth things over by inviting them to the Sinn Féin Ard Fheis.

Reacting to the IRA's statement on behalf of the government, Justice Minister Michael McDowell said: 'If people were in any doubt about the malign influence which the IRA represents in the community, this statement should for once and for all set the record straight. It shows that their only response to crime is to offer to commit crime. Their reaction to murder is to offer to shoot people. The Provisional movement clearly represents the greatest threat to freedom and democracy on this island,' adding that the IRA seemed to be 'in some kind of freefall' by offering to murder and break the ceasefire. In a separate statement, the Justice Minister also said Gerry Adams and his deputy Martin McGuinness were members of the IRA's ruling Army Council.

Sinn Féin and IRA had been determined to disassociate themselves from criminality. Such associations had a detrimental effect on the former's political credibility. They had denied the 2005 Belfast Northern Bank robbery, the large-scale money laundering operation that followed and the murder of Robert McCartney. However, this offer to kill put a remarkable and sickening twist on their credibility and dedication to the peace process. It seemed unfathomable that the IRA went from denying involvement in the killing of Robert McCartney to then offering to shoot those involved. This move has lost the two organisations all credibility and trust. They knew they had to act fast, to back-track, to make a gesture.

Thereafter, following intense media pressure from the McCartney family, three IRA members who were involved in the McCartney murder were expelled from the organisation. This was followed by the suspension of seven Sinn Féin members. A dramatic move on the part of the IRA and Sinn Féin — more especially since Gerry Adams instructed a solicitor to convey the seven Sinn Féin names to the Police Ombudsman, Nuala O'Loan, and by association to the police.

Adams's move broke new important ideological ground since the republicans never recognised the legitimacy of the Northern Irish police force. The IRA murdered 260 Northern Ireland police men and women (RUC) during the Troubles.

The McCartneys noted the symbolic significance of this gesture but believed that Sinn Féin could hardly be commended for suspending members involved in a crime. Such actions would be standard and immediate in any other electoral party. It means nothing; not until people could feel safe enough to walk into a police station and reiterate what they saw when Robert was killed; not until people could feel secure enough to stand up in court and point-out the murderers without fearing for their own lives. Until this happens the family felt Gerry Adams's actions, along with the IRA's, were nothing more than a cynical PR exercise.

'Expulsions, suspensions, it sounds like something out of the classroom. This is a murder inquiry, not misbehaviour in the classroom,' add the sisters. Two months later the McCartneys learned that the most senior provo of the three who had been expelled had been allowed back into the IRA. They question if he was ever actually suspended in the first place.

Three Sinn Féin candidates, two past and one current, were in the bar on the night of the murder. They have been identified as potential witnesses who could provide valuable information. Yet they have not been suspended or expelled by Sinn Féin and, in spite of Gerry Adams's earlier promises to help us, they provided statements to the Ombudsman only after their identities were revealed to the media, *says Catherine*, and their statements said that they saw nothing.

The family believes the IRA and their supporters have been 'sheltering' the five men, intimidating witnesses, not co-operating with the police and spreading rumours about their brother. The sisters began to believe justice could not be achieved in their homeland. Consequently they graciously accepted an invitation to speak with the most powerful man in the world, the President of the United States, George Bush.

We were very honoured to get the invitation but we didn't particularly want to go to the States. We held on till the last minute hoping that we wouldn't have to go to the other side of the world in an effort to get justice for a man from the Short Strand.

In the end we had to go. It was around St Patrick's Day, and we were also invited to a special ball in Washington as well as other functions where we could profile our story. We didn't care how others would perceive our trip. We just knew we were going to meet the most powerful man in the world who was interested in helping us. That was all that mattered, *recalls one of the sisters.*

Going to the States was not a holiday for the McCartney family. Each of the women had to make sacrifices in order to go. Donna had to hire someone to run her sandwich bar. Her customers gave her their reassurance and support. They offered £20 or £50 pound notes to an already tight travel budget.

Robert's fiancée, Bridgeen, didn't want to leave her boys. Conlaed and Brandon were confused about what was going on. She had told them their daddy had gone to heaven.

Conlaed seems to understand. He acts like every other kid, smiling, giddy and fun loving but behind closed doors he is different to before. He is distressed at school and sits in the corner crying. He becomes hysterical when he isn't within sight of his mother, fearing perhaps that she will follow his dad to heaven. They ask, 'What happened Daddy?' 'Why was he stabbed?' They wake up during the night and wake their mother to ask, 'Did it hurt Daddy when he was stabbed?' 'Was he crying?'

Bridgeen had never before been separated from her children but felt it wasn't sensible to take them to the States because there would be no one to look after them when she'd be busy with the media and meetings. She told them that as a reward for being so good they were going on a special holiday to their Auntie Catrina's in England. Bridgeen's mother made the trip with the children. They wished mammy could come too but she said she had to stay at home to sort things out. She didn't pretend to them that she was leaving the country because they might get upset.

Those who truly supported us were happy for us to go to the States and meet President Bush and others were less than happy. Martin McGuinness warned us off. He said, 'The McCartneys need to be very careful. To step over that line, which is a very important line, into the world of party political politics, can do a huge disservice to the campaign. In fact, it can dismay and disillusion an awful lot of people, the thousands of people who support them in their just demands.'

His statement was arrogant and patronising. We're not fools, we know our own minds, and we won't be swayed by his words, *says Catherine.*

Our focus for America was to just stick to the central issue, the truth. After that we thought we couldn't go far wrong. What we wanted people in America to know is that any romantic vision they had of the struggle should now be dispelled. The struggle, in terms of what it was 10 years ago, is over. We're now dealing with criminal gangs who are still using the cloak of romanticism around the IRA to murder people on the streets and walk away from it.

We planned to bring that reality home to Americans who have political and financial influence in Ireland.

And it so happened that when Bush heard the truth Adams wasn't welcome in the White House. Instead he invited the McCartneys as a gesture to all those working towards peace in Northern Ireland. Nor was Adams welcome in his traditional role in the Saint Patrick's Day lunch on Capitol Hill. Previously it would have been a bad Saint Patrick's Day when the Sinn Féin leader wouldn't have collected more than $100,000 for his party.

Since 1995 Adams went yearly to the United States to raise money for his party; he travelled to Washington DC, New York, Chicago and other cities where donations were given by generous Irish Americans who wanted to 'help' their homeland. Single donations were often as large as $1,000. Adams had always needed to get permission from the American government in order to fundraise. After the murder of Robert McCartney and the subsequent 'cover-up', he didn't dare ask.

We weren't sure what to expect in the States but in the weeks before we had grown a lot from been thrown into the spotlight. There were accusations before we went that there was someone behind us pulling our strings. I think that statement was sexist. It wouldn't have been said if we were five brothers. The only man behind this campaign is Robert. He is the only one pulling strings for us.

We travelled from Belfast to Dublin to get our flight to Washington DC. We were waiting on the run-way at Dublin airport, about to board the plane, when the stewardess approached us and asked, 'Are you the McCartney sisters?' 'We are,' one of us said. Gemma thought we were going to get kicked off the plane before we even got in the air. 'The captain would like you to sit in first class,' said the stewardess. We were delighted and surprised as we took our seats.

The relative silence of the plane was a welcome relief to the mayhem of media scrums and constant interviews. Paula was especially relieved with the rest. Her house in the Short Strand has acted as the campaign's headquarters, a house in which the phone rings every five minutes. The sisters take turns to answer it, to speak with the journalists on the other end of the line who are calling from all over the world. They won't turn down any interviews. They need to keep the pressure on so that those who can might be forced into helping them. And in between the myriad of radio, television, and print interviews the women deal with their children who are wondering who's making dinner . . . This is the first quiet time the women have had, where there is no guilt in taking a rest.

———

The captain's welcome is a sign for what is ahead of them in the States, apart from a small hiccup at immigration when they land in Baltimore/Washington International Airport.

Paula remembers the immigration officer politely asked,

'What is the purpose of your visit to the States, business or pleasure?'

'We're here for meetings,' one replies.

'Then you need a work permit,' the officer replies, looking at their passports which have no such permits.

In a clear Belfast accent Bridgeen tells him, 'We've come to see the President.'

He asks, 'Which President are you here to see, Mam?'

'Mr Bush, you know, George,' Bridgeen says.

'And where are you going to meet President Bush?'

Bridgeen shouts over to Catherine, 'Do you know where we're meeting Mr Bush?'

'In the White House,' Catherine replies.

'And how are you going to get there, Mam?' the immigration man asks, not sure if he should arrest the women there and then.

'By taxi,' Catherine replies.

He asks who is meeting them at the airport. The women aren't sure of exactly who'll be there. They don't realise that the world's media is waiting for them some ten feet away at the other side of the partition.

Finally, the now exasperated man at immigration asks the women if he can see their invitation to the White House. When they say they don't have an actual written invitation but were told their passports would be enough to gain entry, the immigration man has heard enough and he asks them to follow him for further questioning because he isn't sure about the veracity of their story. The sisters tell him to ring Senator Ted Kennedy. He'll sort this out. They offer his number. Soon the officers have verified their story. They wish them luck with their campaign. The sisters leave the office to be met by a hundred photographers.

The next day the sisters meet Mitchell Reiss, the president's US envoy to Northern Ireland, the man who can get things done. He talks to the family and arranges to meet the sisters back in Belfast. Then they visit Senator Ted Kennedy who greets them outside with his two dogs. Then he brings them to his office. On the wall hang photos of JFK and Bobby Kennedy.

We tell the Senator that our mother greatly admired his brother John F. and how she followed his career. Without hesitation the Senator asks for our mother's number and before we know it he is chatting away to her and extending his sympathy and compassion. I'm sure those moments give her a great lift. He couldn't do enough for us. He understands our grief because he lost two brothers of his own. We have tea with him and we tell him our story.

Senator Kennedy cancels a planned meeting with Gerry Adams. A Kennedy spokeswoman, Melissa Wagoner, tells the media: 'Senator Kennedy has decided to decline to meet with Gerry Adams, given the IRA's ongoing criminal activity and contempt for the rule of law.'

We're joined by Senator Hillary Clinton. She wants to hear in our own words what happened our brother on the night he died. We haven't prepared what we're going to say to Senator Clinton, but the truth is spontaneously reiterated. She is horrified by our account, most especially by the fact that senior Sinn Féin officials were in the bar on the night of the murder, officials who haven't come forward with real information. She asks us to e-mail her the details.

That night they attend the American Ireland Fund gala dinner. The Taoiseach is also there. A speech is delivered by Senator McCain, whom the McCartneys met earlier. His speech condemns the IRA and Sinn Féin and applauds the courage of the Belfast women. The six are pleased that everyone applauded. They feel it's in their brother's name. Donna looks at Gerry Adams as everyone else is applauding. She notes he sits still, expressionless, and does not applaud. If there were a camera watching he might have acted differently but this shows privately he isn't behind the sisters. 'He isn't sincere in his promise to help us get justice for our brother.'

The sisters are busy talking to anyone who could help them. There are powerful Irish-Americans present, but all eyes are focused on the McCartneys and Bridgeen. They are the ones everyone wants to speak with. Bertie Ahern seems proud. 'I want to say here, rarely have I met braver people,' he enthused, not wanting to be left out of the gang. An awakened, more discerning, more sophisticated Irish-American who might on previous occasions have scrambled to shake the hand of Gerry Adams feels ashamed and sick to death about the murderous behaviour of provo thugs. Those present at the dinner realise they inhabit the same moral space as the McCartneys, not Gerry Adams.

The following day begins at 8 a.m. with a series of interviews, including CNN. The sisters travel all over Washington DC, doing interview after interview. They arrive by taxi at the White House to meet President Bush. They join a line of people who are queuing outside the White House. They're freezing but they know it will be worth the wait. One sister comments it's like queuing to see Santa Claus on Christmas eve. You hope he'll give you what you want but all you can do is hope that your belief will be enough. The six are shown into a reception room where grand portraits of past first ladies adorn the walls. Catherine describes what follows:

Three of us are permitted to meet Mr Bush. He has a lot of people to meet. We are among one group of twelve. It's agreed that Bridgeen, Paula and myself will go in to meet the President. We're ushered into another room. There is no confusion as to where we should stand. Our names are clearly marked out with labels on the floor. Bridgeen moves hers because she wants to stand between us.

We're not left waiting long. President Bush arrives. He asks who is Robert's widow, and then asks Bridgeen how her children are coping. He clearly knows what happened to Robert but Bridgeen feels too nervous to talk very much. Paula tells him about Robert, that he was a good father, brother and son . . . he was gentle and quiet. I tell him that I hope he will be able to help by using his influence to do good. I explain that Robert's killers need to be brought to justice and that this is a real test of Sinn Féin's sincerity. He promises that he is fully behind us and our campaign. He assures us that justice will be done.

A weight has been lifted from the women's shoulders. They pop out of the White House for a quick smoke, relieved things went so well. When they want to get back in they realise they've been locked out and have to wait for the secret service to find them wandering about the garden. The women laugh out loud as they remember back. It's easy to see they laughed a lot as a family before this happened. They're comfortable and in tune with one another, each relying on the other for strength and guidance.

The sisters fall into bed each night, weary from their gruelling schedule. They're staying at a Jury's Inn. They have borrowed money from the credit union, clothes, shoes and luggage for the trip. Six of them are sharing beds in one room, and even sleep on the floor as funds are tight.

The next day is once again filled with meetings and interviews. A photo journalist from *Time* magazine has asked them to travel with him to the other side of the city where he wants to take some photos of the sisters at the sculpture garden of the National Gallery of Art. The sisters see such artistic photos as unnecessary.

'Can't they find an archive photo? They must have hundreds,' says one of the sisters in a tired voice. She's thinking of her children at home. This would be their bed time in Ireland.

'They say it will only take twenty minutes,' replies another one of the other sisters.

'But they always say that and it always takes much longer!' says the former. Then there is silence. One by one the sisters pull their weary bodies and tired feet from the couches and meet the photographer.

You just keep thinking 'Robert, Robert' and you come back to your senses again. There is a reason why we're here.

The trip was hailed a success but the family say: 'Until we get the people who murdered Robert into a courtroom and inevitably into a cell I can't feel anything.' They know they have a long road ahead of them. They don't see themselves as particularly brave.

Had this happened five or ten or fifteen years ago — at the height of the Troubles — we as a family would have spoken out. But the difference is we would not have been listened to because a lot of families who suffered injustice spoke out and were not listened to. No time is a good time for your brother to be slaughtered but yes, the timing is probably in our favour.

We came to Washington dc to see if anyone would listen to our story but by the time we left we realised there was no one left to tell.

The family leave in the same unassuming fashion in which they arrived, impervious to the pomp and ceremony.

———

As the sisters flew home the American media continued to back their campaign. *The Boston Globe* wrote, 'The IRA have shown itself no different from the fictional Mafia family by offering to shoot the men who killed McCartney.' In an unfortunate analogy *The Times-Picayune* of New Orleans referred to Adams's ratings as 'dropping like a knee-capped Protestant'.

The sisters' campaign isn't the only reason the media have sided firmly with the McCartneys. They have strong allies in the Bush administration; Reiss demanded that the IRA disband, while a Bush official compared Adams to Yasser Arafat, the late Palestinian leader. 'Just as the president labelled Arafat not a partner for peace, the same now goes for Adams,' the aide said. Another White House aide confirmed that Adams could not be trusted in peace negotiations and that his public face of civil democracy hid 'sinister connections'.

A heap of congratulatory post awaited the McCartney family on their arrival home.

We also had a lot of people coming to the house giving us prayers and novenas. I told them that Jesus would approve of our actions. Jesus was an activist, he'd have put his head above the fence, he wouldn't have run for cover, he wouldn't have hid away and hoped for divine intervention, *says Catherine*.

We read each letter with interest and gratefulness until we came to one particular letter. It said, 'You are going to be killed.' It was written in a childish scrawl. The badly spelt single-page letter referred to a 'hit list', to 'bullets being too good for them', and to a threat that we would die in a similar way to our brother — by knife attack. The author signed off on the note that he hoped our brother was rotting in hell. The writer obviously didn't sign his/her name. The letter was handed over to the police for forensics.

This letter was sadly the first in a series of threats, some more sinister than others, but none more so than when the sister of one of the IRA men whom we believed killed Robert, came to our door, *says Paula*. The woman stood at my front door and warned me to 'back off' or I would be 'put out of the area', which meant we would be quite literally driven out.

I'm not afraid of her or of them, *says Paula*. We're not doing anything wrong. We're just telling the truth and asking for the truth to be told in return, so my initial reaction was to stay put. I had no reason to run, but after further incidents I was forced to have bullet-proof glass fitted in my windows.

Sadly, in the end I did relocate because I feared for the safety of my children after they were attacked and intimidated and my house was threatened with petrol bombs, *says Paula.*

My son, Stephen (19), was targeted by the son and nephew of a senior IRA representative. His attackers were travelling in a car when they spotted him walking. There were three of them and they attacked him, punching him. All I can say is thankfully Stephen was in a crowded public place where people intervened and helped him. Otherwise the attackers might have killed him. He was lucky, but this wasn't an isolated incident.

Mark, my other son (15), experienced a similar attack. He was in a chipper with his friend at the time. The son of a senior IRA representative came in. He was about nineteen years old. He stared over at Mark. Mark's friend said, 'What are you staring at?' After that a slagging match began between the two boys. The IRA man's son said, 'Your uncle was scum . . .' Mark didn't answer or take part at any stage until the boy physically attacked him. He was hurt quite badly and had to be hospitalised. He had a concussion. There's a big difference between the strength of a nineteen-year-old and the strength of a fifteen-year-old. We reported it to the police but still the boys were intimidated and threatened, *says Paula.*

We have received threats through the police, from their own intelligence. We have to take them seriously because our children's lives could be at risk. We get poison pen letters, 'You're next', written on an up-to-date picture of Robert's children, pictures of Robert with human excrement smeared across them. You wonder what kind of mentality would do such a thing.

We've also received letters from religious fanatics, saying that Robert deserved to die because he had children out of wedlock. We live in a sick society, from these types of people to the people who are meant to be governing our country. All sides are full of hatred and bitterness; at the end of the day it's only about one thing — power, *says Catherine.*

We constantly come face to face with Robert's killers — in the street, the shops . . . everywhere, *says Paula.* We hear about their holidays, their plans . . . Recently Bridgeen was in the supermarket. She was at the checkout and Robert's killer came and stood in the queue directly behind her. This man had been arrested for the murder of our brother but he was out on bail. She got such a fright that she ran from the supermarket without her change or shopping.

Bridgeen lived in the Short Strand up to recently and was also the victim of intimidation. One night a group of 150 women gathered around her house. Among them were wives and sisters of those who were associates of Robert's killers. Many were from the area. The women read out a letter that listed their demands. Bridgeen was terrified to come out. She was a young mother at home with two wee kids. She turned up the TV and pulled down the blinds. She knew she couldn't get out of the house without facing the mob. The leader continued to read out the letter. Its main demand was that Bridgeen move out of the Short Strand area. Bridgeen phoned Paula. Paula's husband, Jim, came around to her house immediately as did a female neighbour. They stood at her door. Gerry Kelly and the police also arrived. The women dispersed when Gerry Kelly told them to 'go home'. Bridgeen's two little boys of 5 and 3 were hysterical with fear. They were up all night vomiting after the incident and suffer from nightmares ever since.

In the weeks that followed a key witness to the murder was threatened at gun-point to keep quiet. 'And a friend of Robert's, who was with him on the night and who agreed to testify, was also targeted. The IRA came and beat him up quite badly. They thought it would frighten him sufficiently to stop him from testifying,' says Catherine.

Out of ten arrested, all exercised their legal right to remain silent and not to engage with the family during the interview process. One man was charged with the murder of Robert McCartney.

Protected by armed police in riot gear, the McCartney sisters took their seats in the Belfast court to witness a veteran republican being charged with the murder of their brother. Another Belfast man was accused and charged with the attempted murder of Robert McCartney's friend, Brendan Devine. Both men were later granted bail. The accused have denied the murder.

We were happy that the first step had been taken in bringing those that killed my brother to justice. But it has to be remembered that there were a lot more people involved in Robert's murder, and we won't be happy until all those people who were involved are brought to account, *says Catherine.*

Because of the suspects' silence the investigation relied wholly on witnesses coming forward and taking part in the court case. A number of people have come forward but they refused to commit their evidence onto paper. The police have said,

> We need people to provide statements to the police in the first instance and then follow that through and be prepared to give that evidence to a judge in court. These people also need to feel comfortable in the knowledge that, having made those statements, they can return to their own communities and live in their own homes safety, without fear and intimidation.

The McCartney sisters' campaign has shown the disturbing evolution of the IRA. It has been personified and reinterpreted by the likes of those who murdered Robert McCartney. The main perpetrator in the murder of Robert McCartney had become so degenerate and sickeningly violent that he was subject to repeated complaints from Sinn Féin supporters. They knew the likes of him could bring great shame to the party. He was accused of burning a woman's breast with a steam iron during a domestic dispute. Yet his crime was ignored.

Another man involved in the murder has a similar infamous reputation. Four years ago he attacked a pregnant woman by violently kicking her in the stomach. His grievance was not with her but with her boyfriend whom he also attacked. The young woman survived with her life but she lost her baby and required emergency surgery. She had been due to give birth three months later. She did not report the incident because she was viciously intimidated into silence.

It seems the one-time 'protectors' of the Short Strand have turned into their tormentors. The once freedom fighters are now bank robbers and murderers. And the wanna-be political leaders want to be part of a democracy only if they can keep the nuances of fascism.

Had it not been for the McCartneys' campaign Robert's murder would have passed with nothing more than a mention in the paper and his killers would have walked the streets which their chests puffed out just that little bit more than usual.

> If these people can get away with murder there isn't anything that they won't get away with . . . It will basically mean there will still be people walking through the streets of Ireland able to kill because they belong to an organisation. Unless we achieve justice there will be no hope for the wider community who live in fear. If these people are brought to account it will be a sign to the people of Northern Ireland that law and order prevails, *says Catherine.*

——

The sisters looked tired and worn-out but not defeated. 'We're exhausted all the time but we can't afford to stop. We have to keep going. We have no other choice. When we sometimes feel like giving up we just think of Robert. I go to bed every night with the image of those men surrounding our Robert and a knife going into him and him falling to his knees and I wake up with that image again in the morning. That's what makes us carry on,' says Paula, with grief frozen to her face, still unable to cry for the loss of her brother, or bring herself to visit his grave.

That is also what makes these women spend precious time away from their children and husbands; from jobs they once loved; from their own lives. That is what has helped them make the same futile journeys to meet bored politicians and officials who secretly wish they'd just go away. But they won't go away. They're driven not by hate but by moral courage, determination and a love for their brother.

They have begun to realise that their fight to get justice for their brother is going to be a long, hard haul. They are shocked that this should be so.

They believe Gerry Adams has the power to make a real difference. They want him to go personally to the houses of those who were involved in their brother's killing and cover-up, and order them to hand themselves in. It has been suggested if he does so it will be seen as brotherly loyalty being traded for political expediency, yet the rest of the world would see it as 'doing the right thing'.

The McCartney women have been credited with changing the political landscape of the Irish peace process. It would not be an exaggeration to say their campaign has contributed greatly to the IRA's historic announcement to disarm, and they have seen the arrest of one of their brother's killers so their campaign has been anything but futile.

They have also given the country a valuable lesson into the depths and strength of love. They have given the IRA a lesson in the true meaning of the word 'bravery' and have shown the world that murder will no longer be tolerated in Northern Ireland. If the justice system fails this family, if these murderers are allowed to walk the streets, then the principles of civilised society have not been upheld in this strange type of 'peace' that occupies the Short Stand.

The McCartney sisters' journey has been long, with a high price to pay at each crossroad. Their sacrifices have been many and personal rewards few. Yet they continue with their journey onto the European Courts: 'There is no ending in sight. We're not budging and they're not prepared to tell the truth. Do I hate them? No, I don't hate them. I'm more sickened by them,' says Catherine.

Chapter 6
Keeping it in the family

Tara O'Brien

The long drawn-out horror . . . had produced in me a kind of inert anesthesia; it was as if I had been so battered and beaten that I was like some hunted animal which, exhausted, can only instinctively drag itself into a hole or lair.

L. WOOLF

'What the fuck took yeh so long to open the bleedin door?' Short of breath, he roared at Tara's mother.

'I'm sorry, I'm sorry.' Tara's mother's usual and immediate response skipped off her tongue like a well-rehearsed song.

Her mother was an elegant, gentle yet very hard-working woman. People who were acquainted with her considered her a lady. She spoke timidly as she helped him wheel his 'precious' Honda 50 into the small kitchen. Tara was never in any doubt that he loved that old bike much more than he did his wife or twelve children. Tara's mother grappled to explain to her husband the reasons for her 'tardiness'. 'When you rang the bell I was upstairs putting a hot water bottle in your bed . . .' Her voice trembled, her head hung low, she ensured no eye contact was made as she stumbled over her words. He interrupted her sentence to continue his rant of abuse with an anger that could set the room alight.

The strength of Tara's father's voice matched his physical presence. He was broad and muscular. His body was packed tight as if three men had been squeezed into one. The neighbours' children ran when they saw him coming, such was the fear he invoked. He was unashamedly fierce, but more especially when he had the drink on him. The drink turned him into a 'complete animal'.

My mother made sure his Honda 50 motorbike was standing securely before she moved over to the boiled kettle. Her hand continued to shake as she spooned the tea-leaves into the pot. Her tremor caused some leaves to spill on the floor, but she pretended not to notice for fear of drawing his attention to the waste. I moved quietly from where I was standing at the top of the stairs into my bedroom. I had heard enough of his temper. I hid underneath my bed, my escape from the adult world, but soon I could feel the vibrations of his voice reverberating through the ceiling. There was no escaping the reality of the situation.

This was a night Tara would remember for the rest of her life.

'Where is she? Tara, get down here right now!' He yelled in a voice so fiercely sharp it cut her breath in quarters, leaving her gasping to inhale gulps of air. Her body turned limp with fear. Sweat appeared through her clothes.

Jelly-legged she ran quickly yet cautiously into the kitchen. Her eyes searched for her mother. The latter was preparing supper. Her clenched knuckles held the brown, ceramic teapot. She placed it, along with a bread-roll, on the neatly set table in front of Tara's father. He looked at the bread-roll as if it were made of coal. Then he looked at his wife in mock astonishment. Holding the bread in the air he said in a smouldering voice, 'And what the fuck is this?'

Tara's mother opened her mouth as if she was trying to say something, but only a stutter came out.

'Well?' he roared as her stutter grew worse. 'Is this what you expect your husband to eat for his supper? Well, is it?' By now he was standing, shoving the bread-roll in her face. He then turned and slowly walked away from her; when he was about ten feet away he quickly turned back, like a cowboy in the wild-west about to shoot, and fired the roll across the kitchen in the direction of his wife. She put her hands over her head but didn't move. The bread-roll bounced off the wall and crashed against the floor.

We stared at the roll on the floor. Its crust had cracked into pieces on the well-worn lino floor. In my child's mind I was glad the bread-roll couldn't feel pain. My mouth went dry and my breathing quickened, yet I didn't move. I didn't want to draw attention to my presence. Maybe if I stayed very still he wouldn't notice me.

Through her tears Tara's mother tried to explain why there was no other food in the house. In an apologetic voice she reminded her husband that he had promised to pick up some food for the family on his way home from the pub. He did all the shopping because he didn't want Tara's mother to have access to their money, most of which he spent on drink, that night being no exception. Her explanation enraged him further.

He walked up to his wife and smacked her across the face. He said nothing, turned back to the table and poured himself a cup of tea as if what had just happened was normal.

Tara's mother bent down and began to pick up the fragmented bread-roll. She looked at her daughter's astonished face, then in a tone a decibel higher than usual she said, 'If you dare lay another hand on me I will call the police and have you charged.' With that he jumped up from the table. Tara and her mother fled upstairs but he was too quick for them. Halfway up the stairs he grabbed his wife and dragged her down backwards. While he grasped her head of hair with one hand he used the other one to punch her face. Tara watched her mother being systematically punched and kicked. Not an inch of her body was left untouched. Tara grabbed her father's leg and tried to pull him away from her mother but he shoved her away and warned her she'd get the same if she interrupted him again. Up to this point, he had never hit his five-year-old daughter Tara.

Tara ran upstairs and put her hands over her ears to block out her mother's screams and pleas for him to stop. She banged on the wall which connected her house to the one next door. She hoped her neighbours would come to the rescue. But no one came. No one ever came.

Finally, her father either got tired or realised if he kicked his wife anymore he wouldn't have anyone to cook or clean for him. By now she was so weak she had stopped crying out — she was hardly able to whimper. Tara heard him leave the hall and go into the sitting-room.

I waited and waited to hear my mother come upstairs but there was no movement. I wondered was she dead. As I crept out of my room and reached the top of the stairs I heard the front door close. Surely, Mammy wouldn't leave me alone with this monster? I ran to the bedroom window and saw what looked like her shape in the night's darkness. I went back to bed and cried the endless tears of a five-year-old child. I cried hard and loud, willing her to hear me, to come back to me, but there was no sign of her returning. I hoped she was gone to get the police for my father.

It must have been about midnight when my father came into my bedroom. I was still crying. He said, 'Come on, get up! Quick as you can. Mammy is missing. Go look for Mammy.' I hurriedly tried to dress myself but he told me that I didn't have time.

'Quick, quick!' he said. 'You have to find her and don't come back without her!' I ran down the stairs and he ran behind me, half chasing, half ushering me towards the front door. He opened the door to let me out and I continued to run. I heard the door close behind me. I glanced around and was surprised to see he wasn't there. He had locked me out.

Tara knew she was in trouble the moment her bare feet stepped onto the icy concrete slabs of the footpath. She walked quickly. The night's winter wind blew through the light cotton material of her nightdress. The darkness of the street, with sporadic gulps of light from the street lamps, the sleeping houses with blinds pulled, the silence — all combined to intensify the edge of Tara's fear. Fear that she'd never find her mother. Fear that she'd be on her own forever. Everywhere seemed to look different at night. She had never before walked beyond the confines of her own street. As she turned each corner she prayed for her mother to appear. Tara realised she had walked such a distance from her own neighbourhood that she couldn't find her way home even if she wanted to.

Up ahead she saw a church and remembered something her mother had told her: 'If you ever get lost go to a church because it's safe there.' Tara walked up the grand steps of the church and entered the vast building where the last of the candles in front of St Jude burned. She lay down on the red carpet in front of the statue and cried herself to sleep.

She awoke to hear voices outside the door of the church. One of the voices sounded like her mother. Tara ran down the church aisle calling out to her mother, 'Mammy! Mammy!' The oak door was pushed open and a woman appeared, but it wasn't Tara's mother. She was a well-dressed woman wearing a matching green coat and hat. She was in her thirties and was accompanied by a man of the same age. Her voice suggested rich carpets, a two-storey red bricked house, hard-backed books and a privileged life so distant to Tara's. The couple were shocked to see such a young child alone in her night clothes.

The woman asked Tara why was she out on her own so late at night. Tara explained she had lost her mother and didn't know how to get home. The couple chatted between themselves and then the man, who had a Hollywood smile, picked Tara up in his arms. Tara hoped they might bring her home to their house where she could be their orphan Annie, but instead they carried her to the Garda station. The sergeant in charge put Tara sitting on his seat by the fire. He wrapped her in his coat and someone else brought hot drinking chocolate. After a while another guard entered the small room and behind him stood Tara's father.

'There you are. I was looking for you everywhere,' her father said, insincerely. A guard drove Tara and her father home. Not a word was spoken between father and daughter until they reached their front door. As her father opened the front door he said, 'Get up those stairs. I'll deal with you in a minute.'

I sat on my bed. I heard him bolt the front door. As each step grew closer I felt weaker and weaker. By the time he reached the landing my whole body was shaking. I hid underneath the bed. I could see his heavy-booted feet cross the wooden floor. There was nothing to do but wait. He jumped onto my bed, so the metal springs were pushed down against my body. Then his hand appeared underneath the bed. It was coming towards me like a animal's claw, searching down a burrow for its prey. I had nowhere to hide now, nowhere to move, so I buried my face into my body and I lay in the foetal position. He grabbed me by my ponytail and yanked me out from underneath the bed. He held me in the air by my blond wispy hair, the way you'd hold a rag doll. Then he threw me against the wall. He got up and walked to where I lay. In a slow and methodical manner he punched and kicked me in the face. I put my hands up over my face to protect it. I could feel the blood pumping from my nose and mouth. It didn't stop him though. He kicked my body like a football, lap after lap around the room. He stopped momentarily but only to take a penknife from his pocket. He opened it and I saw the shiny blade coming for me. I closed my eyes. In the final moment he changed direction and instead dug the blade into the mattress. He ripped the mattress from head to toe until the horsehair was exposed in pockets throughout.

He seemed distracted by something stuck to his hand. Strands of my hair were webbed between some of his fingers. He flicked his hand as if to rid it of my hair but my blood had adhered it to his skin. He wiped it on the untorn strip of mattress.

Tara's father left her room. She heard him enter his own room. She presumed he was going to bed, but he returned within seconds. This time he was holding a belt. This was no ordinary belt; it was a belt he had custom made for whipping his family. Each inch of the thick leather belt was fitted with heavy, old coins. Tara lay face down in the same spot in which he had left her. She couldn't move or make an effort to escape. He crashed the belt against the wall, and the impact of the coins caused the plaster to disintegrate into white dust which fell onto her little body. He wanted her to hear the degree of pain he was about to inflict. Each crash of the belt sounded like the discharge of a shotgun. He hit the wall for a second and third time. Convulsive fits rolled over her body. Uncontrollable shaking echoed the terror and the reality of the scene. Finally, the burning clash of the belt against her skin came as it would time after time. Each lash was like an electric shock that saw her tiny body yelp from the floor.

'Now that will keep you in your place,' he said with beads of sweat running down the side of his red, heated face.

The belt hung tired in his right hand. He used his left hand to once more pick me up my hair, or at least what was left of it. He threw me on top of the torn mattress.

Tara passed out before her father left the room and remembers nothing else from that night. The next day she awoke, unable to move with the pain that enveloped her body. She looked at her hand that rested beside her face. It had deep cuts and was swollen with blue bruises, an image which was mirrored on her body. Without moving from the bed her eyes searched the room. It told a sad story of the night's events; the wall was spattered with her blood, tufts of her hair were scattered on the floor among the white dust and horse hair stuffing, and the wall bore indents from his belt.

Confused chaotic thoughts wailed inside Tara's head. She was unable to fathom this impossible situation. She felt like an injured animal on the side of the road that no one bothered to rescue. She wondered was she dying. She prayed to Our Lady to take her to heaven.

Some hours later her father came to her room. She closed her eyes and pretended to be asleep. She felt the heat from his breath against her face as he leaned over her. He walked out of the room but locked her bedroom door on his exit.

That evening he returned, opened her bedroom door and carried her to the sitting-room. 'I want to keep an eye on you,' he said, without a trace of regret.

Tara sat and stared out the sitting-room window. She wondered was she hallucinating when she saw her mother coming towards the house. Her mother knocked on the front door. Her husband answered it promptly, and before he could confront her she caught a glimpse of Tara and rushed to her side.

'What happened her?' Tara's mother gasped.

'This one had to be shown that you don't involve the police in a family affair.'

This was Tara's first memory of her father's abuse. In the years that followed, her father continued to inflict his violent rages against his family. Yet during his moments of sobriety he could show acts of kindness, such as building Tara a go-cart. She wanted to trust him, to love him and be loved in return.

Tara strove to be a model child so that her father would have no reason to be annoyed at her. Sometimes it worked, sometimes it didn't. Sometimes he would lash out because his tea was too hot, sometimes it was because it was too cold. Other times he was cruel for no reason other than being cruel. On the night before Tara's Holy Communion her father seemed quiet and calm. He called her to his side. She was giddy with excitement at the hopes and prospects of what the following day would bring. He asked her to kneel before him. As she knelt in front of him he gathered her honey-blond hair back from her face and shaved it clean. 'If you move your head it will be sliced open,' he warned in the same calm voice with which he'd beckoned her.

What Tara remembers most is not his atrocious act of cruelty but rather the shame of not being able to wear a Holy Communion veil. The veil could not sit on her head because she had no hair to attach it to. Her mother sat up late trying to attach some of the cut hair to the veil to make a wig, but it didn't work. Tara remembers how the congregation gasped when she walked up the aisle to receive her first Holy Communion. On the day she was meant to be the centre of attention, her father ensured she was just that, but for all the wrong reasons.

———

Tara has eleven siblings. When each of her brothers and sisters reached the age of eleven or twelve, arrangements were made for them to be sent to industrial schools run by nuns. Tara's mother usually made these arrangements. She told the authorities that the children were too wild and she couldn't cope. Tara knew this wasn't the truth and was soon to find out the real reason.

I was sitting on my father's knee. He was bouncing me up and down. I saw my mother's eyes fix on us. He looked at her as he stood up with me in his arms. 'I'm going to bed and I'm taking Tara with me for company,' he said quite matter-of-factly. She protested but he took me anyhow.

I didn't understand what was happening. He placed me on his king-size bed that had two mattresses. His bed was very soft, the best bed in the house. He dropped his trousers on the floor and awkwardly mounted the high bed. 'Lie down Tara,' he said. 'I'll keep you nice and warm.' I didn't know much about the facts of life. I was eight years old, but I knew something wasn't right. I slid down under the covers and my father asked me to lie on top of him. I didn't move so he pulled me on top of him. He pulled down my underpants and placed me in a certain position. I was hurting inside. I told him he was hurting me and I screamed for my mother. He told me to shut up or he would give me a beating. I knew my mother could hear me screaming but she didn't come into the room to defend me. After a while he stopped and told me that I could go to my bedroom and sleep. When I left my father's room I went straight down to the bathroom to clean myself. I sat on the toilet. I was still hurting and now I could see I was bleeding as well. I went to my room and sobbed. There was no chance of sleep that night. I wanted to die.

In the subsequent years the mental, physical and sexual abuse continued. 'My father seemed to think it was his parental right to abuse me and my mother kept pretending everything was okay. I felt betrayed by her. I couldn't understand how she allowed this to happen.'

When Tara turned ten her mother finally took action. Perhaps she was fearful that Tara would become pregnant. Whatever her reasons she got in touch with a social worker and asked to arrange a place for Tara in the Holy Angels Boarding School. She didn't tell the social worker about the abuse. She merely told her that Tara wasn't happy living with them. The next day the nuns came to collect her. Tara was thrilled to be getting away. She grabbed a plastic bag, filled it with her few processions and gave her mother a goodbye kiss.

'There is no time for that carry on,' her father barked. 'The nuns are in a hurry.'

Tara got into the nuns' mini bus and looked out the window to wave goodbye to her mother, but she wasn't there. Her father was walking into the house, laughing. Tara hated him more than ever for not even allowing her mother to wave goodbye.

Tara settled into the Holy Angels School and expected to stay there until she was sixteen. Her parents were given a progress report and told that Tara was excelling in her new environment. Soon after this report her father came and took her home. Because Tara hadn't been placed in the school through the courts her father had the right to take her back whenever he wished.

The abuse became worse than ever. Each time her father tried to rape her she would do her best to fight him off, but she rarely succeeded. Usually he would manage to pin her to the ground and he didn't care who was in the house. Tara thought about telling someone in authority about what was going on, but each time she was about to tell she would hear her mother's voice ringing in her head, 'You don't want to send Daddy to prison now, do you?' On one occasion she threatened her father that she would tell the police what he was doing and she subsequently fled the house to act upon this threat.

Tara returned home and admitted she hadn't told the police. Nonetheless her father tried to lock her into a room so that she couldn't leave again. Tara threw a chair out the window. Her father pulled her to the ground and tried to rape her again. 'This time I'm really going to teach you who is boss of this house,' he said, full of madness. Tara fought him like she had never fought him before, biting and kicking. Her father shouted to her mother to get the doctor, 'Tara is going mad!' He held Tara down by sitting on top of her. When the doctor arrived he gave Tara a sedative in the form of an injection. Without speaking to her or examining her the doctor agreed to her father's request to have her committed to St Ita's Psychiatric Hospital.

———

At ten years of age I was locked into an adult ward with seriously ill psychiatric patients. My memory of arriving is blurred with the shock of the experience. I remember being brought into a large room. I don't remember any colours in this room. It was all grey. Some women were banging their heads against the wall. Someone else was trying to break a window with a fire extinguisher. The window had bars on the inside so her efforts were futile. The only other child in there was a girl, about 12 years of age. If you came within two feet of her she'd bite you. She was like a wild dog. The place terrified me. I knew I didn't belong in a place like this. I wondered was everyone else sane when they came here and only became mad by the surroundings. Would I become mad too? I tried to make a run for the door when it was briefly opened, but I was caught and heavily sedated.

Tara was in the hospital for almost a year. Her family did not contact her during this time but for her eleventh birthday her father sent her a card and a few weeks later he arrived at St Ita's and took her home.

Tara went back to school and it was there that she finally met someone who genuinely cared about her — a teacher by the name of Sister Lucy. Sister Lucy was a kind, middle-aged nun who always smelled of soap. She took a great interest in every aspect of Tara's life and more especially when she noticed that Tara had bruises and a black eye.

'Did your father do this to you?' Sister Lucy asked me. 'No,' I replied with panic in my voice. She didn't question me anymore. She knew I was lying. She told me to go home until I was better. My father was outraged that I should be sent home from school. 'I'm going down to that school to give Sister Lucy a piece of my mind!' he said, slamming the front door behind him. He was gone for over a hour and we were surprised to see that he hadn't stopped off at the pub on the way home. He never spoke of what the nun had said to him but he was quiet and non-abusive for the next few weeks. He didn't even drink.

When Tara returned to school Sister Lucy took her aside and brought her to the living quarters of the convent which felt warm and safe. The solid wood floors were polished to a high shine and fresh flowers filled the communal sitting-room with a faint sweet smell — even the religious statues which usually frightened Tara seemed to be smiling at her. In a corner of the room sat bags and bags of second-hand clothes that had hardly been worn. 'Take what you want,' the nun told Tara.

The following week Sister Lucy brought Tara to the nicest shops in Dublin to pick out a confirmation suit. Tara was in heaven. For the first time she had something new, something that hadn't been passed down. In the changing room she held the fabric to her nose and smelled its newness. Tara asked Sister Lucy to look after her new suit until the day of her confirmation. She knew only too well that her father could easily destroy it if he discovered it during one of his rages.

On Tara's confirmation day she awoke to see the sun streaming in the window. Her father put on his best suit as did her mother and Tara felt proud as they made their way to the church. They were an impressive looking group. Her father stood tall in his dark navy suit. He had the air of a man who believed his presence enhanced the congregation. He liked people to notice him, to consider him. Tara's mother was in an unassuming shade, understated, which blended into the crowd.

Sister Lucy stood outside the church and gave Tara a big welcome while slipping her a confirmation card. Tara knew by the thickness of the card that there was money inside. She admired Tara's attire as if she was seeing it for the first time. After mass her father went from pub to pub. Tara and her mother went with him and watched with sadness as he spent his daughter's confirmation money. Tara says she didn't care about the money and was just happy to have peace, a peace which of course was not to last.

On the bus journey home Tara's father picked a fight with some local lads who were sitting at the back of the bus. The lads were laughing and larking about. Tara's father was having none of it and confronted them.

'What's your fucking problem?' he asked them as if their laughter was intended towards him. He continued to shout at the boys until he looked as if his head was fit to spin off his body with frustration. The whole bus had gone quiet. The boys, who were in their late teens, exited the bus at the same stop as Tara's family. Tara knew they were from their street though she didn't know them by name.

Her father produced a pen-knife from his pocket and ran towards the boys, shouting, 'You're not so tough now, are you!' Tara's mother ran after her husband and grabbed him with her whole strength. Her actions slowed him down enough for the boys to escape. One boy looked back and shouted, 'This isn't over mister, not by a long shot!'

Tara remembers the walk home to their house: My father walked ahead of us. We didn't speak but we both wondered the same thing. Were we going to be in for it when we arrived home? As we turned the corner of our street, I noticed a small crowd of people standing at our front door. As we approached, one man broke away from the group and walked up to my father. 'What the hell are you playing at?' he demanded in a stern voice. My father didn't reply because he wasn't sure exactly what the man was talking about.

The man continued, 'It's not acceptable that you terrorise your family and it's certainly not acceptable that you attack the kids on this street. Do you know the children around here are so afraid of you they won't even walk past your door?'

With that my father tried to lash out at the man but he was too quick for him and got in the first punch. Then the man was joined by the rest of the men in the group. Together they laid into my father. My mother tried to defend my father but she was held back by the other men's wives. One woman said to my mother, 'Why do you bother with a man who beats up on you and your children?' My mother looked away and didn't reply. My father couldn't fight back because there were too many of them beating on him. After a short time they stopped and he lay on the pavement in front of our gate.

My mother ran to his side. He was badly injured and he couldn't get up. She dashed into a neighbour's house and called for an ambulance that arrived quickly and took him to hospital.

I hoped he would die that night but of course his injuries weren't as bad as he let on. My mother stayed with him until three o'clock in the morning. When she arrived home she came straight to my bedside. 'I'm sorry things ended up like this on your Confirmation day. I wish that things could be better for all of us.'

The next day he arrived home with a couple of broken ribs. I wasn't happy to see him. I couldn't help but regret that they didn't finish him off, but you know what they say, 'It's hard to kill a bad thing.'

For Tara, incidents of abuse were an almost daily occurrence. She saw her mother miscarry due to beatings. She saw her siblings being abused so badly that one still remains in a mental institution today. She saw the authorities turn a blind eye and she saw things that no child should ever see. She wondered would her death or the death of one of her brothers or sisters be enough to make her mother leave this terrible 'home'.

Tara's answer came clearly when her father tried to murder his family by locking them in an upstairs bedroom and setting the house on fire. There was no reason for his act of madness; he just did it. The family survived thanks to a neighbour who came to their aid. Yet instead of Tara's mother reporting her husband's attempted murder she decided to put all her children into care, to keep them 'safe'. Each went to a different state-run boarding school — though Tara was soon fetched home by her father.

On her fourteenth birthday Tara's father decided it was time for her to leave school and begin work in the local Tayto factory. At the end of each week she had to hand over her wages to her father. She began to work over-time and hid this fact from her father — the extra money she earned from over-time she gave to her mother and used the remainder to buy cigarettes for herself.

Tara was a good worker and her employer was fulsome in his praise of her. Soon her confidence began to grow. In the months that followed, she used this confidence to run away from home and start a life on her own, but her father quickly tracked her down and brought her home. This was a pattern that would repeat itself. Each time Tara ran away her father would find her and either blackmail her to come home because her mother was 'sick' or create such a scene with her flat-mates or with those with whom she worked that she was left with little choice but to leave. She knew if she didn't obey him the repercussions for her mother would be far greater.

On her fifteenth birthday some of Tara's workmates arranged to take her for coffee after work. On the way to the coffee shop they stopped off at Dunnes Stores to look at the season's new arrivals. Tara always wore the same second-hand clothes that had been handed down from sibling to sibling. Buying new clothes was not a luxury she could afford, not when she had to hand over her wage package each week. She watched her friends open their wage packets and pay for new outfits. Tara admired a top and bellbottoms and after much persuasion from her friends she agreed to buy them. This would be the first time she had spent her own wages.

Tara's mother was waiting at the sitting-room window for her daughter's arrival home. She had bought her a surprise birthday cake and card. She rushed to open the door but when she saw that Tara was carrying a clothes bag her smile changed to a worried frown.

'Oh my God, Tara, what have you done? You've spent the wages! He'll kill you . . .'

'I'll tell him I'll pay him back,' Tara pleaded.

'Tara, you know he won't listen to that. He won't be able to hear anything once he finds out what you've done.'

Tara's mother made her a cup of tea and put the small cream cake with unlit candles in front of her on the table and handed her daughter a beautiful card. Her gesture meant more to Tara than any clothes and she told her that. She felt guilty for the mayhem that would undoubtedly ensue. Mother and daughter sat and sipped their tea. Neither felt like cake and the candles didn't beckon to be lit.

They sat until they heard his motorbike pull up outside the house. Tara's mother told her to hide the cake and card in her room because her father would want to know how she could afford to buy it. Tara's father was already angry when he got home because the Gardaí had fined him for drink driving and for not having a licence.

That night he quite literally almost killed Tara. He hit her with a fire poker, and then he stamped on her head and body. There was no end to his fury. It was primeval and uncontrollable and it was the first time Tara's mother ever went to a neighbour's house for help. She returned with Mrs Hanly. Her family were nicknamed the 'hurricane Hanlys' partly to differentiate them from the other Hanlys who lived on the street and partly because they weren't a family to cross. If you offended one of the Hanlys, the whole family would descend upon you like a hurricane. Mrs Hanly was the matriarch, an iron woman who demanded respect and if you failed to give it her sons would beat it into you the next time.

I was in mid-air being thrown down the stairs as she entered the hallway of our house. Mrs Hanly shouted at my father, 'Get into that sitting-room.' He knew better than to disobey a hurricane Hanly, and he also knew that if she was here her sons wouldn't be far behind.

My mother got a wet cloth to clean my face which was covered in blood. She took off her coat, wrapped it around me and helped me to my feet. She put her arm around my back and half carried me out of the house. Once we got to the street another neighbour, Mrs Finn, took us into her house.

Mrs Finn lived alone, so if my father had seen us enter he wouldn't think twice about coming to take us home. Mrs Finn seemed unperturbed and said she wouldn't open the door if he came and would call the Gardaí if necessary. Her house was warm and homely. She made me a mug of hot milk with a drop of whiskey in it to 'strengthen my nerves'. My hands were swollen and numb and hardly able to hold the mug of hot milk. I pushed my hair off my face and felt lumps on my head the size of golf balls. The skin on my face was red raw, my eyes were swelling and bloodshot and my nose was bleeding.

Mrs Finn told Tara's mother, 'It's only a matter of time before you or Tara end up in a grave. Your husband is a madman . . . you have to get away.' Tara was shocked to hear my mother agree. It was probably the first time that her mother ever spoke to anyone outside of the family about the situation at home. Her impenetrable loyalty to her husband and her sense of keeping her problems inside her own front door had previously prevented her from turning to anyone for help or support.

It was agreed that Mrs Finn's brother would come after nightfall and take Tara and her mother to a shelter near the docks. Tara's mother put her hand on her daughter's head and made a suggestion that would alter Tara's destiny for ever.

'We should go to England?'

'Oh, Mam,' Tara said, 'how can we go to England? I have only five pounds to my name. That wouldn't even buy one ticket.'

Tara's mother smiled at her. 'Let's just say your father has a lot of back-pay due to the Council. I have seven weeks' rent money which was to be paid once the rent strike ended!'

Tara didn't reply. She just hugged her mother.

After dark Mrs Finn's brother came and took Tara and her mother to a hostel run by Father O'Connor. Tara had stayed there once before when she ran away from home. Father O'Connor recognised Tara immediately and welcomed her. He brought her and her mother into his office where they told him what had happened and what the situation had been like at home for the previous twenty years. This was the first time Tara's mother had opened up to someone in authority about her experiences and life of hell with her husband.

The priest agreed to give Tara a bed for the night but her mother would have to find somewhere else as the hostel was only for teens.

I told him that I wouln't stay without her. 'If that is the case,' he said, 'you'll both better leave.'

In the end my mother convinced me to stay because it would be better if she only had to pay for one person in a 'B&B' down town. She wrapped a scarf around my head to try and conceal the swelling and dried blood. I lay on my bed and prayed that my mother wouldn't change her mind and want to return home in the morning.

The next morning I awoke to find my mother standing over my bed.

'Are you ready for our new life?' she smiled.

————

That morning we sailed for Liverpool, England, where we knew a large Irish community lived. In my mind everything would be better in Liverpool. I felt like I was coming home even though I had never set foot in England.

Within a few weeks Tara and her mother had organised a modest flat. Their social welfare payments weren't vast, but nevertheless they felt rich in comparison to their situation in Ireland. Tara and her mother had been living in their new home for about a month when her mother received a letter from social welfare asking her to notify the Irish social welfare office of her new address because Tara's father had continued to claim benefits for both Tara and her mother — pretending that they still lived with him. Tara's mother gave the Irish social welfare office the necessary information, including her new address.

The following week Tara and her mother went shopping for new wallpaper, paint and curtains. They managed to buy a lot on a tight budget. Tara's mother was particularly excited at the prospects of decorating the flat. They went home loaded down with parcels and got a taxi to the door. Distracted by the job of carrying their shopping they didn't notice there was someone standing at their front door in the night's darkness.

It was Tara's father. He had got their new address from the social welfare office in Dublin. Tara's heart sank when she saw him. She looked at her mother's face and could not understand the joy that flickered in her eyes.

That night my father got around my mother and convinced her that he'd changed so she allowed him stay. The following week he went home to Dublin and returned with my sisters and brothers who had been in various institutions in Ireland. I felt let down by my mother. I couldn't believe that we had managed to escape from him. We had gone through so much and here was my mother inviting him back into our lives.

Tara began dating the older brother of a friend who lived near by. His name was Darren. Her father did not approve because he was quite a bit older than Tara. Tara liked Darren because he was everything her father was not. He was gentle and kind and protective of her. Yet Tara's mother pleaded with her to break off the relationship. She said it was aggravating her father and would drive him back to violence. Her father hadn't lost his temper since arriving in England and she wanted family life to remain stable. So Tara gave into her mother's wishes and told her she'd break up with Darren there and then. But she didn't. She needed time to think about the best way to explain it.

When my parents were out at the pub I sneaked across the road to Darren's house to break up with him. I arrived home just before my parents. I didn't realise my father had seen me crossing the street. He was angry and so was my mother because they thought the relationship had already ended.

'Why did you have to disobey your father! Things were going so well. Why did you have to ruin it!' my mother said in dismay. I tried to explain myself but it fell upon deaf ears. My father stood firm beside my mother. He held a plank of wood with nails sticking out of it in his hands. He had picked it up on the way home and had intended adding it to the fire but now he had a new plan for the plank of wood. He began to beat me across the legs with it. Then he moved onto my upper body and finally my face. Darren's mother could hear my screams from her house. She knew of our situation in Ireland and why we'd fled to Liverpool. She came to our front door which had been left unlatched and let herself in.

'What the hell do you think you're at?' she screamed with shock.

'Get out, what da fuck do you think comin' in here throwing your weight around,' he shouted back.

'If you lay another finger on Tara or if you dare shout at me again I'll have my boys over here before you know what has hit you,' she said.

By this stage my father didn't know our neighbours but he knew Darren's mother had several sons, so he reluctantly backed off.

'If I hear as much as a shout coming from this house I'll call the police and have you locked up. Do you understand what I'm saying?'

My father didn't answer her. After she left he went into the sitting-room and didn't say a word. He realised that people around this area wouldn't put up with his antics.

After that night my father kept his fists in check but became more verbally abusive. He told the rest of the family not to talk to my mother and me because we were runaways. He would humiliate my mother and myself in front of the family and in public. Sometimes it was something as simple as locking us in the back garden all day.

It was only a matter of time before Tara's father found a way to regain full terror and control of the house. One night just before the family were about to eat he said he had an announcement to make:

'Tara,' he said, 'I want you to go right now to your room, pack your bags and leave this house.' There was no explanation or dialogue, no trigger to the event. The family stared at him in amazement. Tara's mother interrupted. 'This is Tara's flat and my flat. It's not your flat and we decide who lives here, not you!'

He looked at his wife and said mockingly, 'Ah yes, I forgot, like mother like daughter! Listen "Mammy", I don't give a damn about the neighbours. There is one boss of this house and it's me and what I say goes. End of story.'

'You don't have control of this house anymore. You're only here because we allow you to be,' Tara blurted. He jumped up out of his chair and dashed towards her. He was getting on in age and Tara was now too quick for him, but her mother wasn't so lucky. He began to beat his wife unmercifully. Tara's two young brothers ran from the house screaming for help.

'If you don't stop hitting her I'll hit you with this,' Tara said, holding a chair high in the air.

'Oh will you, you little bitch!' he said pinning Tara to the wall.

At that very moment Darren appeared with Tara's two young brothers. He pulled Tara's father away from her and pushed him against the wall, pinning him to the spot.

'Well, do you like that, do you?' he asked her father. He held him to the wall until he calmed down.

Tara's mother pleaded with Darren to let her husband go and not to hurt him. When Darren finally let him go, Tara's father walked calmly to the kitchen where he picked up a glass bottle, turned and ran towards Tara with it. Darren grabbed him by the arm. He didn't fight Darren. He simply put the bottle down on the table. It was the first time Tara saw her father succumb to anyone else's authority. Darren sat with the family for hours until Tara's father went to bed.

When Darren was leaving, he asked me why we didn't have a television. I told him we did but my father kept it locked in his room. It was only for his use. 'Your father is a selfish man. He needs to be taught a lesson,' he said. 'You know you and your mother deserve a lot better than him.'

I guess it was on that night that I began to fall in love with Darren and we continued to see each other. On my sixteenth birthday we celebrated it together. We had a wonderful night in a pub where Darren got up to sing. He had a great voice and he tried to persuade me to sing. My mother has always told me I had a voice that would bring the rain down so I faked a sore throat. As we walked home, hand-in-hand, he told me he was in love with me. I was shocked and didn't know what to say, so I said that I might feel the same about him some day. I didn't want things to move so quickly; I didn't want to end up with a house full of children like my mother.

We arrived back at his sister's house. He told me again that he loved me, and he asked me to marry him! I couldn't believe what I was hearing. It was all too quick. I told him I had to think about marriage — it was only yesterday that I was fifteen and marriage wasn't something I was ready to contemplate.

The next day I told my mother. She thought I was having her on. 'Have you lost your mind?'

That night Darren came over to our flat and asked my father for my hand in marriage. My father nearly choked on his mug of tea, spitting some of it on the ground. 'You what?' he said.

Darren repeated the question. My father burst out laughing and then shouted for me to come into the sitting-room. 'Are you in the family way?' he asked accusingly.

'No, there's no baby on the way,' I said, with mortification flowing over my voice.

'Then why the fuck do you want to marry her?' he said, looking at Darren.

I felt angry with Darren for asking my father for permission when I hadn't even given him my answer yet. If my father said 'yes' it would put me under pressure to say 'yes' out of loyalty to Darren.

'I haven't given my answer to Darren yet,' I said to my father, 'so there is no need for you to say anything. Darren, please leave, I will come over to your house later and give you my answer. You shouldn't have come here until you had my answer.'

'Someone had to ask because you were too scared to ask him yourself.'

'Ask! My father doesn't own me, he doesn't need to be asked! I own me. This is my decision!'

'What?'

'Get out,' I shouted.

'I'm sorry, I'm sorry,' he said over and over. 'I love you, you know

I love you. You know, Queenie, I'd do just about anything for you.'

By now, my father was shouting at my mother. 'Mammy, get in here. Did you know about all this carry-on? Am I the last to find out what is going on under my own roof? With my own daughter? What else have you been keeping from your husband?'

Finally Darren left and I locked myself into my room. When I heard my father go to bed I came downstairs and brought in a mug of tea to my mother. We sat by the fire and she talked very seriously to me. She warned me that I would be very sorry if I married Darren because he was almost thirty and I was just sixteen. I didn't tell her my final decision but I'm sure she felt that I would be led by her advice.

By the end of that week Darren came to see Tara. He apologised once more and explained he had just been anxious to get a decision because he loved her so much.

'If you marry me you'll be free from your father. All I want to do is make you happy,' he pleaded.

Though Tara knew she didn't truly love Darren she did love the idea of being free from her father so in the end she agreed to marry him.

Tara's father did everything to stop the wedding but Tara went ahead with it anyhow and Darren's family organised everything for the young bride. After the wedding Tara's father banned the family from speaking to her. At last Tara had the freedom she'd always longed for but it was at a high cost. She was married to a man she didn't love the way she should and she had lost the only people she did truly love.

——

Darren and Tara moved into a council house which they did up together. Darren's mother gave Tara cooking lessons. Tara took pride in looking after Darren, who didn't work. Three months into their new house Tara found she was pregnant. Darren was overjoyed and he went to tell his mother who shared in her son's happiness. Tara announced the news to her father. He was disgusted and told her that as far as he was concerned she didn't exist. Tara desperately missed her family and when some months later her siblings arrived unexpectedly on her doorstep she was overjoyed. She was happy that her brothers and sisters thought so much of her that they would go against their father's wishes of not visiting.

That night Darren arrived home from the pub and was angry to see Tara's family in his home. He didn't welcome or acknowledge them.

'Where's my dinner?' he demanded. 'And what the hell are this lot doing here? Get them to leave,' he said as if they couldn't hear him.

Darren had never shown Tara such disrespect; she couldn't believe what she was hearing.

'What are you saying? I want my family to stay. I invited them into our home.'

'Shut your gob or I'll shut it for you!' he said.

'I have just left the grasp of one man who beat me since I was a baby. I'm not going to stand by and let another man do the same!'

Tara's sisters and brothers sat very still on the couch while Darren and Tara continued to argue. Finally she turned to her family. 'Let's get out of here. I'm not staying here to be spoken to like this.'

Tara tried to leave but Darren held her back. He hit her as she struggled to be released from his grip.

'You were nothing till I met you, remember that, you were nothing but a twat,' he said. Tara lashed out at him because his words hurt and shocked her so much. He caught her by the hair and swung her around the kitchen like a cat in a cartoon. One of Tara's brothers picked up a stick and hit him over the back until he let her go. Tara and her family fled the house and went to her parents' house. She told them what had happened and that she didn't want to go back to Darren. Her father listened and then asked her to leave his house.

'You've made your bed and now you have to lie on it. Don't expect us to help you,' he said without emotion.

Darren's mother contacted me and asked me to come home with her so that we could talk. I had nowhere else to go so I went with her. When I arrived at her house Darren was waiting for me. When I saw him I felt fear well up inside me. I knew how my mother felt when she would hear my father's motor bike pull up outside the house. I understood why that fear so was pronounced that she would wet herself when she heard him coming.

Darren jumped up from his chair as soon as Tara entered the room. He offered his hand to Tara and apologised.

'Did you forget that I'm carrying your baby? Do you think I'm going to let you do to me what my father has done?' Tara turned and walked out the front door. She didn't know where to go. She had nowhere to go. Darren followed her.

'Queenie, please stop. I promise you that I will never do anything like that again. You can even have your family up to see you. Believe me I'm so sorry.' Unknowingly Tara ended up outside their home, and he ran ahead to open the front door.

I walked into our house but it didn't seem like home anymore. I went to bed and he cleaned up the mess he had made by knocking me about. He slept on the couch that night. For a while things went back to normal or as normal as they could be. Then after a month another beating ensued. Once again it took place while my brothers and sisters were present.

The mistake that ruined my mother's life was now my mistake; I had married 'my father'. I knew the time to leave him was now, not when my baby was born. I turned once more to my family but they couldn't help me. I was a frightened, pregnant teenager. I felt I had nowhere to go. I thought about what my father had said, that this was my problem and I had to sort it out. I thought about why I first liked Darren. I tried to concentrate on the good in him and I thought that perhaps we could work things out.

Tara gave birth to a healthy baby boy whom she named Darren after his father. She saw baby Darren's birth as a new beginning but the relationship deteriorated further. Darren would go out drinking every night and would come home and lash out at Tara. She took as many beatings as she had taken with her father. And on top of that she felt unable to cope with the demands of a newborn baby. She felt unready to bring up a child in a situation so much like her own childhood. By this time her family had moved back to Ireland so she was left alone with no support.

I wished I knew someone who was my own age in my situation so that I could see how she coped. It was as if God was listening to me because soon after I was befriended by a local girl called Janice. She was the same age as me and was married to a man 14 years her senior and she too had a baby. We became firm friends, spending every other day in each other's flat.

On New Year's Eve, Darren, Janice, her husband and myself went out to a bar. We had so much fun dancing, singing and laughing together. When twelve o'clock struck I looked around for my husband. My eyes focused on the dance floor where he was kissing Janice. I ran to break them up but her husband pulled me back and tried to kiss me. I spat in his face and left the building. When I got home I bolted the door so that Darren couldn't get in but he arrived before I could even gather my thoughts. He screamed through the letterbox, 'Let me in!' When I didn't he broke the kitchen window with his fist. He left a trail of blood as he entered through the window.

'I'm leaving you,' I said.

'No, you're not,' he said grabbing me by the throat.

He was trying to choke me. I could feel the blood on his hands which caused him to readjust his grip and gave me the chance to gasp a breath. I saw the monster breaking out in his eyes, eyeball to eyeball matching my every flicker, waiting for the life to be extinguished from my eyes. I put up a fierce struggle to break free from him. I kicked and dug my nails into his hands, but he continued to increase his grip around my throat. He staggered, lost his balance. We fell on the coach. The arms of the couch were made of wood and he wedged my head underneath one of them. I couldn't breathe. I felt as though my head was going to explode. Blood was streaming from my nose and I was falling into unconsciousness.

I faintly heard a banging in the background. My friend and neighbour who lived upstairs had got her husband to break down our front door. He pulled Darren from me and his wife took me to their flat where I spent the night. That night I promised myself that baby Darren and I would escape from him.

When we returned the next day I found Darren sitting there with the baby in his arms. I tried to take him from his arms but he grabbed me by the wrist. 'Were you planning on going somewhere, Queenie?' he asked.

I feared that the baby would get caught up in the fight that was brewing. 'If you ever take him I will chase you down and there won't be a court in this land that would deem you a fit mother. Think of the background you came from!' he shouted.

I didn't reply. I felt he was right. How could anyone think I was a fit mother, a child rearing a child? Who was I kidding? My self-esteem and confidence were at rock bottom. I knew it would be quite some time, if ever, before I would muster up the courage to leave him. And even if I did leave I had no access to our money. I wouldn't get very far without money. I was a prisoner.

In the year that followed Tara found out she was pregnant again. Around the same time she found out that Darren was still having an affair with Janice. Tara felt his adultery gave her the higher moral ground and the confidence to once again try to flee from his control. But this time she had a plan. She confronted Darren about the affair and gave him an ultimatum.

'Finish it with Janice and move our family to Ireland or I'll tell your mother how you've been treating me,' Tara said with conviction.

Darren's mother was a good woman who would have been appalled by her son's behaviour. Darren desperately sought his mother's approval and wouldn't want to do anything to upset her. In the end he agreed to his wife's demands.

Once her second baby, Lisa, was born the move was organised. Darren sold the furniture and put his prized stereo in storage at his mother's. Tara felt Darren would be too homesick in Ireland and would promptly return to England, with or without his family, and even if he didn't it would still be easier for her to escape with the children in Ireland than in England. At least in Ireland she knew the geography of the country and she felt she had her mother and siblings to rely upon.

———

Tara stood on the deck of the boat holding her new-born baby Lisa. She saw the Irish coast and she felt like a child who had just woken from a nightmare and was about to be hugged by her mother. On arriving in Dublin, Tara secured a caravan in a halting site for herself and Darren and the children to live in until the housing authorities could provide a house for them. Darren didn't know his way around Dublin, so he had to rely on Tara in a way that was foreign and uncomfortable for him.

Tara reconnected with her mother who hadn't yet met her grandchildren. Tara was distraught to learn that her father still hit her mother and younger siblings. She wished she could take them away from this violent man. When she returned home her husband was in a foul mood so Tara quickly prepared dinner.

'Why the hell do you visit them. Sure your father's a wife beater!'

'Well, that would make him no worse than you,' Tara muttered in response.

He leaned over the table to slap Tara across the face but she moved out of his way and threw her fork towards him.

'I've had it with you,' he said.

'Good, you can get the hell out of here, then,' she replied.

Darren walked to the press and started to pack clothes. Tara's happiness turn to panic when she saw he was packing baby Darren's clothes as well as his own.

'What in God's name do you think you're doing?' she asked.

'I'm taking him back to Liverpool and you're never going to see him again,' he said as he grabbed baby Darren from his cot.

Tara fought to get him back but Darren kicked her in the stomach. As she fell to the ground he said, 'I'll be back for Lisa.'

It took Tara a couple of minutes before she could even stand up. By the time she got to her feet and rushed out the door, she saw him getting into a taxi. She ran after the taxi, screaming, 'Stop, stop! He's taking my son!' Darren looked out the back window of the taxi as it scurried down the laneway, its lights fading quickly into the darkness.

Tara ran over to a man who was standing beside his jeep in the halting site. She tried to briefly explain what had happened.

'Hop in quick,' he said with decency in his voice.

They drove towards Dublin port as quickly as traffic would allow. When they arrived at the port the man dropped Tara outside the door. She pushed through the crowds and skipped the queue to the attendant.

'My husband is trying to kidnap my child. He must be on the boat about to leave for Liverpool,' she gasped with her heart beating so loudly she could hardly talk.

The attendant contacted the Gardaí and made an emergency announcement over the loud speaker. Within minutes the Gardaí arrived, and soon afterwards Darren was spotted. The Gardaí held him and took a statement. Tara felt hopeful they would soon return to her with baby Darren.

'Miss, it is with regret that I am going to have to let your husband and son board the boat for Liverpool,' the garda said to Tara.

'But he's kidnapping him!'

'Because you are still married he has every right to take your son home to Liverpool. You'll have to fight this one through the courts.'

Tara screamed and wailed for Darren to give back her son. People stared at her as she collapsed on the ground.

The next morning Tara awoke to see baby Lisa looking searchingly around the caravan, confirmation that the previous night's events were a reality. Tara heard her father's motorbike outside the caravan. She got out of bed and opened the door.

'He left ye.'

'How d'you know that?' she asked.

'Sure, he called into myself and your mother to tell us that we'd never see the baby again. I think your mother was glad to see the back of him. Oh, and he said he'd be back for *her*,' he said pointing at Lisa.

'I know.'

'You'd better get a house. Otherwise the courts will give him custody. They see living in a caravan the same as living on the street.'

'But I've no money to get a house.'

'Can't help you there.'

Tara knew Darren wouldn't bother going to court if he could just as easily snatch his daughter. It was imperative that she moved to a new location, somewhere Darren couldn't find them. Tara had no money to rent anywhere else so she decided to squat in a vacant flat in Ballymun. Squatting was more common then and it was a way of being fast-tracked into a proper flat.

Shortly after moving in, Tara's younger brother and sister came to live with her because they were being beaten so badly at home by their father. Tara's father continued to collect benefit for them but Tara had to feed them and look after their needs. The weeks passed and Tara loved her life with her little family. She felt safe, knowing there was no way Darren could find her and she enjoyed the company of her family. They were at ease with each other.

Early one morning she awoke to hear unmerciful banging on her front door. She was surprised to find her parents standing there.

'He's coming for Lisa. He knows where you live,' her mother blurted in haste.

'How is that possible?' Tara asked. 'No one knows where I'm living.'

'I don't know,' replied her father unconvincingly.

As they were leaving her mother stepped back and caught hold of her daughter's arm. When Tara turned around to see what was wrong her mother put her finger to her lips, then pointed to Tara's father. She was trying to tell her that her father had informed Darren of her new address. He's a turncoat, thought Tara.

That morning Tara went and bought in enough food for the week. She warned her brother and sister not to answer the door no matter who came knocking. For the next week Darren came and went daily. Tara thought at times he would manage to break down the door but he wasn't on his own turf so he didn't feel quite so brave and Tara had already warned her neighbours to watch out for him.

I felt trapped once more but this time it wasn't metaphorically. I really was a prisoner in my own home. I felt so angry, mostly angry with myself for bringing children into this type of chaos. I also thought a lot about my mother. I had come to know intimately the pain she had endured. I wished we could talk frankly but I knew she couldn't help me when she wasn't even able to help herself. I kept catching myself looking at Lisa. Children learn what they see. She would grow up to be me and marry someone like my father if I didn't take control of this situation.

On the last day Darren brought Tara's father with him. Her father pretended he was on his own and tried to trick his daughter into coming to the door. She knew if she did Darren would simply have burst in and taken Lisa.

The next day her mother arrived up to her flat and through the door she told Tara that Darren was gone back to Liverpool. Tara trusted her mother and let her in. They had tea together but Tara noticed her younger sister was very quiet when her mother was there. When she left Tara confronted her sister.

'Why are you in a snot?'

'I'm not!'

'Well, there's something eating you?'

'It's her.'

'Who?'

'Mammy!'

'Why, what did she do to ya?'

'She's pretending to be all on your side but it was her who gave Darren the money to take the baby.'

'Don't talk rubbish! Why would she do that?'

'Because she wanted him out of your life.'

'But not at the cost of losing my son.'

I couldn't bear to confront my mother. I would be too let down if I had complete confirmation that this was the truth, but at the same time I felt it was the truth so I stopped visiting her. I wanted her to feel the loss of a child.

My younger brother who lived with me still visited my mother and returned one day to tell me that Darren had got a court order and was coming the following evening with my father to take Lisa back to Liverpool. I felt like I was at the end of the road. I was so tired from trying to survive. I felt as if my whole life had been about survival. I felt like I needed a miracle to save me. I had no money. No family to stay with. No friends. I was at a dead end.

My younger sister and brother sat quietly with me. They knew if Darren took Lisa I would follow them back to England and that would mean they'd have to go home to our father. I wasn't sure whose fate was worse, theirs or mine.

As I sat there with my head in my hands thinking hard about the possible options, two envelopes fell through the letterbox on the ground before me. I opened the first one which was from a social worker who said she was going to visit me because she had received a complaint from my husband and my father. I felt so angry that the men who were meant to protect and love me just wanted to destroy me. I opened the second letter quickly and ripped the envelope in two. It was from my local welfare office. Inside was a cheque for £350, money I was owed in back pay. I didn't even realise I was due this money. It may as well have been beamed directly from heaven that's how welcomed it was. It offered me an escape route.

Tara went back to the halting site and asked an old man, a Traveller, if he knew anyone who would help them out with a cheap caravan. When she told him why, he was only too glad to help. He took Tara over to a big caravan, which was very nice but needed a lot of cleaning. His daughters spoke up and promised to have it spotless by the morning. Tara gave him half the money up-front, and told him that she would give him the other half if he would bring the caravan to the flats so that she could pack it with her belongings and then drop her and the caravan down the country somewhere.

In all I had paid two hundred and twenty-five pounds for an eighteen-foot caravan. We had three pull-up beds and a long seat that turned into another double bed. We also had a shower and a toilet. The kitchen was a good size, with plenty of presses for storage. There was also a large wardrobe beside the fireplace. The fire itself had a big boiler on top which heated the water when the fire was lighting. I felt elated, that I had done something right, that we were going to be okay.

The next morning we packed the caravan and set off. We sped by familiar streets. I feel a calmness descend as we put distance between our old life and our new one. We were passing through Glasnevin when we heard a loud bang as if we'd hit something. The caravan came to a halt and we got out to see that one of the tyres had blown out and there was no spare. The Traveller manoeuvred the caravan into a lane beside Glasnevin cemetery. He told me not to worry. He would be back first thing in the morning with the tyre.

I was almost hysterical because I knew my father drove past this stretch of road each morning and evening. That night I slept little, anxious for morning so that we could get moving. But the Traveller didn't return that morning, or the next day, or the day after that. I was beside myself with panic and fear. I forbade my brother and sister to leave the caravan in case my father saw them. We sat looking out the window willing the Traveller to appear, but the only person we saw was my father who passed our caravan each morning and night.

On the seventh morning the Traveller returned. I was angry with him but I didn't show it as I just wanted to get going. He claimed he had trouble getting the tyre fixed. I didn't know if he was telling the truth but I didn't care as long as we were on the move. By nightfall we were beginning a new life outside Dublin. Every few weeks the kind Traveller came back to see if we were doing okay, then he'd tow us to a new location. We moved all around the country and made great friends. We felt a type of freedom, happiness and safety that was alien to us even as children.

————

Offaly was the last town Tara and her family lived in and it was there that she met a man called Seán. He was a soldier. She began to see him on a regular basis and she thought she was falling in love with him. He showed her the respect and kindness she'd always yearned for. But then things changed. He began to make demands on Tara. He tried to control her life, from dictating what she should wear to where she should go. One night he threatened to hit her. Tara's brother came to her defence. He pushed her brother who fell out the door of the caravan. That was the end of Seán. Tara packed up her 'house' and went on the move once more.

As we travelled I wondered was it me who was driving these men to violence. I felt confused and sad. Why me? Why was I attracted to men who ultimately turned out to be like the very men I was running away from? When I left Seán he didn't know I was carrying his child. I wasn't going to have two men chasing me for their children.

I worried about how I'd manage near the end of my pregnancy. I worried that Darren would use the opportunity to snatch back Lisa or to declare me an unfit mother because I had no fixed address. I returned to Dublin, sold the caravan back to the Traveller for the same amount that I had paid and told my sister and brother they would have to go back to our family home until I got myself sorted. I couldn't afford to keep them with a baby on the way. I think they resented me for making this decision.

I stayed in a homeless hostel for the first week and visited the social housing office each day. After a week there was still no sign of a flat. I told the man in social housing that I wasn't leaving his office until he found me a flat. By the end of the day I had the keys to a flat in Ballymun and by the end of the next day my younger sister and brother were back living with me. A week later I gave birth to a beautiful daughter.

Tara discharged herself from hospital the day after the birth. She was anxious to get home to make sure Lisa was safe. She had left Lisa in the care of her fifteen-year-old sister. Tara was delighted to see Lisa and her siblings were safe and well. However, this happiness was short-lived because Tara's father arrived at her flat the next morning. Tara was distraught because either her younger sister or brother had given him their new address. She felt she had done so much for them and they had let her down. Her father told her he was going to help Darren take Lisa because she had taken his children. Tara's siblings begged their sister to believe that they didn't tell their father of their new address. Wherever the truth lay she knew she had to leave again. But it would take the council up to two years to organise another flat. They weren't in the business of relocating people who already had perfectly good accommodation.

Her sister and brother made an effort to show their sincerity by buying Tara a caravan which they had toed to the countryside. Though the caravan was very basic Tara felt she had no option but to move into it. It was now the depths of winter and the caravan was unbearably cold, not to mention the fact that it leaked. She worried about her children's health. She felt she had no one to turn to so she decided to write a letter to the only adult who was a constant 'friend' in her life.

Dear Gay,
You don't know me but I listen to your radio show each morning and feel I know you as a friend.

I am an 18-year-old single mother of a new born baby and a one-year-old daughter and I have found myself in a desperate situation which is partly due to my own making but partly due to my background.

My childhood was one of neglect and abuse. I was beaten and raped by my father from a young age, and I never had any type of security growing up. I always imagined safety and security was a gift that I would guarantee my children, but I ended up marrying a bad man who beat me.

In order to escape from him and to protect my daughter from him I have been forced to live in a caravan. My caravan is very cold and it leaks. I worry that my children will become ill and will be taken into care. If this happens I will have nothing left to live for. I want to offer them a better life.

Do you think there is anyone out there who could help me? I have no one else to turn to but you, Gay. Please help me.

Yours faithfully,
Tara O'Brien

When Gay Byrne's radio show read out Tara's letter, an anonymous businessman made Tara the offer of a new caravan which was delivered by a women's organisation in Drogheda. The Gay Byrne show also made Tara the gift of one hundred pounds with which she bought a car. She had never taken driving lessons but quickly taught herself to drive.

I can't tell you the excitement I felt at having a car. It was such a luxury to be able to drive to a public water source and get water. Before that I had to go to neighbouring houses to ask for water. Some people thought I was a Traveller and shut the door on my face.

Tara became friends with a local man and was thrilled to be asked out for a drink. She enjoyed her night out because it had been so long since she'd been anywhere. She arrived back home at about midnight. She was surprised to see from a distance that the lights were still on in the caravan. She had left her brother in charge of the children and she'd expected that they would be asleep by now. As she grew nearer she saw the reason for the lights being on. The new caravan had been attacked, the windows were smashed into a hundred pieces and the children were screaming. The engine of her car had also been broken up and Lisa and the baby were screaming in terror.

'Who did this?' Tara asked her brother.

'I don't know. It was dark. I couldn't see,' he claimed.

Soon after, Tara's father arrived with a letter from Darren's solicitor. Tara took the letter but refused to speak with him. His arrival and the act of destruction were too coincidental. Tara was left with no option but to go to a homeless shelter.

She opened the letter and feared the worst. She had lost her home and now she was about to lose her children, or so she suspected. Darren's letter explained that he wanted to legalise their 'arrangement'. If Tara agreed to give him full custody of their son then he would give her full custody of Lisa.

I agreed to this deal. I loved Darren junior as much as any of my children but I hadn't been part of his life and I didn't want to split him away from the only parent and home he had ever known. That would have been too much for a five-year-old to bear. I did hope, in time, that he would ask for me or that his father would permit me to see him, but for now Lisa and I could stop living like convicts on the run.

On the day we legalised the arrangement I felt as if a big weight had been lifted from my shoulders, but I also felt devastated by the likelihood that I'd never again see my beautiful son. It felt like this agreement was going against nature. I hoped in my heart that one day he would learn the full truth and would understand.

From this moment on my life turned around. I got a job. I always wanted to work but I couldn't because I couldn't leave Lisa out of my sight. And with the money I earned I secured a nice apartment and began to build a future for my family.

I no longer had anything to fear from my ex-husband and I only wished my mother my type of freedom. My parents were now pushing on in age and it shocked me to think that my mother was still enduring beatings at the hands of my father. She was, however, so utterly dependent on him there was no convincing her to leave, even with her children's support. She hadn't the independence to stand on her own, not just emotionally but on a practical level as well. She wholly depended upon him to make every decision and her daily life revolved around looking after her husband in the same way you'd look after a child.

One Friday morning Tara's mother arrived at her door. Her face was red and her eyes looked sore from crying. Tara immediately presumed her father had given her another hiding. She began to blast her father for his actions. Tara's older sister stood beside her mother and abruptly interrupted Tara.

'Tara! He's dead. He had a heart attack this morning.'

Like Tara, her older sister couldn't refer to their father as 'dad'. Even in that moment of heart's darkness he didn't deserve the title. Tara felt sorry for her mother because she didn't like to see her upset but she felt no sorrow for her father.

'Is there anything I can do to help?' Tara asked her mother.

'There is only one thing I want from you, Tara. I want you to come to your father's funeral.'

I promised I would, but only for my mother's sake. I hated this man more than any other living thing and that hate didn't die because he had died. I felt absolutely no remorse after his death. As his coffin was lowered into the ground I felt anger well up inside, an anger that only intensified as time went on. I felt he was still controlling me even from the grave. I regretted that I hadn't reported what he had done to my family and me and that now it was too late.

I thought death would finally give me freedom from this despicable man but it had not. Similarly, I felt that the custodial legal arrangement would give me freedom from Darren but it had not. Each day I thought about Darren junior and by association his father. I wondered had his father poisoned him against me. I wondered did my son ever think of me. Did he miss me? Did he need me?

For the next thirty years I was angry, angry with my father and angry at my husband. My anger and sadness were so pronounced that it quite literally made me ill. I was diagnosed with cancer two years ago.

I first became aware of the lump in my breast when I was in the shower. I tried to ignore it, to put it to the back of my mind in the hope that it would just go away. It didn't. One morning I got the courage to tell my daughter Lisa and she made an appointment with our GP. He checked it out and with a kind voice he said it might not be serious. But I knew it was serious because you know your own body. I was sent to Saint Vincent's Hospital for a biopsy. Afterwards the doctor sat me down. I knew what he was going to say so I was calm and strong. He told me I had an aggressive form of breast cancer and that I needed an operation to remove the tumour.

I told my daughters. I knew I had to be strong for them so I just got on with it. I had the operation. I stayed positive even though the recovery was difficult, especially the chemotherapy. The medication wasn't working and I knew I was dying. On some level I knew if I could just let go of my anger the cancer would let go of me. I felt the two were intertwined.

I began to write down my feelings in a diary my daughter Lisa gave me. I wrote and wrote until my hand hurt. At first it was difficult because I've had no education and consequently I couldn't spell very well, but still I found that I couldn't stop writing. I used a dictionary and I also bought spelling books and taught myself. I realised I was writing about incidents with my father, events I had never even been able to verbalise. As one page became two and two pages became two hundred, then two thousand, I noticed that my anger was diminishing. By the time I stopped writing I had a manuscript written of my life. I felt elated.

Today my anger and hate lives inside my manuscript, not inside me. Writing down my feelings was my long-overdue therapy and without it I could never have been truly free from the abuse. It made things clear in my mind. What my father did to me wasn't my fault. And yes I have made mistakes, but when I knew better I did better.

I used to feel ashamed about my background, about what happened to me at the hands of my father and my husband. Deep down inside I felt it was my fault, that I was a bad child or a bad wife. But now when I look inside and see what that 'little girl' and 'young woman' went through I feel tremendous sorrow for her but I also feel empowered by her, because she survived. I find it hard sometimes to believe it was I who got through all that.

My writing has helped me to forgive. You can't underestimate the power of forgiveness. It's like untying yourself from shackles that have kept you bound to fear and sadness.

There were days I was so ill that I couldn't lift my head from the pillow. The pain was so fierce at one stage that I went blind, but still I continued to write. I dictated the words to my daughter.

Slowly the doctors began to see some changes in my health. I was improving, though they warned me I had a long road ahead and acknowledged I was at high risk of the cancer coming back.

During this time I thought a lot about death and I thought about my son, Darren. I wanted to see him. I tried to make peace with myself, to accept that if he hadn't contacted me after thirty years it was unlikely that he would do so now. I wondered would he come to my funeral. What would go through his mind as he stood over my coffin?

My daughters knew how much meeting him meant to me. I felt it was important that he knew where he came from, that he knew my story. And above all I wanted him to know I never forgot about him, not for one day. I wanted to show him pictures of me holding him when he was a baby. I wanted to show him that he had a mother who cared about him then and now.

To my shock my daughter Lisa told me that she had tracked him down and that he wanted to talk to me. The first time he phoned he said, 'Hello Mum. I've been looking for you all my life but I gave up because my family told me you were dead.'

'I've been looking for you too,' I said. My voice was shaking. 'I hope you know I didn't give you away — you were taken from me and later I agreed to your father's suggestion that you remain living with him, not because I didn't love you but because I loved you so much.'

'I want to come to see you, to get to know you,' he said.

'I want to see you too. I want to get to know the son I gave birth to. I can't make up for all the time I've lost with you but I'll do my best,' I promised. When we chatted it made me sad because this man was a stranger to me and I was a stranger to him.

We have been waiting for so long to see each other that I think we're both scared of the actual meeting. I don't want to push him into it, he has to do it in his own time and I have to be patient and accept that he might not be able to bring himself to meet me. We have had a couple of false starts.

Life isn't like the movies. There are no violins playing, no dramatic scene of my son and I running into each other's arms at the airport. Sometimes there isn't a happy ever after but there is a resolution, and sometimes we have to accept that that's enough. I'm glad to know my son is alive and well. I'm glad he knows that his mother loves him. I feel I've a lot to be grateful for and when I write now my words aren't filled with sadness and regret. They're filled with gratitude, contentment and hope. Writing will always be part of my life because, only for it, and of course only for my children, I mightn't be here today.

I know now it's so important to let out your anger but that doesn't mean taking it out on other people. If you can't write down what's making you angry then go out to the mountains and scream until you can't scream anymore.

I had never shown anyone my emotions before. I was afraid of rejection, but now I feel, what's the point in having emotions if you don't share them! It's like keeping a beautiful garment in your wardrobe which is too good to wear and when you do finally go to wear it you realise it has been eaten by moths, wasted by being hidden away for all those years. Don't wait until it is too late to tell people that you love them. Tell them while they're still alive to hear it. Tell them while those words can make a difference. And likewise don't be afraid to share your story. Your story is your strength. No matter how your story started out — no matter what circumstances you were born into — it's up to you to decide the ending. You're in charge of your own destiny.

Chapter 7

'Don't get sick in Ireland'

Janette Byrne

I've learned that people will forget what you said, people will forget what you did, but people will never forget how you made them feel.

MAYA ANGELOU

People are being forced to urinate into plastic bottles because they're too weak to walk to the toilet. No bedpans are available. Indeed it might be safer to use a bottle because male drug addicts use the ladies toilets to shoot up heroin and the door of the toilet doesn't lock. You call for help for your mother because she is having what seems to be a series of strokes, but your calls can't be heard over the drunks' abusive shouts and screams. Your mother turns her head away from the drunks but the girl on the other side of her trolley is projectile vomiting. Now you feel like you're going to vomit too and your mother feels the same. You rush to the nurse to get a sputin container to vomit into, carefully stepping over and around people as you navigate your way to the nurse's station, but 'suprisingly' there are no sputin containers available.

'So where should my mother vomit?' you ask the nurse.

'On the floor,' the nurse replies.

Your mother has no choice. She is too ill to walk to the toilet. She can't even sit up and she can't hold in the vomit any longer. She vomits on the floor. The vomit is left there for the next four days. Your mother, like others around her, is exposed to passers-by while a doctor examines her. She feels humiliated and frightened. The doctor doesn't know what's wrong with her. He can't do the necessary tests until your mother is allocated a bed but there are no beds available. Your mother thinks she is dying. Secretly you think she might be dying too. She closes her eyes and tries to sleep, but she can't sleep because the fluorescent light of the busy corridor burns into her eyes, people are rushing by and her trolley rests beside the door of the sluice room where the commodes and bed pans are emptied. As the door opens and closes it releases a smell that makes her vomit more. She's now choking on her vomit because she's passing out after each 'stroke'. She needs a sip of water, but you're unable to get any water in the A&E. Like sputin containers, water cups seem to be in short supply. You have to go across the road to the shop to buy water for your mother. Your return is delayed because you notice a girl on the fire escape of the hospital about to commit suicide. You talk her down. She appears to be a drug addict. She says she has just lost her mother.

When you return to your mother you find her sobbing. She seems devastated. The vomiting bug which she had contracted since going into A&E has brought with it diarrhoea so your mother needed a bed pan. The busy nurse was angry to be bothered again for a bed pan. 'Open your legs,' the nurse barked at your mother. 'You need a nappy!' And roughly puts it on her.

'How could anyone treat my mother like that?' recalls Janette. Her mother was left on a trolley under these conditions for five days.

Welcome to an accident and emergency (A&E) in the capital city of a country that was voted, according to a 'quality of life' survey by the *Economist* magazine, as the best place to live in the world. (Obviously the surveyors didn't get sick on their visit to Ireland.)

The sad reality is that the story above is not the combined stories of several people's experiences, nor is it unique. It is merely a few hours in the story of Janette Byrne who struggled to get medical care she and her mother had already paid for through their taxes. Her story is one that should be printed on bill-boards because her reality will become yours, if it has not already. No one can escape getting sick or watching loved ones getting sick, and by association sooner of later you too will visit an A&E. We brag that our economy is one of the fastest growing in Europe but we don't shout so loud about our health-care system. Perhaps we're ashamed, embarrassed or maybe we feel it won't make any difference.

Janette Byrne isn't like the rest of us. She's doesn't sit around and moan and wait for the government to fix things; she knows that won't get her anywhere. She knows because she has been through the health-care system, once as a daughter whose mother was sick and once as a patient herself.

——

To start with, Janette's story is similar to that of the vast majority of people in Ireland. She worked hard all her life, set up her own catering supplies business, paid her taxes. She trusted that the system that took almost half her wages in taxes would, if need be, look after her.

In 2001 at 39 years of age Janette was diagnosed with cancer, though the road to this diagnosis was more problematic than the cancer itself. Janette recalls:

I hadn't felt well for about a year and a half before my diagnosis. I was attending my local GP regularly. My illness started out with continuous sore throats, but they weren't normal sore throats. They were so bad I couldn't talk or swallow. I was also getting recurring colds. If someone came into my house and sneezed I would have the cold an hour later. I felt unwell all the time. People kept saying to me, 'What's wrong with you? You're always sick.' That would irritate me because I wasn't making it up. I didn't choose to be sick. I would go back and forth to the doctor taking antibiotic after antibiotic and it got to the stage where I just wouldn't go to the doctor anymore. I didn't see the point but my partner Declan and my parents would drag me there.

Every time I saw the girl in the doctor's reception I felt like she was saying to herself: 'God, here comes your woman again — the hypochondriac,' *Janette says jokingly*. And then other times I couldn't afford to go to the doctor because it's expensive when you're 'a regular'. After loads of visits the doctor still couldn't find anything serious wrong with me so I just tried to move on with my life and pretend there was nothing wrong.

Then things got so bad that I knew I had to go and get a second opinion. I went up to the GP and asked for a letter to see a specialist for my throat. I waited to be notified about my appointment in the Mater Hospital but nothing came, so I went up to the doctor again to make a new appointment but still no notification came through. The Mater had no record of my doctor's request for an appointment. Finally I said to my doctor, 'Give me the letter for the specialist and I'll make the appointment myself.' I got an appointment and the specialist X-rayed my throat. I got no results back but my GP said they'd have let me know if anything had been wrong. So, I wrongly presumed that everything was okay.

My sore throats continued but now they were accompanied with neck swelling, a terrible wheezing and shortness of breath. If I sat in a room with people they'd comment, 'What's that noise?' And it would be my lungs wheezing as if they were crying.

I couldn't accept that there was nothing wrong so I paid to go and see a private throat specialist in the Blackrock Clinic. He said I needed to see a speech therapist, that maybe I wasn't pronouncing some of my words properly and that was putting a strain on my voice. I didn't feel my pronunciation was the problem. There was too much going on for that to be the sole cause of my illness so I decided not to see a speech therapist.

A week passed. Then one morning I woke up to find my face was extremely swollen. I phoned the specialist's secretary to see if I could get an appointment to show him my face. The secretary said there wasn't a chance of an appointment. It would take months even as a private patient.

A week later I found lumps on the side of my neck. I went back to my local GP. She couldn't see me because she was about to go on maternity leave, so the doctor who owns the GP practice saw me. My partner Declan came with me and he had to do the talking because I just hadn't the will to talk about it anymore. The doctor took all my information and said he would talk to my own GP about it before she went on maternity leave. He said he'd come back to me and let me know what she said.

Two weeks passed and I didn't hear anything. By now I couldn't get out of the bed I was so sick. Declan brought me back to the GP again. This time I met my doctor's replacement. She opened my file and there wasn't even a note on my chart that I had been there previously. I couldn't believe this was happening. It was crazy. I was getting mad and my family was mad but I was so sick that all I was concerned with was someone naming what was wrong with me.

The new doctor looked at my whole chart and immediately said, 'I don't like this. I'm going to get you a second opinion.' She apologised for how I'd been treated but what could she say? She was only new to the place. She sent through a letter but as before the hospital didn't get it so there was another delay with my appointment and before I knew it a year and a half had passed since all this began.

Finally Janette got an appointment to go into the Mater Hospital for another scan. They called her back two weeks later and said they wanted to do a needle biopsy into one of the lumps. 'I still didn't think the worst. I didn't even contemplate the notion of cancer and no one mentioned it,' says Janette.

Janette was scheduled to go back for the results of her biopsy three weeks later. She thought if there was anything wrong with the biopsy the hospital would have come back before the three weeks were up.

Two weeks passed and then one morning I woke up to find that I could hardly breathe. I was gasping for air and unfortunately I was on my own in the house. I saw my reflection in the mirror. I looked like the elephant man. I began to cry. That made my breathing more difficult. I couldn't get a breath at all and the room was spinning. I crawled on all fours to the phone. I called Declan and my mam, 'Get here quick. I can't breathe,' I gasped down the phone. This is serious; there is something radically wrong, I thought. En route home Declan called an ambulance. They took forever to come. They couldn't find the house. All the time I was trying to calm myself because by now Declan and Mam were here and I could see they were panicking.

The ambulance men arrived and they were questioning me. 'Did you have sea food?' They thought maybe I had an allergic reaction. I arrived at the hospital and I could see that there was a bit of a panic going on when they saw me. Then they couldn't find the file with my scans so I was left sitting there while they looked for my missing file. The scans were finally found. I got nervous because there were so many doctors around me. One doctor held up my scans and said there was a growth and negative cells in my biopsy. They hoped to operate the following morning so that they could have a proper look at what was wrong. Still cancer was never mentioned.

There was no bed available so I had to spend the most horrendous night of my life in the A&E unit. I will never forget it, I wouldn't wish it on anyone. *Janette shakes her head as if what she is about to tell me is still unbelievable to her.* The only way I can describe it was as if there was a war going on outside and the injured were being dragged unexpectedly into the hospital. Such was the chaos. It was like a mad house.

I was left on a trolley in an alcove off the corridor, and there were two male patients on either side of me. One was Chinese who was accompanied by a large family and the other one was a young guy. He was 'rough and ready' and talked loudly on his mobile. He seemed to be phoning all his mates. His phone calls went on through the night. I felt vulnerable lying there in public in my nightdress with two strange men on either side of me and people rushing by all night. My trolley was beside a room where the bereaved mourned their losses and when they vacated it other people were brought there to be told bad news about their loved ones. I could hear people crying, wailing with sadness. The crying went on and on. It made me think about my own death because by this stage the thoughts of cancer had come into my head. I had lost my grandparents, a very young aunt and uncle to cancer so my family and I were right to be worried.

Then this woman came to talk to Declan and myself. I had seen her earlier and noticed whenever she talked to anyone she made them cry. I named her 'Dr Death', so when I saw her heading in my direction I wanted to run. I disliked her even before she spoke. She didn't introduce herself and she wasn't wearing any type of uniform. She just said to Declan and me, 'Now, does anyone have any questions?'

Questions about what exactly? I thought, though I didn't answer her.

'No. Well let's see what happens tomorrow then,' she said and left in the same abrupt fashion in which she came. I knew I was waiting to be operated on so that they could find out what was wrong but I didn't know what she meant by 'Let's see what happens tomorrow.' Did she mean we'd wait and see if I had cancer? Was she trying to prepare me for some news? I guessed she was some sort of counsellor but she brought me no comfort.

I went to use the ladies toilets. I got a fright when I walked in because men 'greeted' me. They were junkies shooting up heroin or whatever. There was no lock on the cubicle door but I had no choice other than to use this toilet. There was no alternative available, unless I used the men's toilets. I remember a breeze blew in the door and I felt so exposed in my nightdress with these junkies standing there. I felt degraded and humiliated, but most of all I felt frightened. To see men in the ladies toilets sticking needles in their arms isn't something I'd ever seen before. It was shocking and disturbing.

I ran back to my bed, or rather to my trolley. There were a lot of people around, drunks coming in from late night bars, homeless people and junkies. People were roaring and shouting. I felt unsafe. None of the nurses came near me. No one came to see if I was okay, to see if I was still breathing, if I was still alive. No one was giving me a second thought. I was just taking up a space. Most of the nurses were in the main area near their station so even if I'd shouted they couldn't have heard me from where they were based. I needed a glass of water. My throat was parched. I called to a nurse as she rushed by. I knew she heard me but she kept going.

I didn't sleep a wink that night even though I knew I needed my sleep so that I'd be strong for my operation the following morning. The trolley was so narrow that you couldn't turn left or right. You had to just lie on the flat of your back, staring into the fluorescent light. When I did manage to manoeuvre my way onto my side I was looking into the face of a strange man who stared back at me. I was so frightened by my surroundings that I wouldn't let Declan, my partner, go home. He spent the night sitting on a plastic chair with his head resting on my trolley. I thought the morning would never come. But I was lucky, I was only there for one night. I can't imagine how people spend days on end in A&E and may not even have a trolley.

———

The following afternoon Janette was told that the surgeons had found time in the operating schedule for her. Janette was happy. This operation would at last give her some answers. She needed to get to the bottom of her illness. The process of getting to this point had taken a year and a half and near-strangulation by a tumour. You'd think there must be an easier way of securing adequate medical attention.

Janette was taken to her long-awaited hospital bed. She looked forward to getting a little rest before her operation but she was only in the bed ten minutes before she was brought to the operating theatre for her eight-hour operation.

I remember being wheeled down the corridor after the operation and seeing my family waiting there. I thought I was waving and smiling at them but they told me later that I could barely lift a finger. I was brought into the intensive care unit (ICU) and the first thing I saw was the patient in the bed next to mine. He had a big frame around his head and neck and didn't look well at all. I looked at him and thought to myself, 'Well, he's done for!' He looked at me and I'm sure he thought the same.

I had tubes down my throat and other tubes inserted into my chest which ran down into my lungs, I couldn't breathe on my own. I was hooked up to machines. I remember at one point there was gurgling coming from the tubes in my chest. The nurse rushed over and cleared out the tubes that went into my lungs. I think there was fluid in them which could have smothered me. The nurses in the ICU were fantastic. I need only look and there was someone by my bed.

My bed faced the door and every time it opened I could see a member of my family straining to try and see in. I lay there and it was surreal because the previous day I was at home.

My son Graham was the first to come in to see me. He's 24 now and was 20 at the time. He walked over to me and his whole body was shaking. I knew he was taking it hard. The worse part was that I couldn't talk to him. Usually I'd be very flippant and made a joke that would have taken the tension and sadness out of the situation. I didn't want him to be upset. He said, 'Are you alright, Mam?' I couldn't say anything in response because of the tubes down my throat. I was worried about what would happen Graham if I died. His father had never been in his life and though Declan loves him like a son it wouldn't be the same as having me. I have since found out if I had died he wouldn't have even been entitled to my half of the house because Declan and I aren't married.

The next day a doctor came to talk to me. He said it was cancer of the lymphatic system and that the nodes they removed were cancerous. One of them was 11.3 cm in size so that was quite big by any standard. It was wrapped around my windpipe and was closing in, basically choking me, so that was why I had trouble breathing. They were rapid growing tumours so everything had to be done very quickly. I took the words on board — 'rapid growing', 'tumour', 'cancer'.

I was on my own when they told me. I felt they should have asked a member of my family to be with me while they broke the news — they were after all only a few feet away in the corridor. I remember when they told me I just shook my head and told myself, 'Don't cry, don't cry', because I was sure if I started to cry I'd start to choke. Then I was told I'd have to have chemotherapy straight away.

Though it's strange the way you think when you're in a vulnerable situation like this, the cancer wasn't bothering me as much as silly things — like I was very conscious that I had my period and I was thinking of my modesty, thinking of the nurses having to wash me when I had my period.

I signed to the nurse for a pen because I needed to communicate with Declan. I wrote single words: 'shock', then I wrote 'afraid' and 'water'. He kept all my notes.

Janette's family had been doing 24-hour vigils in the corridor. They thought she was going to die. They were told that hours would determine her fate. Janette, however, had already made up her mind that she was going to live. She wouldn't entertain death. She was anxious to get the tubes removed from her throat so that she could get back to breathing on her own. However, she was told that the doctors weren't sure if she would be able to breathe on her own so the tubes had to be left in until she was stronger. When the tubes were removed she was able to breathe on her own.

Within a few days I was moved to St Vincent's ward. There is no designated cancer ward in the hospital but they try and put all the patients with cancer into this ward. When I was brought in I saw all the patients had bald heads. Others were wearing bandanas. I just didn't want to be there. I said to my family, 'I don't care what happens. Just take me home. I don't want to be here. I want to go home.' It must have been hard on my family because obviously they would have loved to take me home but of course they couldn't. A doctor came in to try and calm me. She asked, 'What's wrong?' I said, 'I don't want to stay here. I don't want to die.' For the first time I was hit by the realisation of having cancer. I looked at the other people in the ward and I knew that was going to be me in a couple of months. The doctor was brilliant. She calmed me down and said, 'You're too young and lovely to die.' She was being real girlie and kind, which was what I needed. When I asked her if I could have it in writing, we laughed.

I got settled in the room but I felt weak, feeble and drained. I was conscious that I could hardly walk. The physiotherapist came and helped me out of the bed. She helped me put on my slippers and took me for a little walk. I took baby steps. I walked the way you see little old ladies walk down hospital corridors. I thought to myself, What have I become? How did I go from being a normal woman to being like a little old lady? I stooped as I walked; I wondered if I would ever be able to straighten up again.

In total I was in hospital for 90 days. I'd go in for a couple of weeks of chemotherapy and then go home for two or three days. But if I was unwell in between the chemotherapy I mightn't go home at all. Some people can be treated in a day ward but my cancer was in stage two so that wasn't an option for me. The cancer had been left too long and it had really taken hold of my body. The chemotherapy gave me side effects like bad headaches, vomiting, sick stomach, diarrhoea, pains in my body. I was basically a wreck. And then I was on steroids. Steroids made my face puff out, so it was moon-like in shape. All the patients in the ward started to look alike. Visitors would walk into the ward, stop at the door and look around thinking, 'Damn, now which one is she?' Sometimes people would come to my bed and say 'Hi-ya Elaine.' And I'd have to say, 'No, Elaine is over there!'

After each chemotherapy treatment Janette was given a return date for her next appointment. She had been told she needed to receive her treatment in a timely manner — this would help to ensure its effectiveness. When her return date grew near she would ring to make sure a bed was available. Sometimes the hospital would bring her in for the weekend to hold a bed so that she could start treatment the following Monday. This system meant precious family weekends would be put on hold. Janette didn't really mind. She was prepared to do whatever it took to get better.

Janette worked very hard on staying positive throughout her illness because she believed it would be key to her recovery. She told her family and close friends:

'Don't tell anyone how ill I am, or that there is a chance I could die. I need everyone to be positive.' It's very important to believe you're going to get well. I felt if I was negative or if I was getting negative vibes or pity from other people it would impede my recovery. A friend gave me a diary. She wrote on the inside cover, 'For positive thoughts only and I'll be checking your "home-work!",' so I began to write some positive notes.

_____

Things were going well for Janette but a major set-back was around the corner:

I was due back in the hospital for chemo but my treatment was postponed because there was no bed available. It was a major delay and I feared the worst because I had been told that I had to receive my treatment in a timely manner and that subsequently there was a good chance I would make a full recovery. When there was a delay with my treatment I worried that the tumour would start to grow again. I thought maybe they're not bringing me back in for my treatment because there is no hope for me and they believe it's better to give my bed to someone who has a chance.

Up until this time I had told myself to focus on the positive: Yes I have cancer but it's curable if I get my treatment. I had left the treatment of my body in the hands of the professionals and had been aware that the treatment of my head, my mental state, was just as important and that was something I myself had to look after. But the delay knocked some of the positivity out of me.

I phoned the hospital 17 times a day for nine days, trying to get a bed. It was like some sort of torture. 'Can you ring back in the afternoon when the doctors have done their rounds,' the hospital would say. So I'd ring and ring. By the third day I was at my wits-end. I said to the girl who answered the phone in the hospital, 'What the hell is going on? I'm sitting here terrified that this thing has started growing again because I haven't got my treatment. I was told by my doctor I had to get it according to my schedule and this isn't happening!'

She replied, 'Well you're a priority on the list.'

'Where exactly am I on the list?'

'Number twenty-three,' she replied.

'Number twenty-three!'

Then I phoned the ward nurse and said to her, 'Am I in danger by not getting my treatment on time?'

She didn't answer directly. She said, 'There is nothing I can do. There just isn't a vacant bed. Try not to worry.'

Try not to worry! I'm sitting here crying my eyes out because I have gone through so much and now because there isn't a bed it's going to be all for nothing. I felt like arriving down to St Vincent's ward with my own bed! By the time it got to day five or six I was a total wreck. I was so upset and weak. I knew things were getting serious. I had to have my treatment.

These type of experiences changed me, changed how I looked and responded to the world. For example, if someone told me their mother had just died in the Mater Hospital, I would reply, 'That's terrible,' but inside I'd be saying, 'Oh God, that's great — there's a free bed!'

Isn't that terrible? But that's the truth because when it comes to saving your life you'd trample on anyone.

The wait exhausted me. Each time the phone rang I thought it was the hospital. If I let myself I could have got very down. I could have easily stayed in my bed all day and not got up until someone told me my hospital bed was ready. But I'm not that type of person, thank God. I'm not one to sit back and cross my fingers and hope for the best. When I saw there was no bed being made available I took action. I got out the phonebook and began to call anyone I thought had a public voice or influence. I started at 'A' and I didn't stop until I got to 'Z'. I said to myself, I'm going to let everyone know this is how cancer patients are being treated. Surely the rest of the country hasn't a clue that this could happen, that you could have a curable cancer but couldn't get the necessary treatment because there isn't a bed available.

I phoned every organisation that I thought could help: Women's rights organisations, The Cancer Society, TDs, Senators,

Councillors, Ministers; offices, the Citizens Information Bureau, the Department of Health, the Health Boards . . . no one could do anything. I came off the phone knowing for certain that no one actually cared if I lived or died. No one except my own family and a few close friends gave a damn. It's a sad reality but that's the society we live in.

I wondered how regular people would react if they knew this could be their reality so I contacted Joe Duffy's radio show 'Liveline' and I told him and his listeners my story. I told him how I had never taken time off work . . . how I had paid my taxes all my life, how I had supported 'the system' because I thought that when I needed its support it would be there for me. Surely to God I have a basic human right to have a life-saving treatment? I was very emotional. I broke down and cried on the national airwaves.

I wanted people to know the truth about our health-care system. I was shocked to find out that this wasn't just happening to me. It was happening to lots and lots of other people.

There was a huge response to Janette's interview on 'Liveline'. One woman rang in who had been in hospital for three weeks recovering from an operation. She was so upset that she had taken up a bed that Janette could have used. 'I just said, What type of system makes people feel guilty for being sick?' says Janette.

I remember one cancer patient who phoned in to 'Liveline' said he had been waiting for a bed for so long that he pretended to be sick so that he could be admitted to A&E. That was his way of getting back into the system to get his treatment. The health system had turned us into liars, actors, and campaigners — all to get treatment that was already our right.

After hearing all the callers to 'Liveline' I didn't feel so alone, though it didn't help me get a bed. Finally I got my treatment and I thought that it would never again be postponed. I presumed it was a once-off incident.

——

I was distraught when I was made wait again. By this stage I had heard many horror stories of other people waiting for dangerously long periods. One woman told me her daughter had to wait three weeks. I said, That's not going to be me! So I contacted solicitors to see if someone would take my case on the grounds that I have a right to treatment. I phoned a number of solicitors in the phonebook and no one would touch my case. Then I phoned someone I knew in the Law Society and he recommended James McGill.

James McGill told me to come in to talk with him straight away. He asked me to write a statement listing out the events, from my first GP visit up to the present day. He agreed to take the Mater Hospital, the Eastern Health Board and the Department of Health to the High Court in an effort to secure my treatment.

I think my parents and family were shocked by my radical action. My family said, 'Let's forget about the hospital in Dublin. Let's get you to France or America where you'll be treated properly in a private hospital.' But I knew that wouldn't work. I needed my family around me and I knew they wouldn't be able to come if I went abroad. And that would have meant extra stress, not to mention the huge cost. And secondly, I'd made great friends in the cancer ward. We depended on one another's support. We needed one another.

You form friendships very quickly when you're in a ward for weeks on end, with the same people, 24 hours a day. There is no escaping and you can't hide anything, most especially the truth. You can't hide your tears, your fears, your regrets, your hopes. You tell your personal stories. There are no holds barred because you think you're going to die. Life in the ward was hard — your friends die. One day we were all chatting and I looked over at one of the girls who was sitting out on her chair. I called her name but she didn't respond. She was dead. Those were moments that bonded the rest of us together. I guess we'd wonder the same thing, 'Am I next?'

So I told my family that I wanted to proceed with my case, though I was worried about costs because you hear of people losing their homes when they go to court and lose. The solicitor reassured me and said, 'We'll take it to the stage where there are only minimum costs for you and I will keep you informed. If it gets to a stage where the costs are going to increase, you will be notified first and can decide if you want to proceed.'

I felt safe in my solicitor's hands. His uncle had died of cancer. He had been through the system. He knew what I was talking about and he seemed to be humane, but most of all I liked that he wasn't afraid. When I went into the office the first thing he said was: 'Well, what is your prognosis? Are you going to live or die?' He was straight in there and I liked that because there was no crap. There was no time for crap.

On the day of the court case the media found out where I lived and they were at my door. I did interviews but it got too much for me in the end. I remember that night I was looking at RTÉ news and I saw myself! I made a laugh of it and said, 'Would you look at the state of me making my television debut.' You have to try and see the funny side. As I sat there watching myself it was as if it was someone else. 'How could this be me on the Nine O'Clock news? I was only at work a while back, leading a normal life and here I am on TV talking about the government and the health board!

There were people who thought, 'Why are you bringing this on yourself at a time when you least need it?' I felt, Well I have the energy to do it right now and I might not be able to fight in the future, and what if they just leave me here and forget about me? I felt I could get lost in the system and I felt no one else had the right to judge me. If you want to sit at home when you have cancer and wait for the treatment that's fine, but that's not me. That's not who I am. There will always be the few who let on not to know you in case their name will be tarnished in some way by being associated with yours, but I don't give those people a second thought.

Sadly, in this country we are still very much ruled by fear, fear of what people will say or think, fear of rocking the boat, of standing up . . . I didn't know that then but I know it now. I don't know if it's been engrained in us by our history of oppression or if it's just part of us . . . I remember I would have said to the girls in the ward, 'We're going to have to get together. Think what we can do if we fight this battle together!' But they would be too afraid. They feared if they 'caused trouble' they wouldn't be able to get into hospital for their treatment. But I pointed out that we were already being denied treatment.

My court case took place the day after my first visit to the solicitor. My full statement was read out in court. Thankfully I didn't have to be there in person. The bottom line of my statement read, 'Just give me my treatment and stop messing me around.' Justice Kelly presided over my case. He said you'd have to have a heart of stone not to realise this woman had been very badly treated from start to finish.

The judge said a bed had to be provided for me. The Eastern Health Board said that while they couldn't provide the treatment they would write the cheque for me to receive it in the Mater Private Hospital. Then complications arose because The Mater Private couldn't give me the treatment over the weekend because they only worked Monday to Friday and we were coming into a weekend. So my treatment was delayed for the weekend and then by Monday a bed was made available in the Mater Public.

I realised after the court case that there is nothing in the Health Act that says the hospital can be forced by law to give me treatment. That law should be changed and it's something I hope to work on.

———

I felt a bit awkward and really nervous going back to the hospital after the court case. I thought maybe there will be nurses or consultants who will be angry with me. I worried in case they thought I was putting them down by slating the system. Then I said, So what? They have to use the same system as I do. If their mam or sister gets cancer they wouldn't want her to be treated the way I was treated. I told myself I hadn't done anything wrong.

As Declan and I entered the hospital I saw the husband of one of the cancer patients coming towards me. His wife Pauline was in my ward. He walked almost the length of the corridor with his hand out towards me. *Janette takes a deep breath and puts her hand over her eyes. Her voice breaks and she holds back the tears. She composes herself and apologises.* I don't cry so much talking about myself but when I think of the other women I can't help it. I think, I'm here, and they're not. I think a lot about their families. How do they cope with the loss?

Pauline had breast cancer. She was doing great but then she found more lumps. The prognosis wasn't good. When I had last seen her she was very sick. Her husband shook my hand and said, 'Fair play to you. My wife has been in your situation loads of times and it has caused her huge stress.'

I asked, 'How is she?'

He replied, 'We've only hours with her now.'

She had been moved to another room away from our ward.

Then her daughter came up to me and said, 'Fair play to you. We saw you on TV. You're really brilliant.' I wanted to get away from her because I was going to cry and I thought she is being strong and it's her mam who is going to die.

Janette was happy to be back on the ward getting her treatment even though the ward wasn't a happy or comfortable place to be.

The hospital ward was dirty. Filthy. Excrement on the floor. Overflowing sanitary bins. No hand soap. We had to bring our own. There was a problem with the drains that caused a vile smell on the ward. The cancer patients had to bring in scented candles and air fresheners. The toilets had no windows so there was a smell in there too. There was no ventilation, nowhere for the smell to escape to except into our ward. Unfortunately chemotherapy causes vomiting and bowel problems, either constipation or diarrhoea, so the toilets were in constant use and this smell was constant. Inside the toilet cubicles there were splashes on the wall and around the toilet, splashes of vomit and god knows what. It was never cleaned properly.

After chemotherapy you're wide open to infection so this environment was detrimental. I got septicaemia, an infection of the blood. I thought I was a goner at that stage. I thought, How sad to have gone through all this and to die from an infection which could have been prevented.

The hygiene employed by the nurses wasn't best practice either. The nurses would wear gloves but they wouldn't change them between patients. Maybe they'd fix a drip that was falling out of one patient who had one type of infection and then they'd go and change another patient's drip without washing their hands or changing their gloves in between. I remember one young nurse had to take samples from a patient's excrement in a commode. When she finished handling that person's bowl movement she proceeded to adjust someone's drip without washing her hands. These might seem like little things but they're not. They're very big things when other people's germs can kill you.

Sometimes we'd be too weak to make it to the loo, so we'd have to use a commode beside our bed. Afterwards no one would be available to take the commode away so it would stink the room out. This was naturally very embarrassing for the user. Then when someone would come to take the commode they would just wheel it into the toilet beside the shower and it would sit there full of waste. Then if one of us wanted to take a shower we'd have to first navigate our way around the dirty commodes. Often the smell from the commode would make you gag in the shower. There was no curtain on the shower so anyone who used the loo could see you. This loo was used by visitors as well as patients.

As if looking after ourselves under these conditions wasn't enough, we also had to look after an elderly lady in our ward. She hadn't cancer. She had senile dementia I think. She shouldn't have been in hospital. She should have been in a nursing home but there was no place available in a nursing home. She was in the ward when I arrived and she was still there when I left. She was in her 80s and her only family seemed to be her sister who would visit her. She was also in her 80s.

The elderly woman would take her pants and nappy off while she was sitting on the chair beside her bed. She'd sit there naked with her legs open and exposed to everyone in the ward, including the visitors — small children and men. She would have a bowel movement on the floor and then play with it. This was allowed to happen even though we were all wide open to infection. She would go into the toilet every few minutes and accidentally lock herself in. We'd have to let her out. We basically were left to look after her. Sometimes she'd take all our magazines and she'd scream if we tried to take them back. Of course we didn't really want them back after her dirty hands had touched them.

I felt so guilty because I came to hate this elderly woman. I hated her because she was vulgar and horrible. I hated her because I saw her as my potential killer.

Her uncleanliness and her actions could infect Janette at a vulnerable stage of her treatment. Such an infection could be enough to cause her death.

I was utterly disgusted by her. Obviously you're going to be disgusted if someone is playing with bowel movements on the floor. At night when I'd be lying in bed I'd start to think about her; she was someone's daughter once; maybe someone's mother; she was loved and cherished once. I'd get upset. Who knows, any of us could end up like this woman, forgotten, without a voice.

As far as the nurses were concerned it was as if this elderly woman didn't exist. We all found it hard because when you're not well you don't want to have the strain of having to look after someone else. It was like having a child to look after. Apparently there were 80 such elderly people in the hospital who needed nursing home care at that time, but there were no nursing home facilities for them to go to. I've been told people like her end up in wards for up to a year and a half. The lack of nursing home facilities is a huge problem.

Yes it's sad, but it's also sad that cancer patients are pushed into that situation of having to look after her. We complained about how this woman was forgotten and we complained about everything else but it made no difference, even when our complaints were put in writing.

Death was never far from anyone's mind in St Vincent's ward. We were surrounded by death. I will never forget the night that I experienced the first death on the ward. A man was dying from cancer. His daughter was screaming for her dad. 'I want my dad. Daddy, don't die. Don't die!' Over and over again she cried out for him. She was in agony with the pain of losing him. We were in our beds like little children with the covers pulled up to our chins, crying. No one said a word. Eventually he died. Then the whole family came in. They were all hysterical.

After many more deaths I asked if there was a counsellor available to the ward. It's hard to cope with so much death, especially when you've built close friendships with those who have died, but there were no counsellors available to us.

There was also nowhere on the ward to get away from death. The only communal room was a tiny TV room where smoking was permitted. If Janette or any of the other patients were well enough to go there they couldn't stay long because of the smoke. It was also the place where family members of those who died went to plan funerals and fight over wills. So Janette would go for little walks around the corridors with the other patients. Sometimes she even went outside so that she could go somewhere quiet to have some 'head space'. No one seemed to miss her.

One night one of the girls who had a particularly difficult cancer went with a friend for a drink. She just had to get away. She was missed and got into terrible trouble. She was diagnosed with cancer while she was pregnant. Her family would bring her new born baby in to see her. There was great excitement when the baby came to visit. The poor girl had a terrible cancer. Her skin was falling off. The nurses had to bandage her whole body and she would scream each day when the bandages had to be changed. Her skin would have wept and the bandages would be stuck to her raw skin, so you can imagine it was very painful for her. She died since. I think about her baby growing up without ever knowing her mother.

Janette's family and other families wrote letters of complaint about conditions in the hospital but nothing changed.

After Janette's court case she thought there certainly wouldn't be any more delays with future treatment. However, there were delays but never as long as before.

———

Janette had her last and most difficult chemo sessions in July 2001. She was happy because she had been told she was in remission. That was until a young doctor announced otherwise. He said that she might need a bone marrow transplant. He made the statement but couldn't offer any further information and said that she and her family should go to see her doctor to discuss it. That indicated to Janette that there were obviously still problems.

Janette and her family met in advance of her doctor's appointment. Each family member offered bone marrow. Then Janette, her six bothers, sister, parents and son all went into the doctor's little office.

He said, 'My God I've never had so many people in my office at the one time.' Nonetheless, no one was leaving. We all squashed in and I sat before him with my family standing behind me. He looked at the scan and shook his head. Time seemed to slow down. He had a second look at the scan and seemed surprised. Then he said, 'I can't believe this. Your scans are clear.'

We couldn't believe it.

'I don't know — prayers, medications — put it down to

whatever you like but the scans are clear,' he said with shock in his voice.

We were ecstatic, bawling and crying, *says Janette.*

I went home and thought I would pick things up where I left off before I got sick, but I couldn't. At this time when I should have been full of the joys of life, I found myself miserable. I hit rock bottom. It was as if the negativity I had been suppressing was now bubbling up to the surface. I was cross, sad, angry and snappy with the people I loved most. I didn't have depression. It was more like an unyielding anger. It was in the pit of my stomach and it was eating away at me the whole time. It was like having PMT that never went away. I felt guilty for being alive and angry that they were dead. Why them and not me?

After a few months Janette make the decision to do something about it. She began counselling in ARK which offers free services such as aromatherapy, meditation, Tai-chi . . . to cancer patients. 'It's a fantastic place for anyone who is diagnosed with cancer — they look after your "head", says Janette.

Janette had previously gone to ARK in between chemo sessions. She had made friends there with other cancer patients, they'd sometimes go for lunch together, but slowly, one by one these friends died and those who remained were very ill.

I had previously stopped going to ARK. I wanted to move away from all the sickness because I was better, but I couldn't move away because I was still sick, sick in my head and my soul. I knew I had to go back to ARK if I was going to find a way back to myself, to who I was before all this.

Life, post-cancer, was different to what I'd become accustomed to — the extra affection, support, attention, the cards and gifts that come with being sick — these were all gone. Everybody was getting on with their lives and expected me to do the same. After all, my hair was growing back, I was getting back to looking like my old self, so why couldn't I start acting like the old Janette?

I shouldn't complain that people expected me to get on with things. While I was ill I had insisted that everyone 'pretend everything is okay' even though it wasn't. But now everything wasn't okay and I didn't want to pretend anymore.

When Janette first went to the counsellor she was even angry
with the counsellor because she wanted to talk about her
experiences of cancer while the counsellor started back at Janette's
childhood, growing up . . . Janette felt the counsellor was making
things worse. She was making her think about things she didn't
want to think about, giving her new problems to worry about. But
Janette stuck with the counselling and soon saw the bigger picture.
She realised that she needed to understand how she viewed herself,
her family, the world . . . before she could understand where her
cancer fitted in.

> The counsellor told me, 'It's okay to be negative and let your guard
> down.' There has to be a place for negativity, a place I hadn't allowed
> for before, otherwise things are unbalanced. So I had to let myself
> vent that negativity. 'Go to the countryside and scream out loud. Go
> to the end of the garden and break some plates,' she told me, 'Let it
> out.' I wanted to scream at the world. I felt angry at the health-care
> system. At the health service. At the Government.

On a practical level life had also changed for Janette. She hadn't
the energy to socialise the way she used to. She had to take things
easier. She had to sell her business because dealing with pressure,
traffic, travelling became too much. She feels she'll never again be
able to do nine to five, nor does she want to. At the moment she is
trying to redirect the profit from her business and the lessons she
has learned from overcoming cancer and the system, into
something that will help other people who are going through
similar problems.

Consequently her focus remains firmly on 'Patients Together', a
non-political group of patients who came together with a
common goal: to highlight the horrors of A&E and to work for
change in the A&E departments across the country.

> This campaign had kept me from everything. It's all-consuming
> and so frustrating. We all use the hospitals so we should all stand
> together and demand a proper health service. I need people to join
> us on the streets and protest, to stand up and shout, 'This isn't good
> enough!'

You think having VHI or BUPA will save you? That you're secure? It means nothing, absolutely nothing. No one is safe. Private health insurance won't get you a bed when you're lying on a mattress or a chair dying in A&E.

The best advice I can give patients who are trying to get treatment in A&E is, Don't be afraid to be vocal. Stand up for your rights. The nurses have support with their unions and hospital security. You don't have to feel sorry for them. They have a way of feeling safe. For them, it's just a job, in and out, but you're sick and you're entitled to proper care.

Janette doesn't claim to have the solution. I always avoid saying what the solution is to the problem. I don't think it's up to patients to come up with the solution. There are experts the Department of Health can turn to. They can see what worked in other countries and apply it here. At the most basic level it seems obvious that drug-addicts, drunken, abusive and mentally ill people shouldn't be cared for in the same place as everyone else because the care they need is very different.

Today my fear of going back to hospital is far greater than my fear of cancer. My experience of the hospital caused me more stress than cancer ever did. I could manage the cancer but I couldn't handle how the system failed me, how I was treated, and above all how I was made feel. I kept thinking this could be my last few months in the world and this is how I'm going to spend it — without dignity. No one should die under those conditions. *Certainly not in the country which ironically boasts that it is the best place in the world to live.*

Janette's website is *www.patientstogether.com*

Chapter 8
Marrying a murderer
Marie Gough

We either make ourselves miserable, or we make ourselves strong. The amount of work is the same.

CARLOS CASTENEDA

Mary Gough (26) was planning a fairy-tale wedding to the man she had been in love with since the age of 19, Colin Whelan. Mary's mother Marie Gough loved Colin like a son and was happy to help her only daughter with the wedding arrangements. She diligently made the wedding cake. Her only regret was that Mary's dad was not alive to see the happy union on that fine September day in 2000.

Colin was busy planning too. Like Mary, he was concerned with every detail of his big day. But his big day was not his wedding, it was the day of Wednesday, 29 February 2001, the day he would murder his new bride.

––––

Mary's arrival into the world was in sharp contrast with how she left it:

She was my first and only daughter and I had lost a baby before her. I remember I was overdue on that cold winter's day when I felt things just weren't right. I said to my husband Jimmy that maybe I should go to the hospital to make sure everything was okay. He wanted me to wait until the match on tele was over . . . but I got around him and he drove me to the hospital unaware that the birth was near. He had only arrived back home when he was greeted with the news that Mary had been born by emergency Caesarian section. I was lucky that I got to the hospital on time because otherwise it could have been a different story. Back then Caesarean sections weren't as common as today. I remember there was a particular nurse in the hospital who would stop each time she passed Mary's cot. She would look at Mary and say, 'Now that's one lucky little girl.'

Marie smiles at the irony of the words and of how they've stayed with her.

Mary grew up in the peaceful village of Stamullen, nestled on the north Dublin-Meath border; a rural place where neighbours looked out for one another and everyone knew everyone else in the community. Marie's home where Mary grew up is full of love and care; the freshly painted bungalow is neatly kept; the tea pot rests on the stove covered by a warmer in the immaculate but homely kitchen; a well-used easy chair stands at the side of the cooker; the kettle is on the boil and the dog is barking outside the back door.

It's easy to imagine the family squeezed in around the small kitchen table having dinners and chatting endlessly. Marie is the type of woman anyone would instantly warm to. Her manner is gentle, kind and open but at the same time her voice is strong and certain. Her face is unlined and shows little sign of the terrible anguish she has been through, though her eyes are distant, searching and constantly moving as she holds tightly a folded tear-stained tissue.

As a child, Mary loved the carefree ways of country life. Growing up with five brothers, Gerard, David, James, Peter and Cyril, meant she was inevitably a bit of a tomboy and felt she could do anything as well as the boys. She had a sense of daring adventure which is often more common in little boys. Her mother laughs as she thinks back:

When Mary was about three years old she got into an old buggy and pushed herself down a big hill. When it came to a halt she rolled out head over heels. She was fearless and utterly in love with life. By the time she made her Holy Communion she was totally independent. She knew her own mind. I remember once she said: 'Mammy, do you see these hands?' She held out her hands before me as if I hadn't seen them before. 'Now', she added, 'these hands are the same as the boys' hands, aren't they?' I agreed they were. 'If that is the case they can do the exact same work, and that includes washing up!' She wasn't one to let the boys slack off around the house, *smiles Marie.*

Marie glances towards the bin and says everything reminds her of her daughter. She wasn't one for school, you know. I remember the day she finished her leaving cert she made a grand entrance into the kitchen, hurriedly went to the bin, took her school-bag off her back and dumped it into the bin. 'Now that's that!' she exclaimed joyously. All you could do was laugh.

After school Mary went to work in The Huntsman, the local pub. It was there, in 1993, that she met her future husband, Colin Whelan. Colin didn't usually socialise locally, but he had broken his leg at a concert in Slane so he was somewhat confined to where he could go. Marie knew his family. They lived just a short distance away in Gormanstown. When Mary arrived home at Christmas she announced that she and Colin were going steady. She was as happy as she had ever been, recalls Marie.

The first time I met Colin was over that Christmas period. He called to the house on St Stephen's Day. He struck me as a gentleman. He was well mannered and there wasn't anything not to like about him. He treated Mary well and continued to do so until . . . *Marie's voice trails off, unable to finish the sentence.* That day they went to the Funderland amusement park in Dublin. Mary had a fantastic day and Colin won her a selection of soft toys. Mary loved them and arranged them around her bedroom.

During the next two years Colin was a regular visitor to Marie's home. He would call into Mary's on his way home after work. He would always be in a pristine suit. He loved designer suits. Mary's brothers' gave him the nickname the 'McKenna Man' after a local store that specialises in tailored suits. He seemed dedicated to his job in information technology but didn't seem to have any friends, or rather never mentioned work friends. He was a bit of a loner.

Nonetheless, he swept not just Mary, but her entire family, off their feet and he was like a brother to Marie's sons. For the next two years, things went well with Mary and Colin's relationship. They seemed happy and suited to each other.

But then something happened, the full facts of which I do not know, *recalls Marie*. All I know for sure is what Mary told me. She said that they arrived home to Colin's parents' house after a night out. They were sitting down at the kitchen table having a cup of tea and biscuits when Colin turned to Mary and suddenly said, 'It's over.' There had been no argument so Mary couldn't understand where this was coming from. Then he repeated, 'We're finished.' Mary was devastated.

Marie takes a deep intake of breath. One can only suspect she is thinking how things might have turned out if Colin had remained out of her daughter's life.

Mary didn't see Colin for the next six months. Marie is unsure if Colin saw other women during this period but she knows that Mary certainly didn't see anyone else. Colin seemed to be the only man for her. After a time Marie noticed Colin driving up and down past the house. He never stopped but Marie felt he was hoping that he might bump into Mary. One night he was at a party Mary was attending. They got chatting and before the night was out they were back together. 'I think it was from this point that he started planning Mary's murder,' says Marie.

———

Once Mary and Colin rekindled their relationship, things began to get serious. In that year, 1997, they moved into a house on Clonard Street, Balbriggan, a few miles away from Mary's family home. Colin's grandfather had owned the house and Colin purchased it after his death. Mary and Colin went abroad on holidays every year and it was while they were abroad that Colin produced a surprise engagement ring.

Mary phoned me to announce the news, *says Marie*. She was elated, crying down the phone. She was crying with happiness. She couldn't believe she was really going to get married. I decided to have a surprise engagement party to welcome them home. Myself and Colin's family arranged it. We decorated the house. They opened the front door and we switched on the light and cheered and celebrated their engagement. Someone asked had they set a date? Colin interjected quickly to say that it wouldn't be until 2000, two years time. My son's now wife passed a comment to me, 'That wouldn't have been Mary's doing.' She was right. Mary would have got married there and then if she could have. It was a great night. The only thing I can say is that we were like one big happy family.

After the engagement, Mary and Colin set about doing up the house Colin had bought. They built an extension at the back which was practically the size of a new house. Marie was a regular visitor, helping anyway she could: hanging curtains, cleaning up after the builders and so on. When the house was being renovated, the engaged couple lived with Colin's parents. Mary went back to college to do a secretarial course. She'd had enough of bar work and wanted to better herself. She got a secretarial job quickly and when the company moved she decided to look elsewhere for work and settled on Wades Solicitors in Swords. She loved working there and was well respected and liked among her colleagues.

Mary and Colin's wedding date was set for 9 September 2000. She asked her childhood friend Sinéad Byrne to be her bridesmaid. The two girls had been like sisters and were inseparable from the age of five when they met on their first day of school. Sinéad had been reluctant to even venture beyond the school gates of St Patrick's in Stamullen that day, but five-year-old Mary doubled back and took Sinéad's hand. The two girls were by each other's side from that day onwards and Sinéad stood proudly by Mary's side on the day of her wedding.

After the wedding ceremony Marie noticed that her daughter was missing from the crowd. She found her inside the church crying hard. She was inconsolable, recalls Marie. Her friend Ashling who works in a beauty salon was there too, trying to repair Mary's make-up. Soon everyone knew that Mary was upset. She couldn't say what was wrong but her mother presumed it was because she was missing her father who had died when Mary was sixteen.

Colin didn't come into the church to comfort her. He was outside the whole time. He didn't seem to care; he didn't even check to see if she was okay. I thought it strange even then. Now, thinking back, I wonder was she crying about her dad or was she was crying about something else? Had it something to do with Colin?

The one thing I know for sure is that she had no idea about what he was planning. She was like me in that way. She wouldn't tolerate any man who would hit or bully her. Her own father was a kind and gentle man and she expected the same from Colin. At that stage Colin seemed to be that gentleman. There was nothing sinister about him, *says Marie.*

The wedding day went off as Mary had planned it. There was nothing to fault and certainly there was no hint of the havoc that lay ahead, although Colin's father's wedding speech did border on uncomfortable ground for Colin, as Marie recalls:

Andy, Colin's father, said that when his youngest son was a child he refused to play outside with other children. He spent his time upstairs working on his own ... Colin interrupted his father's speech and made him sit down. Colin was very embarrassed. It was as if his father had hit a raw nerve.

Perhaps it was as early as childhood that this loner child established a conviction that it was him against the world and it didn't matter who he had to hurt along the way.

People excused Colin's oddness, putting it down to a tragedy that had afflicted the Whelan family when Colin was just a boy. Colin's brother Andrew committed suicide when he was 19 years old. He drank Romoxone, a weed killer. Andrew was a lovely chap. Colin never spoke about his death, *says Marie.*

Marie remembers how, after her daughter and Colin got married, things changed. I was never allowed stay over at their house. Colin would always insist on driving me home. Previously I would stay the odd Friday night and Mary and I would go into Dublin the next day shopping or we might go to the theatre. Mary loved the theatre. Sometimes Colin and his mother or sister would come with us.

Something else unusual happened after the wedding. One day Mary came to my house with her wedding album and told me to keep it. She didn't want it. Now of course hindsight is a wonderful thing and it was funny that she didn't want to keep her own wedding album, that she wanted to forget about the day. I wish I'd asked her why she didn't want to keep it.

By Christmas 2001 I noticed that Mary wasn't herself. She was somewhat withdrawn but when I asked her about it she just put it down to tiredness. I think she copped that something was wrong before she died. I don't know what. She never said but I could tell she was miles away in thought.

There were other reasons why the new bride might have begun to suspect Colin. An insurance policy which had been taken out in May 2000 prior to their marriage had been increased so that on the death of either spouse the other would receive IR£400,000 (€508,000) but only if the death occurred within 10 years. Strangely the policy did not include a provision for critical illness, a clause that would have been standard for a young couple. After Mary's death, the policy was assessed by an independent financial analyst who said it was 'inappropriate and highly questionable'.

Just three months after his marriage in December 2000, Colin began an on-line relationship with a Welsh woman, Helen Sheppard (38). He was spending increasing amounts of time bombarding the fundraising manager, who worked for a national charity, with e-mails and long phone calls. He instructed Helen to call him by his internet name 'Celtic Tackle'. He even superimposed his head on the body of a male model and e-mailed it to her trying to win her favour. He planned to meet up with her on 2 March, the day after he killed Mary.

Helen, a single mother of two, was wooed by Colin who pretended to show empathy with the loss of her mother to cancer. He claimed he too had suffered a loss — that his fiancée had died of cancer. He also claimed that he had collected IR£500,000 in insurance after her death. In his fantasy world on the internet he wasn't a common computer analyst, he was a high-flying businessman. Frighteningly — though Helen didn't know at the time — Colin gave clues of his horrendous plan to kill Mary. He wrote that he was thinking of getting rid of a gym he owned. However, his plan to terminate his contract of ownership with the 'gym' may really have been his plan to terminate his wife's life. He went on to say:

> 'It's been getting a bit too much lately. It's nearly time to renew the insurance so I have to make up my mind fairy quickly. I'll be sorry and glad to see it go, if you know what I mean. Need a bit of free time.'

When police later visited Helen's home in Wales they found a picture of Colin stuck to her refrigerator door. She was unaware of his plan to kill his wife.

Finally, the one thing that would have really alerted Mary would have been a look at the history of searches on his computer. It would have shown lists of ways to murder someone. These searches began within the month of the insurance policy being taken out.

———

On the day before Mary died, a snow-fall covered Stamullen and the surrounding areas. Mary cancelled an arrangement which was planned for the following day with her best friend Sinéad. She felt it was unsafe to travel because of the snow. Sinéad was engaged to be married and was anxious to see her friend because she wanted to show her some material she'd picked for her bridesmaid's dress. But Mary had become increasingly difficult to stay in touch with. She wouldn't return calls and there was often no answer when Sinéad and her future husband called to her door. When Mary phoned Sinéad on her mobile that morning, Sinéad was driving and she pulled into the side of the road to talk to her friend. That was the last time they spoke.

Sinéad wasn't the first friend from whom Mary had distanced

herself since she got married. Another friend of Mary's had known a secret about Colin, a secret from his past which he was adamant that Mary would never find out about. The friend in question knew that in 1991 Colin had viciously beaten up his then girlfriend, kneeing her in the stomach and causing her to lose the baby she was carrying for him. Previously, he had tried to run her over in his car and he had force-fed her aspirin and vodka so that she would abort the baby. The girl was young at the time, Colin was her first real boyfriend and she had not reported the incident to the guards. Mary's friend wanted to share this secret but at the same time she didn't want to take away from Mary's happiness.

Finally, Colin confided a 'secret' of his own to Mary. He said that Mary's friend was *mad after him*, that she had made passes at him, so it would, presumably, be best if she wasn't around him in future. Mary believed her husband's lies. She was naturally shocked and one can only suppose that she wouldn't have trusted this friend again even if the latter had told her the truth about Colin. The friendship consequently dwindled.

When the phone rings in the middle of the night it is never good news and for Marie it was no different.

At 1.30 a.m. on 1 March I awoke to hear the phone ringing but by the time I got to it, it had stopped. I was just pulling the covers back to return to bed when the phone rang again. This time I reached it before it went off. My son Peter was on the other end of the line. 'I'm here in Beaumont Hospital,' he said. 'Mary has been in an accident. She has fallen down the stairs. You'd better come up here and bring the lads with you.' My sons were living with me at that time and when Peter told me to bring them with me I knew Mary was in a bad way. I thought that maybe she was in a coma but I didn't want to question Peter on the phone because I could tell he was very upset. The boys heard the commotion and were awake. The boys drove in one car and my daughter-in-law Liz came to drive me, though we all arrived in the hospital together.

We headed towards the accident and emergency department. There were a lot of people around, waiting to be treated, I presume. I walked down a long corridor. I remember there was a man standing inside the first set of doors. At the time I didn't know he was Superintendent Tom Gallagher, the man who would investigate my daughter's murder. He looked at me and I thought he might be waiting for me but he just nodded his head and didn't stop me as I went by. After I passed him I thought to myself, 'That man has sorrow on his face.'

As I walked on I saw the local fireman. He nodded to me as well but didn't smile or say a word. Then I turned around the corner of the corridor and I saw my son Peter, and Colin Whelan's family. There was a little room off that corridor. I could see Colin was inside this room. I walked in but he didn't get up. His sisters were there with him. They were all crying but still no one said a word to me. I walked up to Colin. He was sitting down hunched over his hands holding a hankie. I asked, 'How's Mary?' He snapped, cold as could be, 'She's dead.' What a way to answer me. His tone and attitude was such that I didn't ask anything else.

I thought it strange that this newly married man of five months was so composed. I have seen men whose wives have died and you'd have to pick them off the floor with grief. Not Colin. I walked away from him and a nurse approached me and said she wanted me to come down and see Mary. Liz, my daughter-in-law, came with me. I was in such shock it's hard to remember the detail. We walked in through closed doors to a room where each bed was curtained off. Mary was lying behind one of the curtains. A crisp white sheet was pulled up to her chin. There was another nurse there and she was very kind to me. I stared at the sheet. She pulled it down to Mary's waist.

I looked at Mary's hands and noticed how thin her fingers had become. I noted that she wasn't wearing her wedding or engagement ring. It emerged later that her wedding band was found on the ambulance floor and her engagement ring was found on the landing of her home.

I asked the nurse, 'Did she suffer?'

For the first time Marie breaks down as she remembers the details of that night. After a few seconds she composes herself and continues.

The nurse said, 'No, she would have just gone asleep.' Then I saw a mark on Mary's neck and I thought that must be the fatal injury which broke her neck when she fell down the stairs. She had a cat called Muffin and I was sure that her cat, Muffin, accidentally tripped her because he was always at her feet following her around.

She was wearing her pyjamas. They were made of fleece material which was typical of what she would wear even though she had other beautiful nightwear. As I sat there looking at her, something caught my eye: the right-hand sleeve of her pyjamas was torn at the seam. I thought to myself, if she fell down the stairs how could the right-hand sleeve be torn, because the banister is on the left and that's the only thing that could snag the sleeve? The only way she could have torn the right-hand sleeve would be if she fell up the stairs which wasn't likely. But I put this out of my mind and continued to look at her face which was unmarked.

After some time the kind nurse brought me back to the small waiting room. There was a priest there who sat with me all the time. I thought it strange that he never went to sit with Colin, though oddly this young priest kept looking over at Colin. He stared him in the eyes. I noticed that. Then Colin was called out by the guards. They had called him out several times but on this occasion they took his car and house keys and told him he couldn't return to either. Someone told me this was normal procedure, *says Marie, breathing out a deep sigh.*

When I got up to go home the nurse who had been particularly nice to me walked me to the door of Beaumont Hospital. It was around six in the morning and it was quite cold outside, more especially for the nurse who was just in her light uniform, but nonetheless, she waited with me while my son and his wife went to get the car which was at the other end of the car park. She told me to look after myself and my family, *says Marie, grateful to the nurse who took the time to ease the worse day of her life.*

Marie didn't know then that this nurse, Sr Catherine Galvin, had already played a major part in bringing her daughter's murderer to justice. Colin had chosen not to go in the ambulance with his wife and instead travelled in his own car behind the ambulance. When Colin arrived at the hospital, Sr Catherine Galvin was there to meet him. As Mary was being seen to by the doctors she set about looking after Colin. It was then that eagle-eyed Catherine noticed a couple of his shirt buttons were undone. Then something else caught her attention. She could see marks on his chest that looked like fresh wounds. She raised her suspicions and brought those remarks to the attention of the Gardaí.

Supt Gallagher said this information was absolutely vital, more especially because most people wouldn't have noticed it. Colin agreed to be examined and when he was questioned about the scratch marks he claimed they were made by Mary when she threw out her hands while gasping for air at the foot of the stairs. When Dr Junada conducted his examination of Colin he noted further scratch marks on his shoulders and ribcage. These marks would later indicate that his wife fought ferociously for her life.

The doctors who had been standing by for Mary's arrival were struck by the fact that her body was particularly cold to touch and this brought into question the timeframe that Colin had given to the ambulance crew.

However, at this stage no one concerned Marie with such details. On the way home from the hospital Marie called in to see Colin's parents in Gormanstown. She knew they would be genuinely concerned. As Marie pulled up to the house, Colin's father Andy was at the door to meet her. He had tears in his eyes. Marie was welcomed into the sitting-room. She chatted and drank tea with Colin's family. They discussed the tragedy and comforted each other. Then Colin arrived home with his sister and brother-in-law.

Marie puts her hand up to her flushed face as if what she is about to say next still shocks her.

Colin walked into the sitting-room. He was so shocked to see me there. He gave me a terrible look, letting me know that he didn't want me there. He didn't stay in the room. He left immediately and went into another room, the kitchen I think. So we got up and left. I didn't want to stay where I wasn't welcome.

Back at my house people kept calling to offer me their kindness and support. That evening Colin arrived up at my house. He walked into my kitchen which was filled with people. I was sitting on the easy chair beside the cooker. He came over to me and threw his arms around me. But it wasn't a real hug. Even then I realised that he was just doing it for show. The hug was cold, stiff and uncomfortable. I don't know what, if anything, he said to me but he left immediately afterwards.

I also had a visit from two detectives. They were trying to prepare me as gently as they could for what they were going to tell me the following day. The superintendent paced up and down the room. He was agitated as if he had something on his mind. He kept asking me questions like: 'Did Mary and Colin have many fights? Did they get on well? Did he ever hit her?' I couldn't believe his questions but I answered them as best I could. The next day, which was Friday, passed in much the same fashion: people called and offered me their sympathy and support. My son and his wife had to go and identify Mary's body but they hid this from me. They didn't want to cause me any further strain. It was that same day that the two detectives once again called to my house. This time they asked me if they could come in and if I wouldn't mind sitting down because they had some sad news for me. 'Mary was murdered,' the more senior detective said. They said they were sure because Dr Marie Cassidy, the State Pathologist, had completed her autopsy. The results were conclusive. I was shocked.

The detectives were only out the door when there was another knock. This time it was from Colin's father Andy and his brother Martin. Andy was indignant. He said, 'What is all this about murder? Colin wouldn't touch a hair on Mary's head.' He was in a terrible state, crying and everything. Martin was upset too. I stood at the door of the sitting-room. Andy was standing at the window and Martin was just in front of me. I listened to them and then I looked straight into their eyes and said, 'Mary can't ever be hurt again. I'll never be as hurt again. But your nightmare is only beginning.' That's what I said to them. They didn't say anything. I'm sure poor Martin always remembers what I said. He's married with three lovely daughters of his own. But Andy just wouldn't believe that Colin could have done anything wrong. The guards were wrong, everyone was wrong, in Andy's mind. At this stage I knew the truth was that Colin killed Mary. There was no doubt about it because the autopsy proved it to be so.

Then I called a family meeting with my boys and our extended family. I wanted them to hear the truth about Mary's death from me, not through hearsay.

At the time my eighty-year-old father was living with me. He had the 'flu. He wasn't in great form so I hid my announcement from him. I didn't want to upset him any further. The next day, my cousin Elizabeth came to take my father to her house. He needed to get away from everything. By Monday night, six days after Mary's death, he said to my cousin, 'What's wrong? Why haven't they buried Mary?' before adding, 'There is something funny going on in Balbriggan.' Still no one said anything to him and I'm glad he didn't know the awful truth.

————

Mary's funeral finally went ahead on Thursday, 8 March 2001. More than a week after she died, she was buried with her dad, Jimmy. Colin and his family were at the funeral. He didn't come near me or try to carry the coffin. It was just as well because if he did I wouldn't have been able to hold back my lads. By now the rumours about Colin had circulated around the village. People knew he was the main suspect, yet some people still sympathised with him.

In our local church when someone dies the priest always puts the coffin at the left-hand side and the family sit behind it at that same side. That is the way it has always been. However, on this occasion, Fr Daly, who was burying Mary and who was indeed the same priest that married her five months previously, placed her coffin inside the altar, exactly centred so that it wasn't at either side. I said to myself — Mary would be laughing her head off. She'd say, 'Mammy, look where Fr Daly put me!' My family and I sat at the left-hand side as is tradition and Colin and his family sat at the right-hand side. When Colin walked up the aisle to receive Holy Communion a huge gasp went around the church. Colin was calm and didn't look like he was under any type of pressure as he walked up to the altar.

It was an altar where, just five months previously, he had promised to love and protect Mary. His demeanour was much the same as when he had been at the mortuary. Marie remembers him wearing a spanking suit in which he stood serenely and calmly.

When they were about to put the lid on the coffin, he walked over to it, bent down and gave Mary a very quick kiss on the forehead. Then he stood back, composed as could be, showing no emotion. All the men were clenching their fists. My brother-in-law Raphael had to leave the mortuary and go outside where he vomited, such was his upset and grief. I will always remember what he said to me, 'Marie, there was no one there to help her,' and he was right, *says Marie regretfully.*

At the funeral Marie thought she noticed people were talking about her behind her back. She felt them looking at her and then looking away. After the funeral, family and friends went for some food and Marie noticed that her cousin Elizabeth was missing from the funeral party. She inquired as to her whereabouts. Finally Liz, Marie's daughter-in-law, broke the news that the family had been discussing and hiding from her. She told Marie that she would have to leave to go straight to the hospital. Her father had taken a turn. Marie arrived at the hospital to find her father was dead.

I think when Mary died my father gave up. He was very close to her and they'd have the craic together. Her death was too much for him. He just wasn't able for it. He was buried the Sunday after Mary. He had stayed strong through so many deaths: his wife (my mother) died when she was twenty-four, six weeks after giving birth to my brother; she never came home from the hospital. I was one and a half years old at the time and my father's parents had to raise me; my father lived with us too but he never remarried. Then, his two brothers died of TB and he had a partner in later years who died of cancer. When my husband died later on he took it very badly because they were very close.

I wouldn't say I had a tough upbringing. My grandmother did the best she knew how. She was a very strong, no-nonsense woman. I have thanked God that I take after my mother's mother who was gentle, because if I took after my father's mother I'd have to be dug out of the Whelans. I think my background has made me strong. I've had to stand on my own two feet for as long as I've had them.

Six weeks after Mary's death, her husband, Colin Whelan, was charged with her murder. It still mystifies Marie how he got out on bail:

I don't know why they let him out when they had so much evidence against him. He or his family paid a bail of about €13,000. He had to sign on every Tuesday and Thursday in the barracks while another condition was that he had to live with his parents in Gormanstown. He rented out the house in which himself that Mary had lived. We saw him regularly when he was out on bail. Sometimes we would find ourselves driving behind him in the car on the way into town or we would physically pass him on the road. Nothing would be said. We wouldn't put any pass on him.

Nine days after Mary's funeral, Marie planned to go to the annual blessings of the graves. Each year the community came to the graveyard where they prayed for deceased relations. Marie knew there was a chance that Colin would be there because his granny and grandfather were buried in that same graveyard. Marie warned her sons not to go near Colin and if he said or did anything they were to turn their backs because if they got into a fight they would be arrested and held in prison and that would be no help to Marie. She needed them by her side. The boys respected their mother's wishes and held firm when they saw Colin approaching their mother as she stood in the graveyard saying her prayers.

He walked up to me and grabbed my hand; he didn't say anything and I didn't say anything but I almost broke his fingers I squeezed them so hard — as hard as I could! I never moved an inch because if I did, the boys would have been on him. So I just stood there, waiting until it was over because you couldn't have any type of disagreement or words in the graveyard of all places. At the time I thought it was so very cheeky of him to come over to me but now that I know the full facts, I simply can't believe it. He held my hand, knowing in his heart and soul that that same hand had killed my daughter. At this time I knew he had murdered her. I didn't know the full extent of what had happened. I presumed it was a spur of the moment mistake, that he had lashed out in an argument and accidentally killed her.

Colin came to Mary's 'month's mind' and a year later to her anniversary mass. His sisters went to the priest outside the chapel and complained because I had 'Mary Gough' prayed for instead of 'Mary Whelan'. She was 'Mary Gough' as far as I was concerned and there was no way the lads (her brothers) would let her be called 'Mary Whelan'. After talking to Colin's sisters the priest was upset and annoyed, as was I. On the following year's anniversary I got 'Jimmy Gough and his daughter Mary prayed for', so that no one was put out.

———

When the Gardaí questioned Colin, the first thing he said was 'I love my wife. I even brought her a present on the day before she died.' The latter was true. On the day before Mary's death Colin went to the exclusive Dublin store of Brown Thomas where he bought Mary a gift; he used his credit card to pay for it so there would be a concrete receipt of the date and time and he made sure he was seen on the CCTV cameras. The couple had, that precious September, received an ornamental boot as a wedding present. What he purchased was the matching boot for the mantlepiece. After he bought the gift, he went back to work in the nearby Irish Permanent on Stephen's Green. He wasn't an employee of theirs but supplied services to them through his own company. When he returned to his workplace he searched the internet for ways to murder his wife. In all, he conducted at least twenty-two internet searches for ways to kill Mary.

His first search began in July 2000 — two months before his wedding. He consulted an online dictionary to check the spelling of a word that was giving him a bit of trouble. 'Asphyxiation'. It is a word that few of us will ever utter, let alone write. He entered two versions of the word into the search engine before he was satisfied he had it correct. This was the first step in a series of actions that would result in the death of an intelligent, bright and bubbly young woman and lead to the ruination and devastation of several families, most pointedly the Goughs. And in the end it would take away every shred of dignity and freedom Colin Whelan had ever enjoyed.

Sadly, once Colin was over the stumbling block of this difficult word there was no stopping him. His searches continued up until the day before Mary's murder. On this day, 28 February 2001, Colin studied sites on 'loss of consciousness' and 'sudden loss of consciousness'. While his first search on 4 July focused on 'asphyxiation' and 'how to asphyxiate', by the new year he was concentrating his searches on words like 'choking', 'smothering' and 'blocking the air supply'. While Colin was meant to be working for Irish Permanent, he was instead spending more and more time on detailed internet searches. On 20 February he did several searches including 'lack of oxygen to the brain' and 'how long does it take to die from asphyxiation?' Two days later he followed up his searches with the phrase 'death by strangulation'.

He also downloaded the transcript of a hideous case of murder by strangulation. The information was on-line and available from the North Carolina Supreme Court.

The case involved Henry Louis Wallace, a young cocaine addict who murdered nine women in the space of two years. Wallace succeeded in covering up some of his murders and Colin wanted to learn his techniques so that he could make his wife's murder look like an accident. Wallace used towels to strangle his victims, as towels ensured there were no marks left on the victim's necks, and then he used bed covers to preserve his victims' bodies. Wallace's first victim was of particular interest to Colin and he employed some of the mechanisms of this murder. The transcript from this murder explains how Wallace broke into Ms Love's home and lay hidden in the bathroom until she arrived home, after which he murdered her.

The transcript reads: 'I kept hold of her until she passed out. And at that time I moved her to her bedroom . . . while still applying the choke hold. She began to fight [so] I used a curling iron that was near her bed and I placed the cord around her neck.' After the murder, Wallace took the bed sheets she was lying on and folded them around her — just as Colin did with the duvet — in a bid to keep her body warm so that the doctors and detectives would have difficulty in identifying the time of death from her body temperature. When ambulance drivers arrived at Colin and Mary's home, they found a towel near Mary's body which lay wrapped in a blood-stained duvet at the bottom of the stairs. Wallace is currently on death row in North Carolina. He was given nine death sentences in January 1997, one for each victim.

Colin arrived home from work on the night before the murder

at his usual time. One can only imagine that Mary was thrilled with her unexpected gift. The following evening, 29 February, Mary and Colin made a trip to Drogheda to buy a herbal, homeopathic, detox drink. They were both anxious to lose weight and decided to see the homeopath together and embark on a recommended programme. They returned home and some time later that night Mary was murdered.

When Gardaí first questioned Colin about what exactly happened Mary, he claimed that she may have snagged the sleeve of her pyjamas on the banister and fallen down the stairs. The truth, however, was much more sinister: Colin had strangled Mary with the cord from her dressing-gown in their bedroom. It is unclear how long she was dead before Colin phoned the police. Due to the fact that her body was quite cold, even though it was wrapped in a duvet and the house was noted to be warm by the ambulance crew, one can presume she was dead for some time before he alerted the emergency services. During this time he cleaned up the crime scene and made sure enough time had lapsed so that his wife couldn't be resuscitated.

After he murdered Mary it is thought that he dragged her body down the stairs backwards, and left her in the hallway; another theory is that he threw her dead body down the stairs to make it look like she had fallen. When, by 12.16 a.m., he thought he had done a good enough clean up, he put the rest of his premeditated plan into action. He phoned 999 to report an 'accident', claiming his wife had fallen down the stairs and was badly injured. However, he overlooked traces of blood upstairs which had come from Mary's bleeding nose as she took her last breaths of air.

When Gardaí questioned Colin about the fact that his wife was wrapped in a duvet, he claimed that the 999 operator gave him the instruction to wrap his wife to keep her warm. A transcript of the 999 telephone conversation reveals no such instruction. The operator did, however, give instructions on how to resuscitate his wife which Colin pretended to execute.

State Pathologist Dr Marie Cassidy was called to do a post-mortem on Mary's body. She said her death had not been caused by a fall down the stairs. If she had died under those circumstances, Dr

Cassidy would have expected to find certain injuries such as bleeding inside the head, broken ribs and punctured lungs. 'She was strangled and I knew that straight away,' said Dr Cassidy.

Whelan attempted to use his computer expertise to wipe away any trace of his searches on the internet but garda computer analysts seized his work computer and managed to retrieve the information from a central server at his workplace where all the data had been stored. His home computer revealed less information because there was no central server to back up the deleted information.

––––

The trial was finally set for October 2003, two years after the murder. Colin attended the anniversary mass in March of that year and then he disappeared the week after. He chose a good week to disappear because the airports and ports were extra busy with people coming and going from Ireland — Cheltenham was on at the time.

His disappearance was a dreadful calamity. His car was found near Howth Head and inside were his clothes, his chain, ring and a suicide note to his family, or so I believe. Someone had noticed that the car had been sitting there all day, from morning till night, so it was looked into and I think that was when it was realised Colin was missing. I don't think anyone reported him missing before that. His family thought he had killed himself and there was a big search of the waters. I knew there was no way he'd kill himself. As big and strong as he looked he was not the type of person who would kill himself. He wasn't one to cause himself pain.

His family continued to search for Colin but no body was ever found. Then some people around Gormanstown stopped talking to me. They blamed me for his 'death' as if I [metaphorically] pushed him over the edge. I remember I was at the funeral of a local person and there were people on either side of me and someone I knew quite well went down the line of people that were on my left and talked to each one, but when she got to me she skipped me, not saying a word, and then continued to talk to each person on my right.

On another occasion I was in the house of a woman I used to do
a bit of cleaning for and there was a workman in her kitchen. I knew
him well; he was a right chatterbox; you couldn't stop him talking.
But when I entered the kitchen he wouldn't say a word. Finally I
said hello and he grunted hello back. When I left the kitchen the
woman of the house followed me to ask me what all that was about,
why was he so cold with me? She thought it strange. So there you
are. They had faces on them because they thought Colin's 'death'
was my fault.

Colin's family continued to maintain his innocence and because
they believed he had drowned, they spent all their time searching
for him. Then a tourist spotted him in Majorca, Spain. But by the
time the police got to the bar where Colin had been seen he had
moved on to work somewhere else and they were unable to trace
him. Finally another tourist, a woman, saw his picture in the paper
when she returned home from holidays in Spain and recognised it
to be Colin. He had served her in Karma cocktail bar in Puerto
Portals, a posh sailing resort, where he worked under the identity
of Cian Sweeney. She reported it to the police.

The Spanish authorities were notified and arrested him on 12
July 2004. They brought him to Madrid. Colin denied his identity
and produced a passport which 'proved' his name wasn't Colin
Whelan. The passport was real. Colin had applied for it through
the post under the name of a neighbour in Gormanstown. His
neighbour didn't know his identity had been stolen until he read
about it in the newspapers. The man in question had never been
outside of Ireland so had never applied for a passport of his own.
However, the police in Madrid were sure they had the right man
because they had checked his fingerprints.

Detective Sergeant Pat Marry from Balbriggan Garda Station
went to Spain to bring Colin back to Ireland. He was surprised that
Colin wasn't an angry detainee but a complete gentleman. He and
others speculated that on some level Colin must have wanted to be
caught because Spain, and Majorca in particular, attracts
thousands of Irish tourists every year. It was inevitable that
someone would recognise him. The bar staff with whom he
worked said that he lived every day as if it was his last. He allegedly

snorted cocaine and frequented upmarket lap dancing clubs.

Marie heard the news that Colin had been found the same way she heard he'd gone missing, through the newspapers. A newspaper journalist phoned me and said, 'Mrs Gough, do you know Colin Whelan has been found?' I didn't say anything. I just burst out crying and put the phone down. Then I phoned my son to see if he had heard anything. He hadn't but he said he would call the Gardaí and find out if it was true. He called me back and confirmed it was true.

Colin spent maybe a couple of weeks in prison in Spain. We thought he would fight the extradition and try to stay there but he was happy to come home to an Irish prison. Another few weeks in a Spanish prison wouldn't have done him any harm. They have a no-nonsense approach over there. As my grandmother would have said, the prison wouldn't exactly be 'Maggie Murphy's home'. When he was found, we learned that he was leading a 'Jekyll and Hyde' type life. He just switched off one life and slotted into another. He had a new English girlfriend, who I suppose had a lucky escape in the end.

——

When Colin Whelan arrived back in Ireland on 23 July 2004 he requested that the trial date be changed. He wanted a time lapse so that potential jurors would forget that he had absconded; he requested a date of November 2005. The judge offered an immediate trial which wasn't accepted and finally April was agreed because the judge felt the Gough family had already been waiting long enough for the trial to begin. Colin still protested his innocence and his family still stood by him, strongly maintaining his innocence.

Marie had so many questions she wanted answered. She wasn't looking forward to the court date on 11 April 2005 but she was looking forward to getting to the truth.

I sat in court with my family around me. Colin sat to the left-hand side of me. I couldn't see him without leaning forward. He sat the whole time handcuffed with his head down; he was motionless and showed no emotion. The judge asked him if he pleaded guilty or not guilty. We had all presumed he was going to plea 'not guilty' because he had always claimed his innocence. He replied, 'guilty'. Suddenly the whole court was in a flutter. There was a huge sense of shock because I don't think even his own barrister knew he was going to plead guilty. Certainly his family didn't know. The judge said he would pass sentence the following day.

The next day we heard in a statement read by a guard that Colin's murder plan had been premeditated, that he had been working on it for months. I had to hear the details of the murder for the first time in a full courtroom. Then we got a chance to say a few words about Mary and how our lives have changed without her.

In a very warm and crowded Central Criminal Court, Marie's eldest sons, twins Gerard and David, emotionally read their victim impact statements. Gerard went first:

Mary was the heart of our family, especially since our father died in 1989. She lifted our spirits at that time. She was very good to our mother and was a sister that my mother never had; they confided in each other. And for my mother, this is a double loss. She has lost her sister and daughter. Mary's birthday was at Christmas and she really loved Christmas. It was a great family celebration when she brought everyone together. Since her death, I can't stand Christmas. She was the life and spirit of Christmas and now it means nothing to me. It's just a reminder of our family's loss and we'll never get over it. The family have been living a life sentence since her murder, one they will always have to live with. We won't get off for good behaviour. Mary is gone forever and we can't run away. Mary won't be coming back, *Gerard said in a voice brimming with heart-wrenching sadness.*

David Gough next took the stand. He directly addressed Colin Whelan some fifteen feet away. He sat facing him and looked straight at him. Colin did not lift his head or look at him.

'You, Colin Whelan, strangled Mary and for that we'll never, ever, ever forgive you. You caused devastation to our family when you brutally strangled Mary and you took a piece of us too. Then you fled the country which shows you for the coward you are. You tried to rob us of justice. You thought you were above the law but you are not. Justice has finally been done here today. Mary's only crime was loving you too much. No time in prison will ever be enough. The one thing you can't take away is our wonderful cherished memories of Mary and the wonderful part she played in our lives. May she now rest in peace.'

Colin's solicitor read an apology on Colin's behalf but Colin Whelan himself did not speak nor did he show any physical signs of regret in court. He remained emotionless. Marie felt the apology was just a show, so that it will be on the record for the parole book. She said he could have asked to see her either before or after the trial and apologised properly. She doesn't expect he will ever write her a letter to explain things. She feels if he did, it would be a miracle.

Colin Whelan received the mandatory life sentence of 15 years. He won't receive any money from the €508,000 insurance policy and he has also lost ownership of the €350,000 house he owned with Mary in Balbriggan. Marie doesn't care about the money. She feels money was at the source of all this pain and is at the source of so many people's pain. However, she does feel that the sentence doesn't reflect the crime in the sense that he will be up for parole in a mere eight years.

Trial Judge Paul Carney, one of Ireland's most experienced judges, described the murder of Mary as 'the most calculating and callous killing that I have ever encountered'. He also said that since Colin had prolonged the suffering of the Gough family by skipping bail through his staging of a 'Reginald Perrin' style disappearing act, he would not deduct from his sentence the days he had already served.

———

Marie says: The truth is Colin is serving a life sentence but the boys and I are serving one too. One day Colin will get out and until then he'll get three square meals a day. When he went in first there was a

24-hour watch on him to make sure he didn't kill himself. I believe it's standard with all such prisoners. But I don't remember anyone calling to see if I'd had three meals a day. I don't remember anyone watching me 24 hours to see if I was okay. At the end of the day, Colin's parents can go to the prison and throw their arms around their son; they can talk to him and one day take him home. He will be a model prisoner and could be out in a few years. All I can do is stand at Mary's grave and talk to my dead daughter. She's never coming back, not after ten years or fifteen years.

I don't hate or hold bitterness towards Colin. I don't carry that burden, thank God. I have known people who went to their graves hating but I'm not going to be one of them. Hate is a terrible thing. If you let it into your life, it will rip your family apart and finally it will turn on you and destroy you. It's so important not to even entertain hate.

Do I forgive him? I'm not sure. What does 'forgive' really mean? I have no feelings for him. He is nothing to me. All I know for sure is he doesn't bother me. I won't let him.

I have never taken a sleeping tablet or anything during this whole ordeal. I feel the best treatment is my family and if I was on medication they would be worrying about me unnecessarily. Four of them have their own families now so they have enough to worry about.

It's important for people who are going through a trauma to make sure they get to the bottom of the truth.

The truth shouldn't frighten you, no matter how bad it appears to be. Once you know the truth you can deal with it and finally move on.

When you are as long in the world as I am you realise a lot of things. Years ago family scandals were commonly covered up. These denials or masking of the truth still causes heartache on families. I have seen so many unfortunate families carry secrets and it rips them apart. I don't know why but since Mary died I have heard more confessions than the priest. People have told me their most intimate and sad secrets. Only the other day I had a woman in talking to me about how she had to give up two little children at birth. She would do anything to see them. She wishes they would try to contact her. That is a heavy secret that she has been carrying.

We should learn from the past and not hide things. The truth, no matter how bad, can be dealt with and from it we can heal.

The best advice I can give is to live for the living, not the dead. Remember everyone is hurting but they have different ways of dealing with it. I find it good to focus on my family. I have five sons and they keep me going.

Just as Marie says this the phone rings. It's Gerard her son on the other end of the line. Marie tells him she can't talk because she's with someone. She assures him there are no emergencies and gives a little chuckle as she puts down the phone.

Yes, the lads take good care of me. And their wives are wonderful too, but they have their own mothers. I have to say I'm lucky to have grandchildren. My five-and-half-year-old grandson brings me back to reality. He shows me what is really important in life and he's a straight talker and tells me how things really are!

I also focus on staying healthy. I see so many good people dying of cancer that I have to feel lucky to be in good health and do everything I can to remain strong both physically and mentally. I have to feel lucky to be alive and enjoy this life that has been given to me.

Not everyone will have sons or grandchildren but they might have a husband or a friend and from them they can get strength. If they find it hard to talk to them or simply don't have special people in their lives then there are still ways to get through grief and be positive. For example, they could go to their local 'Victims' Support'.

I found talking about what I've been through was very therapeutic and that's why I went to my local 'Victims' Support' group meetings for a number of weeks. Every week we each told a different part of our stories and on the third week it hit me that I was just like the other people in the group. I didn't feel alone anymore. I knew in that moment I could take control of things.

It's good to talk about Mary. That's the best thing people did for me: they listened. Others found it too hard to talk about Mary and you have to accept that too. One woman avoided me for a year and half, to the point that she'd cross the street when she saw me coming. Finally she came up to me and told me that she had been avoiding me all this time because she knew if she met me she'd have to mention Mary and she didn't want to because she knew it would upset me. Yes, talking about Mary makes me cry but I like talking about her. And crying is a good thing. A good cry or a good laugh is the natural way to release tension and pressure, so we shouldn't be afraid to cry or to see others cry.

I think it's also important to have time to myself. In the evenings, I like to take the dog up the road for a walk and I have a good cry then. I think about Mary and what I'm missing out on. Sometimes I think of Colin's family. God love them. They are decent people and don't deserve any of the blame. Mary wouldn't have wanted it. I'm glad they took time to write and call and apologise. Mary was their sister-in-law and I believe they were all fond of her. The only one I haven't received a call or apology from is Andy, Colin's father. I think it's very difficult for him to believe what his son did.

Marie's only worry is that Colin might come back and live in the area once he is released. She said some people still sympathise with him.

A few people have said to me, 'Ah sure he's doing his time, the poor fellow.' So, I ask them, 'Do you have a daughter?' They say, 'Yes'. Then I ask, 'Is she dead?' Then, they don't say any more.

Now brighter days beckon. The phone rings again. Sinéad, Mary's childhood friend, is on the other end of the line. She has recently had a baby and Marie says she'll call down to see her and the baby tonight. She plans on going into town first to buy the baby a little outfit. Marie smiles and says, 'The triumph of life goes on.'